DR. BOLI'S ANTHOLOGY
OF AMERICAN HUMOR.

Charles Farrar Browne ("*Artemus Ward*").

Dr. Boli's Anthology

of

AMERICAN HUMOR.

*A generous collection of amusing pieces
for occasional reading.*

PITTSBURGH:
Dr. Boli's Celebrated Publishing Empire,
MMXIV.

Dr. Boli's Celebrated Publishing Empire
An imprint of Serif Press
Pittsburgh
2014
drboli.com
serifpress.com

CONTENTS.

A VERY SHORT INTRODUCTION.

THE SOLE PURPOSE of this book is to give you, dear reader, something to read that will make you laugh, or at least smile. We hope that the selections here are different enough from the ones you have found in most superficially similar anthologies that you will find many surprises, and perhaps strike up friendships with some worthy writers whose names you have never heard before.

In this age of Wikipedia, it is not necessary to preface each extract with a complete biography of the writer. We are vain enough, however, to suppose that our own critical opinions might be entertaining. Seldom will you find us rambling on for more than a page and a half, so that the price you pay for our vanity is small; and you are at perfect liberty to skip any introductory matter that is not to your taste.

On what principle (you may ask) were these pieces selected? Pure whimsy, we answer; which is to say that we had no principle at all, except that nothing went in that did not amuse us. The only set rule was that they must all be out of copyright, for reasons that probably require no explanation.

As for the arrangement of the pieces, it is very roughly chronological, but only very roughly. It would be useless to complain to us that this author ought to have come before that author; we should only reply that to make an accurately chronological arrangement would have been work, and who wants that?

And now, if you will draw a little closer, we shall tell you another secret ambition we have for this book. We should be very happy if one or two readers would close the book and say to themselves, "But everything I was taught about American literature was wrong."

You may have heard that Washington Irving was the first writer to develop a distinctively American style; but here is James K. Paulding, Irving's lifelong friend, writing in his distinctively American way at the same time. You have doubtless been taught that Mark Twain "changed the way Americans write their language" by speaking directly to us in the colloquial language of every day—but here is Fanny Fern writing her breezy and conversational columns while Samuel Clemens is still in knee-pants. It's a safe bet that, as the highest-paid columnist in America, Fanny Fern had some influence on what other writers thought would sell.

Our professors of American Literature draw up a kind of genealogy of American writers, showing how this one led to that one, and that one to the other; but our professors are all wrong, because they have never heard of some of the most influential writers of their day. James K. Paulding, Fanny Fern, Artemus Ward —these are names without which no meaningful history of American letters can be written. How many doctoral theses are lurking in this book, waiting for an enterprising student to tease them out!

THE SUN-CATCHER, OR BOY WHO SET A SNARE FOR THE SUN.

A Myth of the Origin of the Dormouse, from the Odjibwa.

Henry Rowe Schoolcraft married a half-Ojibwe (or Odjibwa) woman who spoke the Ojibwe language fluently; with her help he collected and translated numerous legends—a collection that is still a prized resource among ethnologists today. But we should not leave it to the ethnologists. These stories were told over and over because they were infallibly entertaining; and in the story of the tiny boy who takes his revenge on the sun, we have a fine example of that spirit of humorous exaggeration that will pervade the rest of this collection.

AT THE TIME when the animals reigned in the earth, they had killed all but a girl, and her little brother, and these two were living in fear and seclusion. The boy was a perfect pigmy, and never grew beyond the stature of a small infant, but the girl increased with her years, so that the labor of providing food and lodging devolved wholly on her. She went out daily to get wood for their lodge-fire, and took her little brother along that no accident might happen to him; for he was too little to leave alone. A big bird might have flown away with him. She made him a bow and arrows, and said to him one day, "I will leave you behind where I have been chopping—you must hide yourself, and you will soon see the Gitshee-gitshee-gaun-ia-see-

3

ug, or snow birds, come and pick the worms out of the wood, where I have been chopping" (for it was in the winter). "Shoot one of them and bring it home." He obeyed her, and tried his best to kill one, but came home unsuccessful. She told him he must not despair, but try again the next day. She accordingly left him at the place she got wood, and returned. Towards night-fall, she heard his little footsteps on the snow, and he came in exultingly, and threw down one of the birds which he had killed. "My sister," said he, "I wish you to skin it and stretch the skin, and when I have killed more, I will have a coat made out of them." "But what shall we do with the body?" said she, for as yet men had not begun to eat animal food, but lived on vegeta-bles alone. "Cut it in two," he answered, "and season our pottage with one half of it at a time." She did so. The boy, who was of a very small stature, continued his efforts, and succeeded in killing ten birds, out of the skins of which his sister made him a little coat.

"Sister," said he one day, "are we all alone in the world? Is there nobody else living?" She told him that those they feared and who had destroyed their relatives lived in a certain quarter, and that he must by no means go in that direction. This only served to inflame his curiosity and raise his ambition, and he soon after took his bow and arrows and went in that direction. After walking a long time and meeting nothing, he be-came tired, and lay down on a knoll, where the sun had melted the snow. He fell fast asleep; and while sleep-ing, the sun beat so hot upon him, that it singed and drew up his bird-skin coat, so that when he awoke and stretched himself, he felt bound in it, as it were. He looked down and saw the damage done to his coat. He flew into a passion, and upbraided the sun, and vowed vengeance against it. "Do not think you are too high," said he, "I shall revenge myself."

On coming home, he related his disaster to his sister, and lamented bitterly the spoiling of his coat. He would not eat. He lay down as one that fasts, and, did not stir, or move his position for ten days, though she tried all she could to arouse him. At the end of ten days, he turned over, and then lay ten days on the other side. When he got up, he told his sister to make him a snare, for he meant to catch the sun. She said she had nothing; but finally recollected a little piece of dried deer's sinew, that her father had left, which she soon made into a string suitable for a noose. But the moment she showed it to him, he told her it would not do, and bid her get something else. She said she had nothing—nothing at all. At last she thought of her hair, and pulling some of it out of her head, made a string. But he instantly said it would not answer, and bid her, pettishly, and with authority, make him a noose. She told him there was nothing to make it of, and went out of the lodge. She said to herself, when she had got without the lodge, and while she was all alone, "neow obewy indapin." From my body, some sinews will I take. This she did, and twisting them into a tiny cord, she handed it to her brother. The moment he saw this curious braid, he was delighted. "This will do," he said, and immediately put it to his mouth and began pulling it through his lips; and as fast as he drew it changed it into a red metal cord, which he wound around his body and shoulders, till he had a large quantity. He then prepared himself, and set out a little after midnight, that he might catch the sun before it rose. He fixed his snare on a spot just where the sun would strike the land, as it rose above the earth's disk; and sure enough, he caught the sun, so that it was held fast in the cord, and did not rise.

The animals who ruled the earth were immediately put into a great commotion. They had no light. They called a council to debate upon the matter, and to appoint some one to go and cut the cord—for this was a very hazardous enterprise, as the rays of the sun would burn whoever came so near to them. At last the dormouse undertook it—for at this time the dormouse was the largest animal in the world. When it stood up it looked like a mountain. When it got to the place where the sun was snared, its back began to smoke and burn with the intensity of the heat, and the top of its carcass was reduced to enormous heaps of ashes. It succeeded, however, in cutting the cord with its teeth, and freeing the sun, but it was reduced to a very small size, and has remained so ever since. Men call it the Kug-e-been-gwa-kwa—the blind woman.

BENJAMIN FRANKLIN.

For quite some time, Benjamin Franklin carried on his shoulders the entire intellectual reputation of the young United States. He was strong enough for the burden. As a scientist, he was equal to the greatest minds of the Old World; as a wit, he fascinated the famously witty city of Paris. For American audiences, he produced the famous homespun aphorisms of Poor Richard; for his European friends, he dealt in a more sophisticated form of humor. Here we have examples of both styles.

SAYINGS OF POOR RICHARD.

Here comes the Orator! with his Flood of Words, and his Drop of Reason.

Blame-all and Praise-all are two blockheads.

Serving God is Doing Good to Man, but Praying is thought an easier Service, and therefore more generally chosen.

Three may keep a Secret, if two of them are dead.

To be proud of Knowledge, is to be blind with Light; to be proud of Virtue, is to poison yourself with the Antidote.

7

Many would live by their Wits, but break for want of Stock.

Nothing humbler than *Ambition*, when it is about to climb.

Who is wise? He that learns from every One.
Who is powerful? He that governs his Passions.
Who is rich? He that is content.
Who is that? Nobody.

A learned blockhead is a greater blockhead than an ignorant one.

Fish & Visitors stink in 3 days.

There's more old Drunkards than old Doctors.

God heals, and the Doctor takes the Fees.

A good Lawyer is a bad Neighbor.

The World is full of fools and faint hearts; and yet every one has courage enough to bear the misfortunes, and wisdom enough to manage the Affairs of his neighbor.

How many observe Christ's Birth-day! How few, his Precepts! O! 'tis easier to keep Holidays than Commandments.

Old Boys have their Playthings as well as young Ones; the Difference is only in the Price.

Setting too good an Example is a Kind of Slander seldom forgiven; 'tis *Scandalum Magnatum*.

APOLOGUE ON WAR.

From a Letter to the Rev. Dr. Priestly.

In what light we are viewed by superior beings, may be gathered from a piece of late West India news, which possibly has not yet reached you. A young angel of distinction being sent down to this world on some business, for the first time, had an old courier-spirit assigned him as a guide. They arrived over the seas of Martinico, in the middle of the long day of obstinate fight between the fleets of Rodney and De Grasse. When, through the clouds of smoke, he saw the fire of the guns, the docks covered with mangled limbs, and bodies dead or dying; the ships sinking, burning, or blown into the air; and the quantity of pain, misery, and destruction, the crews yet alive were thus with so much eagerness dealing round to one another; he turned angrily to his guide, and said, "You blundering blockhead, you are ignorant of your business; you undertook to con duct me to the earth, and you have brought me into hell!" "No, sir," says the guide, "I have made no mistake; this is really the earth, and these arc men. Devils never treat one another in this

9

cruel manner; they have more sense, and more of what men (vainly) call humanity."

THE EPHEMERA;

An Emblem of Human Life.
(Translated from the French.)

You MAY REMEMBER, my dear friend, that when we lately spend that happy day in the delightful garden and sweet society of the Moulin Joly, I stopped a little in one of our walks, and stayed some time behind the company. We had been shown numberless skeletons of a kind of little fly, called an ephemera, whose successive generations, we were told, were bred and expired within the day. I happened to see a living company of them on a leaf, who appeared to be engaged in conversation. You know I understand all the inferior animal tongues. My too great application to the study of them is the best excuse I can give for the little progress I have made in your charming language. I listened through curiosity to the discourse of these little creatures; but as they, in their national vivacity, spoke three or four together, I could make but little of their conversation. I found, however, by some broken expressions that I heard now and then, they were disputing warmly on the merit of two foreign musicians, one a cousin, the other a *moscheto;* in which dispute they spent their time, seemingly as regardless of the shortness of life as if they had been sure of living a month.

10

Happy people! thought I; you are certainly under a wise, just, and mild government, since you have no public grievances to complain of, nor any subject of contention but the perfections and imperfections of foreign music. I turned my head from them to an old gray-headed one, who was single on another leaf, and talking to himself. Being amused with his soliloquy, I put it down in writing, in hopes it will likewise amuse her to whom I am so much indebted for the most pleasing of all amusements, her delicious company and heavenly harmony.

"It was," said he, "the opinion of learned philosophers of our race, who lived and flourished long before my time, that this vast world, the Moulin Joly, could not itself subsist more than eighteen hours; and I think there was some foundation for that opinion, since, by the apparent motion of the great luminary that gives life to all nature, and which in my time has evidently declined considerably towards the ocean at the end of our earth, it must then finish its course, be extinguished in the waters that surround us, and leave the world in cold and darkness, necessarily producing universal death and destruction. I have lived seven of those hours, a great age, being no less than four hundred and twenty minutes of time. How very few of us continue so long! I have seen generations born, flourish, and expire. My present friends are the children and grandchildren of the friends of my youth, who are now, also, no more! And I must soon follow them; for, by the course of nature, though still in health, I cannot expect to live above seven or eight minutes longer. What now avails all my toil and labor in amassing

11

honey-dew on this leaf, which I cannot live to enjoy! What the political struggles I have been engaged in for the good of my compatriot inhabitants of this bush, or my philosophical studies for the benefit of our race in general! for in politics what can laws do without morals? Our present race of ephemera will in a course of minutes become corrupt, like those of other and older bushes, and consequently as wretched. And in philosophy how small our progress! Alas! art is long, and life is short! My friends would comfort me with the idea of a name they say I shall leave behind me; and they tell me I have lived long enough to nature and to glory. But what will fame be to an ephemera who no longer exists? And what will become of all history in the eighteenth hour, when the world itself, even the whole Moulin Joly, shall come to its end and be buried in universal ruin?"

To me, after all my eager pursuits, no solid pleasures now remain, but the reflection of a long life spent in meaning well, the sensible conversation of a few good lady ephemeræ, and now and then a kind smile and a tune from the ever amiable *Brillante*.

FRANCIS HOPKINSON.

Signer of the Declaration of Independence, designer of the American flag and our Great Seal, Francis Hopkinson was also known for his wit. Sometimes it was hard for him to get himself taken seriously. For the services of designing flags, seals, currency, and so on, Mr. Hopkinson at first asked Congress for a quarter-cask of the Public Wine. That seems to have been taken as a joke, so he asked for money. It will not surprise anyone familiar with the workings of Congress under the Articles of Confederation to hear that this second request was also treated as a joke.

Hopkinson kept up spirits in Philadelphia during the Revolutionary War with a series of sarcastic satires, of which this letter is a pretty fair specimen. The beginning refers to his previous letter, in which our Tory correspondent had been shocked by the rebel sentiments of a friend whom he had supposed to be a Tory as well. The *Pennsylvania Ledger* was a paper of notoriously Tory sentiments, accused by the rebel side of printing false propaganda planted by British interests.

LETTER FROM A TORY.

Mr. Printer,

It is not easy to conceive how much I was surprised and disappointed at the discourse of my friend, as communicated to you in my last. There are indeed some whom we confide in with safety in these precarious times: and people should be very cautious in opening their minds before persons of a doubtful political character.

It is a rule in our tory society to be very circumspect in this particular—But I confess that, in this instance, I was not as prudent as I should have been; and I have had the mortification of being reprimanded for my indiscretion before a full meeting.

You can hardly imagine what regularity prevails in our board of tories. We are all formed into committees of various denominations, and appointed to various duties. I have myself the honour to belong to *the committee of wiles and stratagems*. It was I, Mr. Printer, who planned the scheme for stealing the mail sent by General Washington to congress.[1]—And my design was so successfully executed, that whilst the committee of congress were searching Bristol for those letters, they were then on their way to our friend General Howe; where they safely arrived, as we have been since informed. You may be sure that I gained great applause for this manœuvre.

We have also a *committee of false reports;*— whose duty is to fabricate and publish such articles of intelligence as may tend to alarm and terrify timid whigs, and distract the minds of the people. These are circulated at such times as the situation of public affairs may

---

[1] By this Mail (which was stole from off the express horse, whilst he was refreshing himself at Bristol) Gen. Howe was informed of the situation of the American army, and of the day on which most of the troops would be disbanded by the expiration of their enlistments. He accordingly came into Jersey with his whole force at the critical time and drove Gen. Washington over the Delaware.

make them most probable. Sometimes they are thrown out in whispers, in so dark and secret a manner that their origin cannot be traced; and at other times openly, by means of the *Pennsylvania Ledger*.

We have, moreover a *committee of true intelligence;* whose business it is to employ a number of spies, who are directed to mix amongst the people in the assumed character of zealous whigs; to hire themselves as servants and waiters in houses and taverns frequented by members of congress. This committee holds a regular correspondence with our friends in the British army; so that we are certainly informed of what passes on both sides, from the best authority, and are thereby enabled to take all advantages. Happily for us, the several ferries and stages have as yet been left free and open, so that our messengers pass and repass without examination, and of consequence this department has been attended with little or no difficulty.

Another committee is called the *committee of lies:* whose duty differs from that of false reports in this— the latter is to circulate misrepresentations of facts respecting the armies, and things of a public nature, on the large scale: whilst the former only frame temporary lies for the use of this city: particularly respecting the deliberations and intentions of congress. These lies must be fresh and fresh every day; and always supported by a strong assertion that the information came from some leaky member of congress; generally without mentioning the name of any individual member; yet, in cafes of urgency, the real name of some leading character may be adduced; when the lie may have had its operation before it can be contradicted.

There is likewise a *committee of extortion;* these are wealthy men, who monopolize, as far as they can, the articles most wanted for the rebel army; buy lip the necessaries of life, and put on them the highest prices they can with any appearance of propriety, in order to make the people discontented and uneasy.

The last committee I shall mention is the *committee of depreciation—as important as any*—they are to take all possible pains, and to exercise every subtile art to run down and depreciate the Continental currency. This committee is very large, and composed chiefly of bro-kers and monied men. They get some of this money, and run with it to discharge any debts they may have contracted, with a seeming anxiety to get rid of it as fast as possible. If they have goods for sale, they openly avow three prices: one, if the purchaser will agree to pay in hard money; an higher price, if in pro-vincial paper, under the old government; and a still higher, if in the present continental bills of credit. But we have many other ways of bringing that currency into disrepute, which I am not at liberty to mention.

I would give a list of the men of most influence in our society—at present this would be improper: but I will be more explicit hereafter, when toryism may be more safely and openly avowed. Some narrow minded people say, that we are doing all we can to ruin our country, and entail a miserable slavery on our unborn posterity. We believe we are doing the best we can for ourselves—and pray what has posterity done for us, that we should run the risk of confiscation and a halter for them? Our fixed opinion is, that the British army must eventually subdue this country—and setting the

16

right or wrong of the thing out of the question, we think we may as well have the reputation and advantage of assisting them in their designs as not. 'Tis true, if the British Generals should succeed in their enterprise we may see our neighbours and friends imprisoned by hundreds, and hanged by dozens; their estates confiscated, and their children turned out to beggary and want; but then we shall ourselves escape, and enjoy in safety our lives and estates—and, perhaps, be even promoted, for our present services, to places of honour and emolument.

I am, &c.

A TORY.

Teague at the President's Levee, by F. O. C. Darley.

HUGH HENRY BRACKENRIDGE.

Hugh Henry Brackenridge was a remarkable man: author of America's first important novel, founder of what became the University of Pittsburgh, state supreme-court justice, and urbane wit in what was still a rather rough little city across the Alleghenies from civilization. *Modern Chivalry*, his rambling picaresque novel, is the first important novel to be published by an American author, and a priceless picture of manners in the area around Pittsburgh in the late 1700s.

A review of an 1847 edition of his *Modern Chivalry* tells us this story of Brackenridge and President Washington: "Judge Brackenridge was accounted a great wit in the days of Washington, whom he endeavored to entertain with his stories upon one occasion at a public dinner, but without effect, the Presidential decorum not relaxing a muscle; but at night when the Father of his Country was laid aside with the buff and blue, the humorist had the satisfaction of hearing the bottled-up laughter of the day explode with many a gurgle through the thin partition which separated their bedrooms. Such was the prudence of Washington, and such the humor of Brackenridge."

LETTER TO THE PITTSBURGH GAZETTE.

Now the *Post-Gazette*, or officially *Pittsburgh Post-Gazette Sun-Telegraph The Pittsburgh Press*, this venerable paper, one of the world's oldest metropolitan newspapers, is still the leading institution in Pittsburgh journalism. Brackenridge financed it and contributed many amusing letters to the paper in its early days. In the late 1700s, dueling was a plague throughout America, and especially in Pittsburgh; a similar challenge and response, much elaborated, makes up an extended episode in *Modern Chivalry*. "Mr. Scull" was John Scull, the editor and founder of the *Gazette*.

Mr. Scull—The Age of Chivalry is not over; and challenges have been given even in the midst of a yellow fever which, one would think, was killing people fast enough already. The fear of God or the law, are usual and just grounds of refusing. But I will give you a sample of the way in which I get off with some of my challenges, in the following letter and answer on a late occasion; but omitting the name of the challenger, as I have no inclination to trouble him with a provocation.

PITTSBURGH, October 15, 1797.

Sir—I will thank you to take a walk with a friend and meet me at the back of the graveyard about sunrise to-morrow morning. After what has happened, you know what I mean.

Your humble servant, &c.

PITTSBURGH, October 15, 1797.

Sir—I know what you mean very well; you want to have a shot at me, but I have no inclination to be hit, and I am afraid you will hit me. I pray thee therefore have me excused.

H. H. BRACKENRIDGE.

FROM MODERN CHIVALRY.

The Author's Address to the Reader.

IT HAS BEEN a question, what would be the best means of fixing the English language? Some have thought of Dictionaries, others of Institutes; and Swift proposed, in his letters to the Earl of Oxford, the forming an academy of men of letters for this purpose, similar to that of France. Reflecting on the subject, it appeared to me that if some work were undertaken with a view to style, regarding thought as of secondary importance, it might do more to effect so desirable an end, than can be accomplished by all the dictionaries and institutes, that were ever made.

Following up this idea, without waiting for some one more competent to undertake the work, I here present the reader with a production in which style, language, and forms of expression, are more regarded than matter; as the unmeaning words fa, sol, la, are used in teaching the science of music. After becoming, in this way, master of musical tune and sound, these may be "married to immortal verse." It is scarcely in the power of human ingenuity, to do more than one thing well at a time. They mistake greatly, who think to have a clock, that can at once tell the hour of the day, the age of the moon, and the day of the week, month, or year; because the complexness of the ma-chine hinders that perfection which the simplicity of the works and movements can alone give. For it is not in nature to have all things in one. If you are about to choose a wife, and expect beauty, you must give up

21

family and fortune; or if you attain these, you must at least want good temper, health, or some other advantage; so, to expect good language, and good sense at the same time, is absurd, and not in the compass of common nature to produce. Attempting only one thing, therefore, we may entertain the idea of hitting the point of perfection. Culling out the choicest words of diction, then, I shall pay little regard to the idea, as it is not in the power of human ingenuity to attain two things perfectly at once. It has been owing to an inattention to this principle, that so many fail in their attempts at good writing. A Jack of all trades, is proverbial of a bungler; and we scarcely ever find one who excels in two parts of the same arts; much less in two arts at the same time. The smooth poet wants strength; the orator of a good voice, is destitute of logical reason and argument. How many have I heard speak, who, were they to attempt voice only, might be respectable; but undertaking, at the same time, to carry sense along with them, they utterly failed, and became contemptible. One thing at once, is the best maxim that ever came into the mind of man. This might be illustrated by a thousand examples; but I shall not trouble myself with any; as it is not so much my object to convince others, as to show the motives by which I myself am governed. Indeed I could give authority superior to all example, viz., that of the poet Horace; who, speaking on this very subject of excellence in writing, says, *Quidvis*, that is, whatever you compose, let it be, *simplex*, *duntaxit et unum:* that is, simple, and one thing only.

It will be needless for me to say any thing about the critics; for as this work is intended as a model of good writing, it cannot be the subject of criticism. It is true, Homer has been criticised by a Zoilus and an Aristotle; but the one contented himself with pointing out defects; the other beauties. But Zoilus has been censured, Aristotle praised; because, in a model, there can be no defect; error consisting in a deviation from the truth; and faults, in an aberration from the original of beauty; so that where there are no faults, there can be no food for criticism, taken in the unfavourable sense of finding fault with the productions of an author. I have no objection, therefore, to any praise that may be given to this work; but to censure, or blame, must appear absurd; because it cannot be doubted that it will perfectly answer the end proposed.

Notwithstanding this candid explanation of the author's design in this work, there will be ingenious readers, who will fancy, that they can discover in it distinct ideas and meaning; just as we distinguish forms in the embers of a fire, or on the accidental scratches on a wall. All that can be said in this case, is, that if the reader finds amusement in tracing such resemblances, let him enjoy it. Others may say, that in spite of the disclaimer just made, they can plainly discover much sound and wholesome doctrine in this book; if so, let them prize the more the treasure so unexpectedly found. Many will, perhaps, turn up their noses, and throw the book away with contempt; saying, "of what use is all this—a book without ideas, or only such as have no other effect than to cause a laugh!" And does he accomplish nothing who can do this? What is there which so much conduces to health? When I get a man to laugh, I put him in a good humour with himself, and his neighbour. Nothing does a man more good than a hearty laugh, and if it does him good, is it not of use to him? Here then is an argument strictly utilitarian, according to the most rigid rules of logic. As to the book having no idea, that will be all the better for those who like light reading, and do not wish to be troubled with the labour of thinking. In conclusion, it may be, after all, that there is a moral in the book, which the reader may discover if he will take the trouble to look for it. Truth is at the bottom of the well, and will remain there unless some one draws the bucket. Wishing the Reader all manner of happiness, for the present,

Vale—Valete,
THE AUTHOR.

The Indian Treaty-Man.

NOT LONG AFTER this, being at a certain place, the Captain was accosted by a stranger in the following manner:

"Captain Farrago," said he, "I have heard of a young man in your service who talks Irish. Now, Sir, my business is that of an Indian treaty maker; and am on my way with a party of kings, and half-kings, to the commissioners, to hold a treaty. My king of the Kickapoos, who was a Welch blacksmith, took sick by the way, and is dead: I have heard of this lad of yours, and could wish to have him a while to supply his place. The treaty will not last longer than a couple of weeks; and as the government will probably allow three or four thousand dollars for the treaty, it will be in our power to make it worth your while to spare him for that time."

"Your king of the Kickapoos," said the captain, "what does that mean ?"

Said the stranger, "It is just this: You have heard of the Indian nations to the westward, that occasionally make war upon the frontier settlements. It has been a policy of government to treat with these, and distribute goods. Commissioners are appointed for that purpose. Now you are not to suppose that it is an easy matter to catch a real chief, and bring him from the woods; or if at some expense one was brought, the goods would go to his use; whereas, it is much more profitable to hire substitutes, and make chiefs of our own. And as some unknown gibberish is necessary to pass for an Indian language, we generally make use of Welch, or Low Dutch, or Irish; or pick up an ingenious fellow here and there, who can imitate a language by sounds of his own, in his mouth and throat. But we prefer one who can speak a real tongue, and give more for him. We cannot afford you a great deal at this time for the use of your man; because it is not a general treaty, where twenty or thirty thousand dollars are appropriated for the purpose of holding it; but an occasional, or what we call a running treaty, by way of brightening the chain, and holding fast friendship. The commissioners will doubtless be glad to see us, and procure from government an allowance for the treaty. For the more treaties, the more use for commissioners. The business must be kept up, and treaties made, if there are none of themselves. My Piankasha, and Choctaw chiefs, are very good fellows; the one of them a Scotch pedlar that talks the Erse; the other has been some time in Canada, and has a little broken Indian, God knows what language; but has been of great service in assisting to teach the rest some Indian customs and manners. I have had the whole of them for a fortnight past under my tuition, teaching them war songs and dances, and to make responses at the treaty. If your man is tractable, I can make him a Kickapoo in about nine days. A breech-clout and leggins, that I took off the blacksmith that died, I have ready to put on him. He must have part of his head shaved, and painted, with feathers on his crown; but the paint will rub off, and the hair grow in a short time, so that he can go about with you again."

"It is a very strange affair," said the captain. "Is it possible that such deception can be practised in a new country? It astonishes me that the government does not detect such imposition."

"The government," said the Indian treaty-man, "is at a great distance. It knows no more of Indians than a cow does of Greek. The legislature hears of wars and rumours of wars, and supports the executive in forming treaties. How is it possible for men who live remote from the scene of action, to have adequate ideas of the nature of Indians, or the transactions that are carried on in their behalf? Do you think the one half of those savages that come to treat, are real representatives of the nation? Many of them are not savages at all; but

26

weavers and pedlars, as I have told you, picked up to make kings and chiefs. I speak of those particularly that come trading down to inland towns, or the metropolis. I would not communicate these mysteries of our trade, were it not that I confide in your good sense, and have occasion for your servant."

"It is a mystery of iniquity," said the captain. "Do you suppose that I would countenance such a fraud upon the public ?"

"I do not know," said the other; "it is a very common thing for men to speculate, now-a-days. If you will not, another will. An hundred dollars might as well be in your pocket as another man's. I will give you that for the use of your servant for a week or two, and say no more about it."

"It is an idea new to me entirely," said the captain, "that Indian princes, whom I have seen escorted down as such, were no more than trumpery, disguised, as you mention; that such should be introduced to polite assemblies, and have the honour to salute the fair ladies with a kiss, the greatest beauties thinking themselves honoured by having the salutation of a sovereign."

"It is so," said the other; "I had a bricklayer once, whom I passed for a Chippewa; and who has dined with clubs, and sat next the president. He was blind of an eye, and was called blind Sam by the traders. I had given it out that he was a great warrior, and had lost his eye by an arrow in war with a rival nation. These things are now reduced to a system; and it is so well known to those who are engaged in the traffic, that we think nothing of it."

27

"How the devil," said the captain, "do you get speeches made, and interpret them so as to pass for truth ?"

"That is an easy matter," said the other; "Indian speeches are nearly all alike. You have only to talk of burying hatchets under large trees, kindling fires, brightening chains; with a demand, at the latter end, of rum to get drunk on."

"I much doubt," said the captain, "whether treaties that are carried on in earnest are of any great use."

"Of none at all," said the other; "especially as the practice of giving goods prevails; because this is an in-ducement to a fresh war. This being the case, it can be no harm to make a farce of the whole matter; or rather a profit of it, by such means as I propose to you, and have pursued myself."

"After all," said the captain, " I cannot but consider it as a kind of contraband and illicit traffic; and I must be excused from having any hand in it. I shall not be-tray your secret, but I shall not favour it. It would ill become me, whose object in riding about in this man-ner, is to impart just ideas on all subjects, to share in such ill-gotten gain."

The Indian treaty-man, finding it in vain to say more, withdrew.

———◦◉◦———

The captain, apprehending that he might not yet drop his designs upon the Irishman, but be tampering with him out of doors, should he come across him, sent for Teague. For he well knew, that, should the Indian treaty-man get the first word of him, the idea of making him a king would turn his head, and it would be impossible to prevent his going with him.

Teague coming in, said the captain to him, "Teague, I have discovered in you, for some time past, a great spirit of ambition, which is, doubtless, commendable in a young person; and I have checked it only in cases where there was real danger, or apparent mischief. There is now an opportunity of advancing yourself, not so much in the way of honour, as profit. But profit brings honour, and is, indeed, the most substantial support of it. There has been a man here with me, that carries on a trade with the Indians, and tells me that red-headed scalps are in great demand with them. If you could spare yours, he would give a good price for it. I do not well know what use they make of this article, but so it is, the traders find their account in it. Probably they dress it with the hairy side out, and make tobacco pouches for the chiefs, when they meet in council. It saves dying; and, besides, the natural red hair of a man may, in their estimation, be superior to any colour they can give by art. The taking off the scalp will not give much pain, it is so dexterously done by them with a crooked knife they have for that purpose. The mode of taking off the scalp is this: You lie down on your face; a warrior puts his feet upon your shoulders, collects your hair in his left hand, and drawing a circle with the knife in his right, makes the incision, and with a sudden pull, separates it from the head, giving, in the mean time, what is called the scalp yell. The thing is done in such an instant, that the pain is scarcely felt. He offered me an hundred dollars, if I

would have it taken off for his use; giving me direc-
tions, in the mean time, how to stretch it and dry it on
a hoop. I told him, No; it was a perquisite of your
own, and you might dispose of it as you thought
proper. If you chose to dispose of it, I had no objections; but the bargain should be of your own making,
and the price such as should please yourself. I have
sent for you to give you a hint of this chapman, that
you may have a knowledge of his wish to possess the
property, and ask accordingly. It is probable you may
bring him up to a half Johannes more by holding out a
little. But I do not think it would be advisable to lose
the bargain. An hundred dollars for a little hairy flesh
is a great deal. You will trot a long time before you
make that with me. He will be with you probably to
propose the purchase. You will know him when you
see him: he is a tall-looking man, with leggins on, and
has several Indians with him going to a treaty. He
talked to me something of making you a king of the
Kickapoos, after the scalp is off; but I would not count
on that so much; because words are but wind, and
promises are easily broken. I would advise you to make
sure of the money in the first place, and take chance
for the rest."

I have seen among the prints of Hogarth, some such
expression of countenance as that of Teague at this instant; who, as soon as he could speak, but with a double brogue on his tongue, began to intimate his disin-
clination to the traffic. The hair of his scalp, itself, in
the mean time, had risen in opposition to it. "Dear
master, vid you trow me into ridicule, and de blessed
salvation of my life, and all dat I have in de world, to

be trown like a dog to de savages, and have my flesh torn off my head to give to dese vild bastes to make a napsack to carry deir patates and tings in, for an hundred dollars or de like? It shall never be said that de hair of de O'Regans made mackeseens for a vild Indian to trat upon. I would sooner trow my own head, hair and all in de fire, dan give it to dese paple to smoke wid out of deir long pipes."

"If this be your determination," said the captain, "it will behoove you to keep yourself somewhat close; and while we remain at this public house, avoid any conversation with the chapman or his agents, should they come to tamper with you. For it is not improbable, while they are keeping you in talk, proposing to make you a Kickapoo chief and the like, they may snatch the scalp off your head, and you not be the wiser for it."

Teague thought the caution good, and resolving to abide by it, retired to the kitchen. The maid at this time, happening to want a log of wood, requested Teague to cut it for her. Taking the axe, accordingly, and going out, he was busy chopping, with his head down; while, in the mean time, the Indian treaty man had returned with one in Indian dress, who was the chief of the Killinoos, or at least passed for such; and whom he brought as having some recruiting talents, and might prevail with Teague to elope and join the company.

"I suppose," said the Indian treaty-man, "you are the waiter of the captain who lodges here at present."

Teague hearing a man speak, and lifting up his head, saw the leggins on the one, and the Indian dress on the other; and with a kind of involuntary effort

31

threw the axe directly from him at the Killinoo. It missed him but about an inch, and fell behind. Teague, in the mean time, raising a shout of desperation, was fixed on the spot, and his locomotive faculties suspended; so that he could neither retreat nor advance, but stood still, like one enchained or enchanted for a moment; the king of the Killinoos, in the mean time, drawing his tomahawk, and preparing for battle.

The captain, who was reading at a front window, hearing the shout, looked about and saw what was going on at the woodpile. "Stop villain," said he, to the king of the Killinoos; "you are not to take that scalp yet, however much you may value it. He will not take an hundred dollars for it, nor five hundred, though you make him king of the Kickapoos, or any thing else. It is no trifling matter to have the ears slit in tatters, and the nose run through with a bodkin, and a goose-quill stuck across; so that you may go about your business —you will get no king of the Kickapoos here."

Under cover of this address of the captain, Teague had retired to the kitchen, and ensconced himself behind the rampart of the maid. The Indian treaty man, and the Killinoo chief, finding the measure hopeless, withdrew, and turned their attention, it is to be supposed, to some other quarter to find a king of the Kickapoos, while the captain, after paying his score, set out on his travels.

SALMAGUNDI.

This irregular paper burst into New York from nowhere in 1807, and it was immediately obvious that the young United States had never seen anything like it. "The sensation produced by this whimsical miscellany," wrote Rufus Wilmot Griswold, "is described by the 'old inhabitants' as exceeding any thing of the kind ever known in New York. Its amusing ridicule of the ignorance and vulgarity of British tourists, and of all sorts of foreign adventurers and home pretenders, with its occasional dashes of graceful sentiment, captivated the town and decided the fortunes of its authors."

The first number set the tone for the rest—a tone of winking overconfidence, pointed sarcasm, and occasionally juvenile humor (would anyone much over college age give his characters names like Launcelot Langstaff and Pindar Cockloft?).

As for the authors, they were three young men of distinct talent. One of them, Washington Irving, would go on to be America's first writer of international repute. James Kirke Paulding would never equal Washington Irving's success; but he was funnier than Irving, and his style is perhaps more distinctively American. (Ten years later, he attempted a revival of *Salmagundi* on his own, which was not as successful as the original.) The third was Washington Irving's older brother William, who did not pursue a literary life, and died fairly young a little more than a decade later. His memory lived on in the name of James K. Paulding's son, William Irving Paulding—an indication of what close friends the Irvings and Pauldings were.

If this paper had accomplished nothing else, it would have earned its place in history by attaching the name "Gotham" to New York City. But the fact that the name stuck shows us that the paper had influence. It gave us Americans a glimpse of limitless possibilities; at a time when the United States had no native literary culture to speak of, *Salmagundi* suggested a future in which American writers had no need to bow down before English models.

NO. I.— SATURDAY, JANUARY 24, 1807.

As EVERYBODY KNOWS, or ought to know, what a Salmagund is, we shall spare ourselves the trouble of an explanation; besides, we despise trouble as we do everything low and mean, and hold the man who would incur it unnecessarily as an object worthy our highest pity and contempt. Neither will we puzzle our heads to give an account of ourselves, for two reasons; first, because it is nobody's business; secondly, because if it were, we do not hold ourselves bound to attend to anybody's business but our own; and even that we take the liberty of neglecting when it suits our inclination. To these we might add a third, that very few men can give a tolerable account of themselves, let them try ever so hard; but this reason, we candidly avow, would not hold good with ourselves.

There are, however, two or three pieces of information which we bestow gratis on the public, chiefly because it suits our own pleasure and convenience that they should be known, and partly because we do not wish that there should be any ill will between us at the commencement of our acquaintance.

Our intention is simply to instruct the young, reform the old, correct the town, and castigate the age;

this is an arduous task, and therefore we undertake it with confidence. We intend for this purpose to present a striking picture of the town; and as everybody is anxious to see his own phiz on canvas, however stupid or ugly it may be, we have no doubt but the whole town will flock to our exhibition. Our picture will necessarily include a vast variety of figures; and should any gentleman or lady be displeased with the inveterate truth of their likenesses, they may ease their spleen by laughing at those of their neighbors—this being what we understand by *poetical justice*.

Like all true and able editors, we consider ourselves infallible; and therefore, with the customary diffidence of our brethren of the quill, we shall take the liberty of interfering in all matters either of a public or private nature. We are critics, amateurs, dilettanti and cognoscenti; and as we know "by the pricking of our thumbs," that every opinion which we may advance in either of those characters will be correct, we are determined, though it may be questioned, contradicted, or even controverted, yet it shall never be revoked.

We beg the public particularly to understand that we solicit no patronage. We are determined, on the contrary, that the patronage shall be entirely on our side. We have nothing to do with the pecuniary concerns of the paper; its success will yield us neither pride nor profit—nor will its failure occasion to us either loss or mortification. We advise the public, therefore, to purchase our numbers merely for their own sakes; if they do not, let them settle the affair with their consciences and posterity.

To conclude, we invite all editors of newspapers and literary journals to praise us heartily in advance, as we assure them that we intend to deserve their praises. To our next-door neighbor, "Town," we hold out a hand of amity, declaring to him that, after ours, his paper will stand the best chance for immortality. We proffer an exchange of civilities: he shall furnish us with notices of epic poems and tobacco; and we, in return, will enrich him with original speculations on all manner of subjects, together with "the rummaging of my grandfather's mahogany chest of drawers," "the life and amours of mine Uncle John," "anecdotes of the Cockloft family," and learned quotations from that unheard of writer of folios, *Linkum Fidelius*.

NO. XI.—TUESDAY, JUNE 2, 1807.

Letter from Mustapha Rub-a-Dub Keli Khan, Captain of a Ketch, to Asem Hacchem, Principal Slave Driver to His Highness the Bashaw of Tripoli.

THE DEEP SHADOWS of midnight gather around me; the footsteps of the passengers have ceased in the streets, and nothing disturbs the holy silence of the hour save the sound of the distant drums, mingled with the shouts, the bawlings, and the discordant revelry of his majesty, the Sovereign Mob. Let the hour be sacred to friendship, and consecrated to thee, O thou brother of my inmost soul!

O Asem! I almost shrink at the recollection of the scenes of confusion, of licentious disorganization which I have witnessed during the last three days. I have beheld this whole city, nay, this whole State, given up to the tongue and the pen; to the puffers, the bawlers, the babblers, and the slang-whangers. I have beheld the community convulsed with a civil war, or civil talk; individuals verbally massacred, families annihilated by whole sheets full, and slang-whangers coolly bathing their pens in ink and rioting in the slaughter of their thousands. I have seen, in short, that awful despot, the People, in the moment of unlimited power, wielding newspapers in one hand, and with the other scattering mud and filth about, like some desperate lunatic relieved from the restraints of his strait waistcoat. I have seen beggars on horseback, ragamuffins riding in coaches, and swine seated in places of honor; I have seen liberty; I have seen equality; I have seen fraternity. I have seen that great political puppet-show—AN ELECTION.

A few days ago the friend, whom I have mentioned in some of my former letters, called upon me to accompany him to witness this grand ceremony; and we forthwith sallied out to the polls, as he called them. Though for several weeks before this splendid exhibition nothing else had been talked of, yet I do assure thee I was entirely ignorant of its nature; and when, on coming up to a church, my companion informed me we were at the polls, I supposed that an election was some great religious ceremony, like the fast of Ramazan, or the great festival of Haraphat, so celebrated in the East.

My friend, however, undeceived me at once, and entered into a long dissertation on the nature and object of an election, the substance of which was nearly to this effect: "You know," said he, "that this country is engaged in a violent internal warfare, and suffers a variety of evils from civil dissensions. An election is the grand trial of strength, the decisive battle when the belligerents draw out their forces in martial array; when every leader, burning with warlike ardor, and encouraged by the shouts and acclamations of tatterdemalions, buffoons, dependents, parasites, toad-eaters, scrubs, vagrants, mumpers, ragamuffins, bravoes, and beggars in his rear; and puffed up by his bellows-blowing slang-whangers, waves gallantly the banners of faction, and presses forward TO OFFICE AND IMMORTALITY!

"For a month or two previous to the critical period which is to decide this important affair, the whole community is in a ferment. Every man, of whatever rank or degree—such is the wonderful patriotism of the people—disinterestedly neglects his business to devote himself to his country; and not an insignificant fellow but feels himself inspired, on this occasion, with as much warmth in favor of the cause he has espoused, as if all the comfort of his life, or even his life itself, was dependent on the issue. Grand councils of war are, in the first place, called by the different powers, which are dubbed general meetings, where all the head workmen of the party collect, and arrange the order of battle—appoint their different commanders, and their subordinate instruments, and furnish the funds indispensable for supplying the expenses of the war. Inferior councils are next called in the different classes or

38

wards, consisting of young cadets, who are candidates for offices; idlers who come there for mere curiosity; and orators who appear for the purpose of detailing all the crimes, the faults, or the weaknesses of their opponents, and speaking *the sense of the meeting*, as it is called; for as the meeting generally consists of men whose quota of sense, taken individually, would make but a poor figure, these orators are appointed to collect it all in a lump; when, I assure you, it makes a very formidable appearance, and furnishes sufficient matter to spin an oration of two or three hours.

"The orators who declaim at these meetings are, with a few exceptions, men of most profound and perplexed eloquence; who are the oracles of barbers' shops, market-places, and porter-houses; and whom you may see every day at the corners of the streets, taking honest men prisoners by the button, and talking their ribs quite bare without mercy and without end. These orators, in addressing an audience, generally mount a chair, a table, or an empty beer barrel, which last is supposed to afford considerable inspiration, and thunder away their combustible sentiments at the heads of the audience, who are generally so busily employed in smoking, drinking, and hearing themselves talk, that they seldom hear a word of the matter. This, however, is of little moment: for as they come there to agree, at all events, to a certain set of resolutions, or articles of war, it is not at all necessary to hear the speech; more especially as few would understand it if they did. Do not suppose, however, that the minor persons of the meeting are entirely idle. Besides smoking and drinking, which are generally practiced, there are few who do not come with as great a desire to talk as the orator himself; each has his little circle of listeners, in the midst of whom he sets his hat on one side of his head, and deals out matter-of-fact information, and draws self-evident conclusions with the pertinacity of a pedant, and to the great edification of his gaping auditors. Nay, the very urchins from the nursery, who are scarcely emancipated from the dominion of birch, on these occasions strut pigmy great men, bellow for the instruction of gray-bearded ignorance, and, like the frog in the fable, endeavor to puff themselves up to the size of the great object of their emulation—the principal orator."

"But is it not preposterous to a degree," cried I, "for those puny whipsters to attempt to lecture age and experience? They should be sent to school to learn better." "Not at all," replied my friend; "for as an election is nothing more than a war of words, the man that can wag his tongue with the greatest elasticity, whether he speaks to the purpose or not, is entitled to lecture at ward meetings and polls, and instruct all who are inclined to listen to him; you may have remarked a ward meeting of politic dogs, where, although the great dog is, ostensibly, the leader, and makes the most noise, yet every little scoundrel of a cur has something to say; and in proportion to his insignificance, fidgets, and worries, and puffs about mightily, in order to obtain the notice and approbation of his betters. Thus it is with these little, beardless, bread-and-butter politicians, who on this occasion, escape from the jurisdiction of their mammas to attend to the affairs of the nation. You will see them engaged in dreadful wordy contest with old cartmen, cobblers, and tailors, and plume themselves not a little if they should chance to gain a victory. Aspiring spirits! how interesting are the first dawnings of political greatness! An election, my friend, is a nursery or hot-bed of genius in a logocracy; and I look with enthusiasm on a troop of these Lilliputian partisans, as so many chatterers, and orators and puffers, and slang-whangers in embryo, who will one day take an important part in the quarrels and wordy wars of their country.

"As the time for fighting the decisive battle approaches, appearances become more and more alarming; committees are appointed, who hold little encampments from whence they send out small detachments of tattlers, to reconnoitre, harass, and skirmish with the enemy, and, if possible, ascertain their numbers; everybody seems big with the mighty event that is impending; the orators, they gradually swell up beyond their usual size; the little orators, they grow greater and greater; the secretaries of the ward committees strut about, looking like wooden oracles; the puffers put on the airs of mighty consequence; the slang-whangers deal out direful innuendoes, and threats of doughty import, and all is buzz, murmur, suspense, and sublimity!

"At length the day arrives. The storm that has been so long gathering and threatening in distant thunders, bursts forth in terrible explosion; all business is at an end; the whole city is in a tumult; the people are running helter-skelter, they know not whither, and they know not why; the hackney coaches rattle through the streets with thundering vehemence, loaded with recruiting sergeants who have been prowling in cellars

and caves, to unearth some miserable minion of
poverty and ignorance, who will barter his vote for a
glass of beer, or a ride in a coach with such *fine gentlemen!*—the buzzards of the party scamper from poll to
poll, on foot or on horseback; and they worry from
committee to committee, and buzz, and fume, and talk
big, and—*do nothing;* like the vagabond drone, who
wastes his time in the laborious idleness of *see-saw-
song* and busy nothingness."

I know not how long my friend would have continued his detail, had he not been interrupted by a squab-
ble which took place between two old continentals, as
they were called. It seems they had entered into an argument on the respective merits of their cause, and not
being able to make each other clearly understood, re-
sorted to what is called knock-down arguments, which
form the superlative degree of *argumentum ad hominem;*
but are, in my opinion, extremely inconsistent with the
true spirit of a genuine logocracy. After they had
beaten each other soundly, and set the whole mob together by the ears, they came to a full explanation;
when it was discovered that they were both of the
same way of thinking; whereupon they shook each
other heartily by the hand, and laughed with great glee
at their humorous misunderstanding.

I could not help being struck with the exceeding
great number of ragged, dirty-looking persons that
swaggered about the place, and seemed to think themselves the bashaws of the land. I inquired of my friend
if these people were employed to drive away the hogs,
dogs, and other intruders that might thrust themselves
in and interrupt the ceremony? "By no means," replied

he; "these are the representatives of the sovereign people, who come here to make governors, senators, and
members of assembly, and are the source of all power
and authority in this nation." "Preposterous !" said I;
"how is it possible that such men can be capable of
distinguishing between an honest man and a knave; or,
even if they were, will it not always happen that they
are led by the nose by some intriguing demagogue, and
made the mere tools of ambitious political jugglers?
Surely it would be better to trust to Providence, or
even to chance, for governors, than resort to the dis-
criminating powers of an ignorant mob. I plainly perceive the consequence. A man, who possesses superior
talents, and that honest pride which ever accompanies
this possession, will always be sacrificed by some
creeping insect who will prostitute himself to familiar-
ity with the lowest of mankind; and, like the idolatrous
Egyptian, worship the wallowing tenants of filth and
mire."

"All this is true enough," replied my friend, "but
after all, you cannot say but that this is a free country,
and that the people can get drunk cheaper here, particularly at elections, than in the despotic countries of the
East." I could not, with any degree of propriety or
truth, deny this last assertion; for just at that moment a
patriotic brewer arrived with a load of beer, which, for
a moment, occasioned a cessation of argument. The
great crowd of buzzards, puffers, and "old continentals" of all parties, who throng to the polls, to persuade, to cheat, or to force the freeholders into the
right way, and to maintain the freedom of suffrage,
seemed for a moment to forget their antipathies, and

joined heartily in a copious libation of this patriotic and argumentative beverage.

These beer-barrels, indeed, seem to be most able logicians, well stored with that kind of sound argument best suited to the comprehension, and most relished by the mob, or sovereign people, who are never so tractable as when operated upon by this convincing liquor, which, in fact, seems to be imbued with the very spirit of a logocracy. No sooner does it begin its operation, than the tongue waxes exceeding valorous, and becomes impatient for some mighty conflict. The puffer puts himself at the head of his body-guard of buzzards, and his legion of ragamuffins, and woe then to every unhappy adversary who is uninspired by the deity of the beer-barrel—he is sure to be talked, and argued, into complete insignificance.

While I was making these observations, I was surprised to observe a bashaw, high in office, shaking a fellow by the hand, that looked rather more ragged than a scarecrow, and inquiring with apparent solicitude concerning the health of his family; after which he slipped a little folded paper into his hand and turned away. I could not help applauding his humility in shaking the fellow's hand, and his benevolence in relieving his distresses, for I imagined the paper contained something for the poor man's necessities; and truly he seemed verging toward the last stage of starvation. My friend, however, soon undeceived me by saying that this was an elector, and that the bashaw had merely given him the list of candidates for whom he was to vote. "Ho! ho!" said I, "then he is a particular friend of the bashaw?" "By no means," replied my friend, "the bashaw will pass him without notice, the day after the election, except, perhaps, just to drive over him with his coach."

My friend then proceeded to inform me that for some time before, and during the continuance of an election, there was a most delectable courtship, or intrigue carried on between the great bashaws and the mother mob. That mother Mob generally preferred the attentions of the rabble, or of fellows of her own stamp; but would sometimes condescend to be treated to a feasting, or anything of that kind, at the bashaw's expense! Nay, sometimes when she was in good humor, she would condescend to toy with him in her rough way: but woe to the bashaw who attempted to be familiar with her, for she was the most petulant, cross, crabbed, scolding, thieving, scratching, toping, wrongheaded, rebellious, and abominable termagant that ever was let loose in the world to the confusion of honest gentlemen bashaws.

Just then a fellow came round and distributed among the crowd a number of handbills, written by the ghost of Washington, the fame of whose illustrious actions, and still more illustrious virtues, have reached even the remotest regions of the East, and who is venerated by this people as the Father of his country. On reading this paltry paper, I could not restrain my indignation. "Insulted hero," cried I, "is it thus thy name is profaned, thy memory disgraced, thy spirit drawn down from heaven to administer to the brutal violence of party rage? It is thus the necromancers of the East, by their infernal incantations, sometimes call up the shades of the just, to give their sanction to

45

frauds, to lies, and to every species of enormity." My
friend smiled at my warmth, and observed, that raising
ghosts, and not only raising them but making them
speak, was one of the miracles of election. "And believe me," continued he, "there is good reason for the
ashes of departed heroes being disturbed on these occasions, for such is the sandy foundation of our government, that there never happens an election of an alder-
man, or a collector, or even a constable, but we are in
imminent danger of losing our liberties, and becoming
a province of France, or tributary to the British islands." "By the hump of Mahomet's camel," said I,
"but this is only another striking example of the prodigious great scale on which everything is transacted in
this country!"

By this time I had become tired of the scene; my
head ached with the uproar of voices, mingling in all
the discordant tones of triumphant exclamation, non-
sensical argument, intemperate reproach, and drunken
absurdity. The confusion was such as no language can
adequately describe, and it seemed as if all the restraints of decency, and all the bands of law, had been
broken and given place to the wide ravages of licentious brutality. These, thought I, are the orgies of liberty! these are manifestations of the spirit of independence! these are the symbols of man's sovereignty!
Head of Mahomet! with what a fatal and inexorable
despotism do empty names and ideal phantoms exercise their dominion over the human mind! The experience of ages has demonstrated, that in all nations, barbarous or enlightened, the mass of the people, the
mob, must be slaves, or they will be tyrants; but their

tyranny will not be long: some ambitious leader, having at first condescended to be their slave, will at
length become their master; and in proportion to the
vileness of his former servitude, will be the severity of
his subsequent tyranny. Yet, with innumerable examples staring them in the face, the people still bawl out
liberty; by which they mean nothing but freedom from
every species of legal restraint, and a warrant for all
kinds of licentiousness: and the bashaws and leaders, in
courting the mob, convince them of their power; and
by administering to their passions, for the purposes of
ambition, at length learn, by fatal experience, that he
who worships the beast that carries him on his back,
will sooner or later be thrown into the dust, and tram-
pled under foot by the animal who has learnt the secret
of its power, by this very adoration.

Ever thine,

MUSTAPHA.

Washington Irving.

WASHINGTON IRVING.

It would be delightful to be able to say that Washington Irving needs no introduction; but the fact is that Irving is almost never read these days, even if his reputation as our first great literary figure is secure. The one story of his that everyone has heard of is his "Legend of Sleepy Hollow," but that has been curiously distorted in popular culture.

The *History of New-York* was Irving's first great success. Before it was published, Irving planted in the New York papers an amusing story of an eccentric old Dutchman, Diedrich Knickerbocker, who had disappeared from his rooms without paying his rent, leaving only a large manuscript behind; supposedly the landlord was printing the manuscript to make up his lost rent. As an advertising stunt, it was inspired; people were seriously worried about the poor old Dutchman, and the public was ready to eat up the book when it came out. The fact that New York still has a baseball team called the Knicks is proof enough that the book was a wild success.

FROM KNICKERBOCKER'S HISTORY OF NEW-YORK.

THE WRITER OF a history may, in some respects, be likened unto an adventurous knight, who having undertaken a perilous enterprise by way of establishing his fame, feels bound, in honor and chivalry to turn back for no difficulty nor hardship, and never to shrink or quail, whatever enemy he may encounter. Under this impression, I resolutely draw my pen, and fall to with

49

might and main at those doughty questions and subtle paradoxes which, like fiery dragons and bloody giants, beset the entrance to my history, and would fain repulse me from the very threshold. And at this moment a gigantic question has started up, which I must needs take by the beard and utterly subdue before I can advance another step in my historic undertaking; but I trust this will be the last adversary I shall have to contend with, and that in the next book I shall be enabled to conduct my readers in triumph into the body of my work.

The question which has thus suddenly arisen is, What right had the first discoverers of America to land and take possession of a country without first gaining the consent of its inhabitants, or yielding them an adequate compensation for their territory?—a question which has withstood many fierce assaults, and has given much distress of mind to multitudes of kind-hearted folk. And, indeed, until it be totally vanquished, and put to rest, the worthy people of America can by no means enjoy the soil they inhabit with clear right and title, and quiet, unsullied conscience.

The first source of right, by which property is acquired in a country, is DISCOVERY.[1] For as all mankind have an equal right to anything which has never before been appropriated, so any nation that discovers an uninhabited country, and takes possession thereof, is considered as enjoying full property, and absolute, unquestionable empire therein.

This proposition being admitted, it follows clearly that the Europeans who first visited America were the

---

[1] Grotius: Puffendorf, b. v. c. 4, Vattel, b. i. c. 18, etc.

real discoverers of the same; nothing being necessary to the establishment of this fact but simply to prove that it was totally uninhabited by man. This would at first appear to be a point of some difficulty, for it is well known that this quarter of the world abounded with certain animals, that walked erect on two feet, had something of the human countenance, uttered certain unintelligible sounds, very much like language; in short, had a marvelous resemblance to human beings. But the zealous and enlightened fathers who accompanied the discoverers, for the purpose of promoting the kingdom of heaven by establishing fat monasteries and bishoprics on earth, soon cleared up this point, greatly to the satisfaction of his holiness the Pope and of all Christian voyagers and discoverers.

They plainly proved, and, as there were no Indian writers arose on the other side, the fact was considered as fully admitted and established, that the two-legged race of animals before mentioned were mere cannibals, detestable monsters, and many of them giants—which last description of vagrants have, since the time of Gog, Magog, and Goliath, been considered as outlaws, and have received no quarter in either history, chivalry, or song. Indeed, even the philosophic Bacon declared the Americans to be people proscribed by the laws of nature, inasmuch as they had a barbarous custom of sacrificing men, and feeding upon man's flesh.

Nor are these all the proofs of their utter barbarism; among many other writers of discernment, Ulla tells us, "their imbecility is so visible that one can hardly form an idea of them different from what one has of the brutes. Nothing disturbs the tranquillity of their souls, equally insensible to disasters and to prosperity. Though half naked, they are as contented as a monarch in his most splendid array. Fear makes no impression on them, and respect as little." All this is furthermore supported by the authority of M. Boggier. "It is not easy," says he, "to describe the degree of their indifference for wealth and all its advantages. One does not well know what motives to propose to them when one would persuade them to any service. It is vain to offer them money; they answer they are not hungry." And Vane gas confirms the whole, assuring us that "ambition they have none, and are more desirous of being thought strong than valiant. The objects of ambition with us—honor, fame, reputation, riches, posts, and distinctions—are unknown among them. So that this powerful spring of action, the cause of so much *seeming* good and *real* evil in the world, has no power over them. In a word, these unhappy mortals may be compared to children, in whom the development of reason is not completed."

Now all these peculiarities, although in the unenlightened states of Greece they would have entitled their possessors to immortal honor, as having reduced to practice those rigid and abstemious maxims, the mere talking about which acquired certain old Greeks the reputation of sages and philosophers; yet were they clearly proved in the present instance to betoken a most abject and brutified nature, totally beneath the human character. But the benevolent fathers, who had undertaken to turn these unhappy savages into dumb beasts by dint of argument, advanced still stronger proofs; for as certain divines of the sixteenth century, and among the rest Lullus, affirm, the Americans go naked, and have no beards! "They have nothing," says Lullus, "of the reasonable animal, except the mask." And even that mask was allowed to avail them but little, for it was soon found that they were of a hideous copper complexion—and being of a copper complexion, it was all the same as if they were negroes—and negroes are black, "and black," said the pious fathers, devoutly crossing themselves, "is the color of the devil!" Therefore, so far from being able to own property, they had no right even to personal freedom—for liberty is too radiant a deity to inhabit such gloomy temples. All which circumstances plainly convinced the righteous followers of Cortes and Pizarro that these miscreants had no title to the soil that they infested— that they were a perverse, illiterate, dumb, beardless, *black-seed*—mere wild beasts of the forests and, like them, should either be subdued or exterminated.

From the foregoing arguments, therefore, and a variety of others equally conclusive, which I forbear to enumerate, it is clearly evident that this fair quarter of the globe, when first visited by Europeans, was a howling wilderness, inhabited by nothing but wild beasts; and that the transatlantic visitors acquired an incontrovertible property therein, *by the right of discovery*.

This right being fully established, we now come to the next, which is the right acquired by *cultivation*. "The cultivation of the soil," we are told, "is an obligation imposed by nature on mankind. The whole world is appointed for the nourishment of its inhabitants; but it would be incapable of doing it, was it un-

cultivated. Every nation is then obliged by the law of
nature to cultivate the ground that has fallen to its
share. Those people, like the ancient Germans and
modern Tartars, who, having fertile countries, disdain
to cultivate the earth, and choose to live by rapine, are
wanting to themselves, and *deserve to be exterminated
as savage and pernicious beasts.*"[1]

Now it is notorious that the savages knew nothing
of agriculture when first discovered by the Europeans,
but lived a most vagabond, disorderly, unrighteous life,
rambling from place to place, and prodigally rioting
upon the spontaneous luxuries of nature, without task-
ing her generosity to yield them anything more;
whereas it has been most unquestionably shown that
Heaven intended the earth should be ploughed, and
sown, and manured, and laid out into cities, and towns,
and farms, and country seats, and pleasure grounds,
and public gardens, all which the Indians knew nothing
about—therefore, they did not improve the talents
Providence had bestowed on them—therefore they
were careless stewards—therefore, they had no right to
the soil—therefore, they deserved to be exterminated.

It is true the savages might plead that they drew all
the benefits from the land which their simple wants required—they found plenty of game to hunt, which, together with the roots and uncultivated fruits of the
earth, furnished a sufficient variety for their frugal
repasts;—and that as Heaven merely designed the
earth to form the abode and satisfy the wants of man,
so long as those purposes were answered the will of
Heaven was accomplished.—But this only proves how

---

[1] Vattel, b. i. ch.

undeserving they were of the blessings around them—
they were so much the more savages for not having
more wants; for knowledge is in some degree an increase of desires, and it is this superiority both in the
number and magnitude of his desires that distinguishes
the man from the beast. Therefore the Indians, in not
having more wants, were very unreasonable animals;
and it was but just that they should make way for the
Europeans, who had a thousand wants to their one,
and, therefore, would turn the earth to more account,
and by cultivating it more truly fulfil the will of
Heaven. Besides—Grotius and Lauterbach, and
Puffendorf, and Titius, and many wise men beside,
who have considered the matter properly, have determined that the property of a country cannot be acquired by hunting, cutting wood, or drawing water in
it—nothing but precise demarcation of limits, and the
intention of cultivation, can establish the possession.
Now as the savages (probably from never having read
the authors above quoted) had never complied with any
of these necessary forms, it plainly follows that they
had no right to the soil, but that it was completely at
the disposal of the first comers, who had more knowledge, more wants, and more elegant, that is to say artificial, desires than themselves.

In entering upon a newly discovered, uncultivated
country, therefore, the new comers were but taking
possession of what, according to the aforesaid doctrine,
was their own property—therefore in opposing them,
the savages were invading their just rights, infringing
the immutable laws of nature, and counteracting the
will of Heaven—therefore, they were guilty of impiety,

burglary, and trespass on the case—therefore, they were hardened offenders against God and man—therefore, they ought to be exterminated.

But a more irresistible right than either that I have mentioned, and one which will be the most readily admitted by my reader, provided he be blessed with bowels of charity and philanthropy, is the right acquired by civilization. All the world knows the lamentable state in which these poor savages were found. Not only deficient in the comforts of life, but, what is still worse, most piteously and unfortunately blind to the miseries of their situation. But no sooner did the benevolent inhabitants of Europe behold their sad condition than they immediately went to work to ameliorate and improve it. They introduced among them rum, gin, brandy, and the other comforts of life—and it is astonishing to read how soon the poor savages learn to estimate those blessings—they likewise made known to them a thousand remedies, by which the most inveterate diseases are alleviated and healed; and that they might comprehend the benefits and enjoy the comforts of these medicines, they previously introduced among them the diseases which they were calculated to cure. By these and a variety of other methods was the condition of these poor savages wonderfully improved; they acquired a thousand wants of which they had before been ignorant, and as he has most sources of happiness who has most wants to be gratified, they were doubtlessly rendered a much happier race of beings.

But the most important branch of civilization, and which has most strenuously been extolled by the zealous and pious fathers of the Roman Church, is the introduction of the Christian faith. It was truly a sight that might well inspire horror, to behold these savages tumbling among the dark mountains of paganism, and guilty of the most horrible ignorance of religion. It is true, they neither stole nor defrauded; they were sober, frugal, continent, and faithful to their word; but though they acted right habitually, it was all in vain, unless they acted so from precept. The new comers, therefore, used every method to induce them to em- brace and practice the true religion—except, indeed, that of setting them the example.

But not withstanding all these complicated labors for their good, such was the unparalleled obstinacy of these stubborn wretches, that they ungratefully refused to acknowledge the strangers as their benefactors, and persisted in disbelieving the doctrines they endeavored to inculcate; most insolently alleging that, from their conduct, the advocates of Christianity did not seem to believe in it themselves. Was not this too much for hu- man patience? Would not one suppose that the benign visitants from Europe, provoked at their incredulity and discouraged by their stiff-necked obstinacy, would for ever have abandoned their shores, and consigned them to their original ignorance and misery? But no: so zealous were they to effect the temporal comfort and eternal salvation of these pagan infidels that they even proceeded from the milder means of persuasion to the more painful and troublesome one of persecution—let loose among them whole troops of fiery monks and fu- rious bloodhounds—purified them by fire and sword, by stake and faggot; in consequence of which indefati- gable measures the cause of Christian love and charity was so rapidly advanced that in a few years not one fifth of the number of unbelievers existed in South America that were found there at the time of its discovery.

What stronger right need the European settlers advance to the country than this? Have not whole nations of uninformed savages been made acquainted with a thousand imperious wants and indispensable comforts of which they were before wholly ignorant? Have they not been literally hunted and smoked out of the dens and lurking places of ignorance and infidelity, and absolutely scourged into the right path? Have not the temporal things, the vain baubles and filthy lucre of this world, which were too apt to engage their worldly and selfish thoughts, been benevolently taken from them; and have they not, instead thereof, been taught to set their affections on things above? And finally, to use the words of a reverend Spanish father, in a letter to his superior in Spain:—"Can any one have the presumption to say that these savage pagans have yielded anything more than an inconsiderable recompense to their benefactors, in surrendering to them a little pitiful tract of this dirty sublunary planet, in exchange for a glorious inheritance in the kingdom of heaven."

Here then are three complete and undeniable sources of right established, any one of which was more than ample to establish a property in the newly-discovered regions of America. Now, so it has happened in certain parts of this delightful quarter of the globe that the right of discovery has been so strenuously asserted—the influence of cultivation so industriously extended, and the progress of salvation and civilization so zealously persecuted; that, what with their attendant wars, persecutions, oppressions, diseases, and other partial evils that often hang on the skirts of great benefits—the savage aborigines have, somehow or other, been utterly annihilated—and this all at once brings me to a fourth right, which is worth all the others put together. For the original claimants to the soil being all dead and buried, and no one remaining to inherit or dispute the soil, the Spaniards, as the next immediate occupants, entered upon the possession as clearly as the hangman succeeds to the clothes of the malefactor—and as they have Blackstone[1] and all the learned expounders of the law on their side, they may set all actions of ejectment at defiance—and this last right may be entitled the RIGHT BY EXTERMINATION, or in other words, the RIGHT BY GUNPOWDER.

But lest any scruples of conscience should remain on this head, and to settle the question of right for ever, his holiness Pope Alexander VI. issued a mighty Bull, by which he generously granted the newly-discovered quarter of the globe to the Spaniards and Portuguese; who, thus having law and gospel on their side, and being inflamed with great spiritual zeal, showed the pagan savages neither favor nor affection, but persecuted the work of discovery, colonization, civilization, and extermination with ten times more fury than ever.

Thus were the European worthies who first discovered America clearly entitled to the soil, and not only entitled to the soil, but likewise to the eternal thanks of these infidel savages, for having come so far, endured so many perils by sea and land, and taken such unwea-

---

[1] Bl. Com. b. ii. c. 1.

ried pains, for no other purpose but to improve their forlorn, uncivilized, and heathenish condition; for having made them acquainted with the comforts of life; for having introduced among them the light of religion; and, finally, for having hurried them out of the world to enjoy its reward!

But as argument is never so well understood by us selfish mortals as when it comes home to ourselves, and as I am particularly anxious that this question should be put to rest for ever, I will suppose a parallel case, by way of arousing the candid attention of my readers.

Let us suppose, then, that the inhabitants of the moon, by astonishing advancement in science, and by profound insight into that ineffable lunar philosophy, the mere flickerings of which have of late years dazzled the feebled optics, and addled the shallow brains of the good people of our globe—let us suppose, I say, that the inhabitants of the moon, by these means, had arrived at such a command of their energies, such an enviable state of perfectibility, as to control the elements, and navigate the boundless regions of space. Let us suppose a roving crew of these soaring philosophers, in the course of an aerial voyage of discovery among the stars, should chance to alight upon this outlandish planet. And here I beg my readers will not have the uncharitableness to smile, as is too frequently the fault of volatile readers, when perusing the grave speculations of philosophers. I am far from indulging in any sportive vein at present; nor is the supposition I have been making so wild as many may deem it. It has long been a very serious and anxious question with me, and many a time and oft, in the course of my overwhelming cares and contrivances for the welfare and protection of this my native planet, have I lain awake whole nights debating in my mind whether it were most probable we should first discover and civilize the moon, or the moon discover and civilize our globe. Neither would the prodigy of sailing in the air or cruising among the stars be a whit more astonishing and incomprehensible to us than was the European mystery of navigating floating castles through the world of waters to the simple savages. We have already discovered the art of coasting along the aerial shores of our planet by means of balloons, as the savages had of venturing along their sea-coasts in canoes; and the disparity between the former and the aerial vehicles of the philosophers from the moon might not be greater than that between the bark canoes of the savages and the mighty ships of their discoverers. I might here pursue an endless chain of similar speculations; but as they would be unimportant to my subject, I abandon them to my reader, particularly if he be a philosopher, as matters well worthy of his attentive consideration.

To return, then, to my supposition—let us suppose that the aerial visitants I have mentioned, possessed of vastly superior knowledge to ourselves—that is to say, possessed of superior knowledge in the art of extermination—riding on hippogriffs—defended with impenetrable armor—armed with concentrated sunbeams, and provided with vast engines, to hurl enormous moon-stones; in short, let us suppose them, if our vanity will permit the supposition, as superior to us in knowledge, and consequently in power, as the Europeans were to

61

the Indians when they first discovered them. All this is very possible, it is only our self-sufficiency that makes us think otherwise; and I warrant the poor savages, before they had any knowledge of the white men, armed in all the terrors of glittering steel and tremendous gunpowder, were as perfectly convinced that they themselves were the wisest, the most virtuous, powerful, and perfect of created beings, as are at this present moment the lordly inhabitants of old England, the volatile populace of France, or even the self-satisfied citizens of this most enlightened republic.

Let us suppose, moreover, that the aerial voyagers, finding this planet to be nothing but a howling wilderness, inhabited by us poor savages and wild beasts, shall take formal possession of it, in the name of his most gracious and philosophic excellency, the Man in the Moon. Finding however that their numbers are incompetent to hold it in complete subjection, on account of the ferocious barbarity of its inhabitants, they shall take our worthy President, the King of England, the Emperor of Hayti, the mighty Bonaparte, and the great King of Bantam, and, returning to their native planet, shall carry them to court, as were the Indian chiefs led about as spectacles in the courts of Europe.

Then making such obeisance as the etiquette of the court requires, they shall address the puissant Man in the Moon in, as near as I can conjecture, the following terms:——

"Most serene and mighty Potentate, whose dominions extend as far as eye can reach, who rideth on the Great Bear, useth the sun as a looking glass, and maintaineth unrivaled control over tides, madmen, and sea-crabs. We, thy liege subjects, have just returned from a voyage of discovery, in the course of which we have landed and taken possession of that obscure little dirty planet, which thou beholdest rolling at a distance. The five uncouth monsters which we have brought into this august present were once very important chiefs among their fellow-savages, who are a race of beings totally destitute of the common attributes of humanity, and differing in everything from the inhabitants of the moon, inasmuch as they carry their heads upon their shoulders, instead of under their arms—have two eyes instead of one—are utterly destitute of tails, and of a variety of unseemly complexions, particularly of horrible whiteness, instead of pea-green.

"We have moreover found these miserable savages sunk into a state of the utmost ignorance and depravity, every man shamelessly living with his own wife, and rearing his own children, instead of indulging in that community of wives enjoined by the law of nature, as expounded by the philosophers of the moon. In a word, they have scarcely a gleam of true philosophy among them, but are, in fact, utter heretics, ignoramuses, and barbarians. Taking compassion, therefore, on the sad condition of these sublunary wretches, we have endeavored, while we remained on their planet, to introduce among them the light of reason and the comforts of the moon. We have treated them to mouthfuls of moonshine, and draughts of nitrous oxide, which they swallowed with incredible voracity, particularly the females; and we have likewise endeavored to instil into them the precepts of lunar philosophy. We have insisted upon their renouncing the contemptible shackles of religion and common sense, and adoring the profound, omnipotent, and all perfect energy, and the ecstatic, immutable, immovable perfection. But such was the unparalleled obstinacy of these wretched savages that they persisted in cleaving to their wives, and adhering to their religion, and absolutely set at nought the sublime doctrines of the moon—nay, among other abominable heresies they even went so far as blasphemously to declare that this ineffable planet was made of nothing more nor less than green cheese!"

At these words, the great Man in the Moon (being a very profound philosopher) shall fall into a terrible passion, and possessing equal authority over things that do not belong to him, as did whilome his holiness the Pope, shall forthwith issue a formidable Bull, specifying, "That whereas a certain crew of Lunatics have lately discovered and taken possession of a newly-discovered planet called the earth; and that whereas it is inhabited by none but a race of two-legged animals that carry their heads on their shoulders instead of under their arms; cannot talk the Lunatic language; have two eyes instead of one; are destitute of tails, and of a horrible whiteness, instead of pea-green—therefore, and for a variety of other excellent reasons, they are considered incapable of possessing any property in the planet they infest, and the right and title to it are confirmed to its original discoverers. And, furthermore, the colonists who are now about to depart to the aforesaid planet are authorised and commanded to use every means to convert these infidel savages from the darkness of Christianity, and make them thorough and absolute Lunatics."

In consequence of this benevolent Bull, our philosophic benefactors go to work with hearty zeal. They seize upon our fertile territories, scourge us from our rightful possessions, relieve us from our wives, and when we are unreasonable enough to complain, they will turn upon us and say, "Miserable barbarians! ungrateful wretches! have we not come thousands of miles to improve your worthless planet? have we not fed you with moonshine! have we not intoxicated you with nitrous oxide? does not our moon give you light every night? and have you the baseness to murmur, when we claim a pitiful return for all these benefits?" But finding that we not only persist in absolute contempt of their reasoning and disbelief in their philosophy, but even go so far as daringly to defend our property, their patience shall be exhausted, and they shall resort to their superior powers of argument; hunt us with hippogriffs, transfix us with concentrated sunbeams, demolish our cities with moonstones; until having by main force converted us to the true faith, they shall graciously permit us to exist in the torrid deserts of Arabia, or the frozen regions of Lapland, there to enjoy the blessings of civilization and the charms of lunar philosophy, in much the same manner as the reformed and enlightened savages of this country are kindly suffered to inhabit the inhospitable forests of the north, or the impenetrable wilderness of South America.

Thus, I hope, I have clearly proved, and strikingly illustrated, the right of the early colonists to the possession of this country; and thus is this gigantic question completely vanquished: so having manfully surmounted all obstacles, and subdued all opposition, what remains but that I should forthwith conduct my readers into the city which we have been so long in a manner besieging? But hold: before I proceed another step I must pause to take breath, and recover from the excessive fatigue I have undergone, in preparing to begin this most accurate of histories. And in this I do but imitate the example of a renowned Dutch tumbler of antiquity, who took a start of three miles for the purpose of jumping over a hill, but having run himself out of breath by the time he reached the foot, sat himself quietly down for a few moments to blow, and then walked over it at his leisure.

JAMES K. PAULDING.

James Kirke Paulding might have been one of our greatest literary figures if he had put some effort into it; or, on the other hand, he might have destroyed everything that is charming in his writing if he had polished it more carefully. We shall never know. At any rate, he had some success as a writer, though nowhere near as much success as his friend Washington Irving; but he wrote what he liked and never worried about whether the public would take to it. All his works seem to have been written once and never looked at again, so that we sometimes find obvious errors that a little revision work would have caught. But, on the other hand, that very carelessness makes reading his writing seem like sitting down to a conversation with the man himself.

KONINGSMARKE.

In *Koningsmarke; or, Old Times in the New World*, Paulding set out to write a parody of Sir Walter Scott's historical novels. At the time (1823) Sir Walter Scott was an unstoppable juggernaut of historical fiction, easily the most popular novelist in the history of the English novel. Paulding found those historical romances laughably implausible. In the first chapter of his parody, therefore, he sets down what he imagines must be the method followed by Scott. After that, he plays a surprising trick on his readers, and quite possibly himself: he uses Scott's method to construct an adventure story of his own that holds our attention and keeps us turning pages to the end.

67

Chapter 1

IN ORDER THAT our readers and ourselves may at once
come to a proper understanding, we will confess without any circumlocution, that we sat down to write this
history before we had thought of any regular plan, or
arranged the incidents, being fully convinced that an
author who trusts to his own genius, like a modern
saint who relies solely on his faith, will never be left in
the lurch. Another principle of ours, which we have
seen fully exemplified in the very great success of certain popular romances, advertised for publication before they were begun to be written, is, that it is much
better for an author to commence his work, without
knowing how it is to end, than to hamper himself with
a regular plot, a succession of prepared incidents, and a
premeditated catastrophe. This we hold to be an error
little less, than to tie the legs of a dancing master, to
make him caper the more gracefully, or pinion a man's
arms behind his back, as a preparative to a boxing
match. In short, it is taking away, by a sort of literary
felo de se, all that free will, that perfect liberty of imagination, and Invention, which causes us writers to
curvet so gracefully in the fertile fields of historical fiction.

Another sore obstacle in the way of the free exercise
of genius, is for a writer of historical novels, such as we
have reason to suspect this will turn out to be, to embarrass his invention by an abject submission to
chronology, or confine himself only to the introduction
of such characters and incidents as really existed or
took place within the limits of time and space com-

prised in the ground work of his story. Nothing can be more evident than that this squeamishness of the author must materially interfere with the interest and variety of his work, since, if, as often happens, there should be wanting great characters or great events, coming lawfully within the period comprised in the said history, the author will be proportionably stinted in his materials. To be scared by a trifling anachronism, in relation to things that have passed away a century, or ten centuries ago, is a piece of literary cowardice, similar to that of the ignorant clown, who should be frightened by the ghost of some one that had been dead a thousand years.

So far, therefore, as we can answer for ourselves in the course of this history, we honestly advertise the reader, that although our hero is strictly an historical personage, having actually lived and died, like other people, yet in all other respects, not only he, but every character in the work, belongs entirely to us. We mean to make them think, talk and act just as we like, and without the least regard to nature, education, or probability. So also as respects the incidents of our history. We intend, at present, reserving to ourselves, however, the liberty of altering our plan whenever it suits us, to confine our labours to no time nor place, but to embody in our work every incident or adventure that falls in our way, or that an intimate knowledge of old ballads, nursery tales, and traditions, has enabled us to collect together. In short, we are fully determined, that so long as we hold the pen, we will never be deterred from seizing any romantic or improbable adventure, by any weak apprehension that people will quarrel with us

69

because they do not follow on in the natural course, or hang together by any probable connexion of cause and effect.

Another determination of ours, of which we think it fair to apprize the reader, is, that we shall strenuously endeavour to avoid any intercourse, either directly or indirectly, with that bane of true genius, commonly called common sense. We look upon that species of vulgar bumpkin capacity, as little better than the instinct of animals; as the greatest pest of authorship that ever exercised jurisdiction in the fields of literature. Its very name is sufficient to indicate the absurdity of persons striving to produce any thing uncommon by an abject submission to its dictates. It shall also be our especial care, to avoid the ancient, but nearly exploded error, of supposing that either nature or probability is in anywise necessary to the interest of a work of imagination. We intend that all our principal characters shall indulge in as many inconsistencies and eccentricities, as will suffice to make them somewhat interesting, being altogether assured that your sober, rational mortals, who act from ordinary impulses, and pursue a course of conduct sanctioned by common sense, are no better than common-place people, entirely unworthy the attention of an author, or his readers. It is for this special reason that we have chosen for our scene of action, a forgotten village, and for our actors, an obscure colony, whose existence is scarcely known, and the incidents of whose history are sufficiently insignificant to allow us ample liberty in giving what cast and colouring we please to their manners, habits and opinions. And we shall make free use of this advantage, trusting that the good-natured public will give us full credit for being most faithful delineators. Great and manifold are the advantages arising from choosing this obscure period. The writer who attempts to copy existing life and manners, must come in competition, and undergo a comparison with the originals, which he cannot sustain, unless his picture be correct and characteristic. But with regard to a state of society that is become extinct, it is like painting the unicorn, or the mammoth;—give the one only a single horn, and make the other only big enough, and the likeness will be received as perfect.

Certain cavillers, who pretend to be the advocates of truth, have strenuously objected to the present fashion of erecting a superstructure of fiction on a basis of fact, which they say is confounding truth with falsehood in the minds of youthful readers. But we look upon this objection as perfectly frivolous. It cannot be denied that such a mixture of history and romance is exceedingly palatable; since, if the figure may be allowed us, truth is the meat, and fiction the salt, which gives it a zest, and preserves it from perishing. So, also, a little embellishment will save certain insignificant events from being entirely lost or forgotten in the lapse of time. Hence we find young people, who turn with disgust from the solid dulness of pure matter of fact history, devouring with vast avidity those delectable mixed dishes, and thus acquiring a knowledge of history, which, though we confess somewhat adulterated, is better than none at all. Besides this, many learned persons are of opinion that all history is in itself little better than a romance, most especially that part wherein historians pretend to detail the secret motives

71

of monarchs and their ministers. One who was himself an old statesman, writes thus:

How oft, when great affairs perplex the brains
Of mighty politicians, to conjecture
From whence sprung such designs, such revolutions,
Such exaltations, such depressions, wars and crimes;
Our female Machiavels would smile to think
How closely lurking lay the nick of all
Under our cousin Dod's white farthingale.

Such, then, being the case with history, we think it a marvellous idle objection to this our mode of writing, to say that it is falsifying what is true, since it is only sprinkling a little more fiction with it, in order to render it sufficiently natural and entertaining to allure the youthful and romantic reader.

Before concluding this introductory chapter, which is to be considered the key to our undertaking, we will ask one favour of the reader. It is, that if on some occasions we shall, in the course of this work, appear somewhat wiser in various matters, than comports with the period of our history, and at other times not so wise as we ought to be, he will in the one case ascribe it to the total inability of authors to refrain from telling what they know, and in the other, to an extraordinary exertion of modesty, by which we are enabled, at that particular moment, to repress the effervescence of our knowledge.

Finally, in order that the reader may devour our work with a proper zest, we hereby assure him, (in confidence,) that our bookseller has covenanted and agreed to pay us ten thousand dollars in Owl Creek bank notes, provided the sale of it should justify such inordinate generosity.[1] We will now plunge directly into the thickest of our adventures, having thus happily got over the first step, which is held to be half the battle.

KILLING, NO MURDER.

I AM A sober, middle-aged, married gentleman, of a moderate size; with moderate wishes, moderate means, a moderate family, and everything moderate about me, except my house, which is too large for my means, or my family. It is, however, or rather, alas! it was, an old family mansion, full of old things of no value but to the owner, as connected with early associations and ancient friends, and I did not like the idea of converting it into a tavern or boarding-house, as is the fashion with the young heirs of the present day. Such as it was, however, although I sometimes felt a little like the ambitious snail who once crept into a lobster's shell and came near perishing in a hard winter, I managed for ten or twelve years to live in it very comfortably, and to make both ends meet. My furniture, to be sure, was a little out of fashion, and here and there a little out at the elbows; but I always persuaded myself that it was respectable to be out of fashion, and that new things smacked of new men, and were, therefore, rather vul-

---

[1] The Owl Creek Bank of Mount Vernon, Ohio, was a notorious failure, and its notes were worthless.

gar. Under this impression, I lived in my old house, with my old-fashioned furniture, moderate-sized family, and moderate means, envying nobody and indebted to no one in the world. I had neither gilded furniture, nor grand mantel-glasses, nor superb chandeliers; but then I had a few fine pictures and busts, and flattered myself they were much more genteel than gilded furniture, grand mantel-glasses, and superb chandeliers. In truth, I looked down with contempt not only on these, but on all those who did not agree with me in opinion. I never asked a person to dinner a second time who did not admire my busts and pictures, considering him a vulgar fellow and an admirer of ostentatious trumpery.

But let no man presume, after reading my story, to flatter himself he is out of the reach of the infection of fashion and fashionable opinions. He may hold out for a certain time, perhaps, but human nature can't stand forever on the defensive. The example of all around us is irresistible, sooner or later. The first shock given to my attachment to respectable old-fashioned furniture and a respectable old foursquare double house was received from the elbow of a modern worthy, who had grown rich, nobody knew how, by presiding over the drawing of lotteries, and who came and built himself a narrow four-story house right at the side of my honest foursquare double mansion. It had white marble steps, white marble door and window sills, folding doors and marble mantel pieces, and was as fine as a fiddle, within and without. It put my rusty old mansion quite out of countenance, as everybody told me, though I assure my readers I thought it excessively tawdry and in bad taste.

But, alas!—such is the stupidity of mankind—I could get nobody to agree with me.

"What has come over your house, lately?" cried one good-natured visitor; "somehow or other it don't look as it used to do."

"What makes your house seem so rusty and old-fashioned?" said another good-natured visitor. "Mr. Blankprize has taken the shine off of you," said Mrs. Sowerby; "HE HAS KILLED YOUR HOUSE!"

Hereupon the spirit moved me to go out and reconnoitre the venerable mansion. It certainly did look a little like a chubby, rusty, old-fashioned Quaker by the side of a first-rate dandy. I picked a quarrel with it outright, which, by the way, was a very unlucky quarrel. I was not rich enough to pull it down and build a new one; and it is great folly to quarrel with an old house until you can get a better. But if I can't build, I can paint, thought I, and put at least as good a face on the matter as this opulent lottery-man, my next-door neighbour. Accordingly, I consulted my wife on the subject, who, whether from a spirit of contradiction, or, to do her justice, I believe from a correct and rational view of the subject, discouraged my project. I was only the more determined. So I caused my honest old house to be painted a bright cream color, that it might hold up its head against the scurvy lottery-man.

"Bless me!" quoth Mrs. Smith; "what is the matter with this room? It don't look as it used to do."

"Why, what under the sun have you done to this room?" cried Mrs. Brown.

"Protect me!" exclaimed Mrs. White; "why, I seem to have got into a strange room. What is the matter?"

---

somehow or other, don't you think THEY KILL THE WALLS?"

Murder again! Killed, four lath-and-plaster walls! But I'll get the better of Mrs. Sowerby yet. So I got the walls colored as bright as the curtains, and bade her defiance in my heart the next time she came.

Mrs. Sowerby arrived as usual. Her whole life was spent in visiting about everywhere, and putting people out of conceit with themselves.

She threw up her eyes and hands. "Well, I declare, Mr. Sobersides, you have done wonders. This is the real French-white"—which, by the way, my unle[arned] readers should know, is yellow. "But," cont[inued the] pestilent woman, "don't you think th[e] colored walls KILL THE CHAIRS?"

Worse and worse! Here [...] arm-chairs, with yello[w...] dered in cold bl[...] shiny walls! But t[...] death. I forthwith p[...] low as custard, and s[...] Mrs. Sowerby the next [...]

But, alas! what are al[...] Dust, ashes, emptiness, [...] not yet satisfied. She thou[...] —"But, then, my dear friend, [...] and appalling pause, "my dear [...] low satin chairs HAVE KILLED THE [...]

And so they had, as dead as Ju[...] ture-frames looked like old lumber [...] my improvements. There was no hel[p...] went the frames to Messrs. Parker and [...]

"You've killed the inside of your house," said Mrs. Sowerby, "by painting the outside such a bright color."

It was too true; this was my first crime. Would I had stopped here!—but destiny determined otherwise. It happened, unfortunately, that my front parlour carpet was of a yellow ground. It was, to be sure, somewhat faded by time and use; but it comported very well with the unpretending sobriety of the old regime. But the case was altered now, and the bright cream color of the out side of my house, under the dingy yellow carpet within. So I bought a new carpet, of a fine orange ground, determined that this should not be killed. It looked very fine, and I was satisfied. I had done the business effectually.

"Bless my soul!" exclaimed Mrs. Brown; "why, you look as fine as twopence!"

"Save us!" cried Mrs. Smith; "what a sweet pretty carpet!"

"Protect us!" Then, casting a knowing look around the room, she added, in a tone of hesitating candor, "Bu... able affair!" cried Mrs. Sowerby; "what a fashion- don't you think, somehow or other, it kills ... tains?"

Another murder! thought I;—... what have I done? What is ... but I can remedy the affa... yellow curtains. I th... Mrs. Sowe... "Well...

---

time they came back, "redeemed, regenerated, and disenthralled." I was so satisfied now that there was nothing left in my parlour to be killed, that I could hardly sleep that night, so impatient was I to see Mrs. Sowerby.

That baleful creature, when she came next day, looked round in evident disappointment, but exclaimed, with great appearance of cordiality, "Well, now I declare, it's all perfect; there is not a handsomer room in town."

Thank heaven! thought I, I have committed no more murders. But I reckoned without my host. I was destined to go on murdering, in spite of me. The spring was now coming on, and, the weather being mild, the folding doors had been thrown open between the front and back parlours. This latter was furnished with green, somewhat faded I confess. I had heretofore considered it the sanctum sanctorum of the establishment. It was only used on extraordinary occasions, such as Christmas and New-Year days, when all the family dined with me, bringing their little children with them to gormandize themselves sick. The room looked very well by itself; but, alas! the moment Mrs. Sowerby caught sight of it, her eye brightened—fatal omen! "Why, my dear Mr. Sobersides, what has got into your back parlour? It used to be so genteel and smart. Why, I believe I'm losing my eyesight. The green carpet and curtains look quite yellow, I think. O, I see it now—THE FRONT PARLOUR HAS KILLED THE BACK ONE!"

The dickens! Here was another pretty piece of business. I must either keep the door shut all summer and

be roasted, or be charged with killing a whole parlour
—carpet, curtains, chairs, sofas, walls, and all.

It would be a mere repetition to relate how this
wicked woman again led me on from one murder to another. First the new carpet "killed" the curtains; then
the new curtains "killed" the walls; the new painted
walls "killed" the old satin chairs; and so, by little and
little, all my honest old green furniture went the way of
the honest old yellow.

"The spell is broken at last," cried I, rubbing my
hands in ecstasy. Neither my front nor back parlour
can commit any more assassinations. Elated with the
idea, I was waiting on Mrs. Sowerby to the front door,
when suddenly she stopped short at the foot of the old-
fashioned winding staircase, the carpet of which, I confess, was here and there infested with that modern
abomination—a darn. It was, moreover, rather dingy
and faded.

"Your back parlour HAS KILLED YOUR HALL," said
Mrs. Sowerby.

And so it had. Coming out of the splendour of the
former, the latter had the same effect on the beholder
as a bad set of teeth in a fine face, or an old rusty iron
grate in a handsome room.

I began to be desperate. I had been accessory to so
many cruel murders that my conscience became seared,
and I went on, led by the wiles of this daughter of Sa-
tan, to murder my way from the ground-floor to the
cockloft, without sparing a single soul. Nothing escaped but the garret, which, having been for half a
century the depository of all our broken or banished
household gods, resembled Hogarth's picture of the

"End of the World," and defied the arts of that mischievous monster, Mrs. Sowerby.

My house was now fairly revolutionized, or rather, reformed, after the French mode, by a process of indiscriminate destruction.

I did not, like Alexander, after having thus conquered one world, sigh for another to conquer. I sat down to enjoy my victory under the shade of my laurels. But, alas!, disappointment ever follows at the heels of fruition. It is pleasant to dance, until we come to pay the piper. By the time custom had familiarized me to my new glories, and they had become somewhat indifferent, bills came pouring in by dozens, and it was impossible to kill my duns as I had done my old furniture, except by paying them, a mode of destroying these troublesome vermin not always convenient or agreeable. From the period of commencing housekeeping until now, I had never once had occasion to put off the payment of a bill. I prided myself on always paying ready money for everything, and it was an honest pride. I can hardly express the mortification I felt at being now occasionally under the necessity of giving excuses instead of money. I had a miserable invention at this sort of work of imagination, and sometimes, when more than usually barren, I got into a passion, which is a common shift of people when they don't know what else to do. More than once I found myself suddenly turning a corner in a great hurry, or planting myself before the window of a picture-shop, studying it very attentively, so as not to notice certain persons, the very sight of whom is always painful to people of nice sensibility.

80

Not being hardened to such trifles by long use, I felt rather sore and irritable. Under the old regime it had always been a pleasure to me to hear a ring at the door, because it was the signal for an agreeable visitor; but now it excited disagreeable apprehensions, and sounded like the knell of a dun. In short, I grew crusty and fidgety by degrees, insomuch that Mrs. Sowerby often exclaimed:—

"Why, what has come over you, Mr. Sobersides? Why, I declare, somehow or other you don't seem the same man you used to be."

I could have answered, "The new Mr. Sobersides has killed the old Mr. Sobersides." But I said nothing, and only wished her up in the garret, among the old furniture.

My system of reform produced another source of worrying. Hitherto my old furniture and myself had been so long acquainted, that I could take all sorts of liberties with it. I could recline on the sofas of an evening, or sit on one of the old chairs and cross my legs on another, without the least ceremony. But now, forsooth!, it is as much as I dare do to sit down upon one of my new acquaintance; and as for a lounge on the sofa, which was the Cleopatra for which I would have lost the world, I should as soon think of taking a nap in a fine lady's sleeve. As to my little rantipole boys, who had hitherto feared neither carpet, chair, nor sofa, they have at length been schooled into such awe of finery, that they walk about the parlour on tiptoe, sit on the edge of a chair with trepidation, and contemplate the sofas at a distance with the most profound veneration, as unapproachable divinities. To cap the climax of

my ill-starred follies, my easy- old-shoe friends, who
came to see me without ceremony because they felt
comfortable and welcome, have gradually become shy
of my novel magnificence; and the last of them was the
other evening fairly looked out of the house by a certain person, for spitting accidentally upon a new brass
fender, that shone like the sun at noonday.

I might hope that in the course of time these evils
would be mitigated by the furniture growing old and
sociable by degrees, but there is little prospect of this,
because it is too fine for common use. The carpet is always protected by a worn crum-cloth, full of holes and
stains; the sofas and chairs are in dingy cover-sluts, except on extraordinary occasions, and I fear they will
last forever—at least, longer than I shall. I sometimes
solace myself with the anticipation that my children
may live long enough to sit on the sofas with impunity,
and walk on the carpet without going on tiptoe.

There would be some consolation in the midst of
these sore evils if I could only fix the reproach of them
on my wife. Many philosophers are of opinion, that
this single privilege of matrimony is more than equiva-
lent to all the rubs and disappointments of life; and I
have heard a very wise person affirm, that he would
not mind being ruined, at all, if he could only blame his
wife for it. But I must do mine the justice to say, that
she combated Mrs. Sowerby gallantly, and threw every
obstacle in the way of my rash improvements, advocat-
ing the cause of every piece of old furniture with a zeal
worthy of better success. I alone am to blame in having
yielded to the temptations of that wicked woman, Mrs.
Sowerby; and, as a man who has ruined himself by his

own imprudence is the better qualified for giving good advice, I have written this sketch of my own history, to caution all honest, sober, discreet people against commencing a system of reform in their household. LET THEM BEWARE OF THE FIRST MURDER!

MAJOR JACK DOWNING.

In Major Jack Downing, Seba Smith created a popular character who foreshadows the later successes of Artemus Ward:
the sense of self-importance, the pride in his own meager intellectual attainments, and the flashes of cutting back-country
wisdom are the same. Taken from rural Maine and thrust
into the comic gold mine that was the Jackson administra-
tion, Major Downing makes himself a close confidant of the
president, usually showing good common sense when the
Washington insiders around him care for nothing but party.

We have almost forgotten Major Downing today, and
much of his humor is perhaps too topical to survive. But in
"A Partisan Question" we recognize the mechanics of Washington politics in every age. The echo of Wolsey in "I and
the president" is rather clever, too.

A PARTISAN QUESTION.

I AND THE President are getting ready to come on that
way this summer. We shall come as far as Portland
and I expect we shall go up to Downingville; for the
President says he must shake hands with uncle Joshua
before he comes back, that faithful old republican who
has stood by him through thick and thin ever since he
found he was going to be elected President. He will either go up to Downingville, or send for Uncle Joshua
to meet him at Portland. There is some trouble
amongst us here a little, to know how we shall get
along among the federalists when we come that way.

They say the federalists in Massachusetts want to keep the President all to themselves when he comes there. But Mr. Van Buren says that'll never do; he must stick to the democratic party; he may shake hands with a federalist once in a while if the democrats don't see him, but whenever there's any democrats round he mustn't look at a federalist. Mr. McLane and Mr. Livingston advise him tother way. They tell him he'd better treat the federalists pretty civil, and shake hands with Mr. Webster as quick as he would with Uncle Joshua Downing. And when they give this advice Mr. Lewis and Mr. Kendle hop right up as mad as March hairs, and tell him if he shakes hands with a single federalist while he is gone, the democratic party will be ruined. And then the President turns to me and asks me what he had better do. And I tell him I guess he better go straight ahead, and keep a stiff upper lip, and shake hands with whoever he is a mind to.

JAMES FENIMORE COOPER.

Cooper is certainly not remembered as a humorist, but he did sometimes show a keen eye for character. Although his Leatherstocking series is most read today, in his own day he was considered the greatest master of the sea story in English. Having reached a success matched by no American writer and few European writers, he was at liberty to indulge his fancy in whatever form of writing he pleased. Thus he turned to satire after the manner of Voltaire.

The Monikins, a strange tale of intelligent monkeys living at the South Pole, was roundly condemned by most critics when it was published in 1835. "What the work is about, passes our comprehension," said a review in the *Knickerbocker*. "It is said to be a Satire; but the eyes of an Argus, were they twice the fabled number, could not discern it. The volumes have neither consistency of plot, nor grace of execution. Every thing is cloudy, distorted, and unnatural." Some of Cooper's admirers thought the criticism was provoked more by jealousy of Cooper's success than by reasoned judgment, and indeed Cooper's reputation remained high in Europe even as it plummeted in America. "While the author of The Spy receives the applause of Europe," wrote Rufus Wilmot Griswold; "while the critics of Germany and France debate the claims of Scott to be ranked before him or even with him, his own countrymen deride his pretensions, and Monikin critics affect contempt of him, or make the appearance of his works occasions of puerile personal abuse."

It must be admitted that *The Monikins* is not a success. It has its moments of inspiration, and it has developed a surprising following recently as one of the roots of American science fiction; but Cooper lashes out too indiscriminately for his satire to have much of an effect. He fires his satire with a shotgun, not a rifle.

Nevertheless, there is one character who almost redeems the whole book. Captain Noah Poke of Stonington, an old seal-hunter drawn into the voyage to the South Pole by the narrator's money, is a superb character looking for a better book to inhabit. He is drawn with such colorful strokes that one is tempted to think Cooper might actually have made a humorist of himself if he had put his mind to it. In his first encounter with the titular monikins, he responds to the news that, in deference to the delicate sensibilities of the monikin ladies, he will be required to strip naked, with a Rabelaisian torrent of arguments, oaths, and pleas. This shows keen observation. It is exactly the response of a man who has been attacked at his most vulnerable intellectual spot: the unexamined assumptions that lie at the base of all social intercourse. Because he can think of no reason for not wishing to leave his clothes behind, he is obliged to think of every reason. Cooper's greatest weakness was that he tended to write just beyond his ability, constructing elaborate sentences that wobble and crash ungrammatically to the ground; but Captain Poke, even in indirect quotation, speaks in his own unerringly natural voice.

FROM THE MONIKINS

PREVIOUSLY TO SEPARATING from my new friend Dr. Reasono, however, I took him aside, and stated that I had an acquaintance in the hotel, a person of singular philosophy, after the human fashion, and a great traveller; and that I desired permission to let him into the secret of our intended lecture on the monikin economy, and to bring him with me as an auditor. To this request,

No. 22,817, brown-study color, or Dr. Reasono, gave a very cordial assent; hinting delicately, at the same time, his expectation that this new auditor, who, of course, was no other than Captain Noah Poke, would not deem it disparaging to his manhood, to consult the sensibilities of the ladies, by appearing in the garments of that only decent and respectable tailor and draper, nature. To this suggestion I gave a ready approval; when each went his way, after the usual salutations of bowing and tail-waving, with a mutual promise of being punctual to the appointment.

Mr. Poke listened to my account of all that had passed, with a very sedate gravity. He informed me that he had witnessed so much ingenuity among the seals, and had known so many brutes that seemed to have the sagacity of men, and so many men who appeared to have the stupidity of brutes, that he had no difficulty whatever in believing every word I told him. He expressed his satisfaction, too, at the prospect of hearing a lecture on natural philosophy and political economy from the lips of a monkey; although he took occasion to intimate that no desire to learn anything lay at the bottom of his compliance; for, in his country, these matters were pretty generally studied in the district schools, the very children who ran about the streets of 'Stunin'tun' usually knowing more than most of the old people in foreign parts. Still a monkey might have some new ideas; and for his part, he was willing to hear what every one had to say; for, if a man didn't put in a word for himself in this world, he might be certain no one else would take the pains to speak for him. But when I came to mention the details of the programme of the forthcoming interview, and stated that it was expected the audience would wear their own skins, out of respect to the ladies, I greatly feared that my friend would have so far excited himself as to go into fits. The rough old sealer swore some terrible oaths, protesting "that he would not make a monkey of himself, by appearing in this garb, for all the monikin philosophers, or high-born females, that could be stowed in a ship's hold; that he was very liable to take cold; that he once knew a man who undertook to play beast in this manner, and the first thing the poor devil knew, he had great claws and a tail sprouting out of him; a circumstance that he had always attributed to a just judgment for striving to make himself more than Providence had intended him for; that, provided a man's ears were naked, he could hear just as well as if his whole body was naked; that he did not complain of the monkeys going in their skins, and that they ought, in reason, not to meddle with his clothes; that he should be scratching himself the whole time, and thinking what a miserable figure he cut; that he would have no place to keep his tobacco; that he was apt to be deaf when he was cold; that he would be d——d if he did any such thing; that human natur' and monkey natur' were not the same, and it was not to be expected that men and monkeys should follow exactly the same fashions; that the meeting would have the appearance of a boxing match, instead of a philosophical lecture; that he never heard of such a thing at Stunin'tun; that he should feel sneaking at seeing his own shins in the presence of ladies; that a ship always made better weather under some canvas than under bare poles; that he might possibly be brought to his shirt and pantaloons, but as for giving up these, he would as soon think of cutting the sheet-anchor off his bows, with the vessel driving on a lee-shore; that flesh and blood were flesh and blood, and they liked their comfort; that he should think the whole time he was about to go in a-swimming, and should be looking about for a good place to dive"; together with a great many more similar objections, that have escaped me in the multitude of things of greater interest which have since occupied my time.

FANNY FERN.

In her time, Fanny Fern (Sara Willis) was the highest-paid newspaper columnist in America, and she deserved every cent of what she made. When her writing appeared in magazines and newspapers, people bought copies; a publisher with the money to pay for Fanny Fern was sure of turning a generous profit on his investment.

It is not hard to see the source of her popularity: she wrote straight to her readers in the way they talked to each other, not attempting any affected style. And she wrote about experiences they recognized. Women readers made up most of her audience; but Nathaniel Hawthorne, who had no use for most American female writers (and it must be said in fairness to Hawthorne that, unlike England, America was not producing many memorable female writers in his time), made a pointed exception for Fanny Fern: "The woman writes as if the devil was in her," he said of her novel *Ruth Hall*, "and that is the only condition in which a woman ever writes anything worth reading."

In her columns, the conversational style is pleasant and easy, and for that very reason the occasional barb strikes with all the more power. She knew how to end a column with a zinger, and she said the things her female readers doubtless would have said themselves, if only they had been clever and financially independent enough not to worry about the repercussions.

Fanny Fern deserves a much higher place in the history of American letters than we give her—indeed, she is all but forgotten, though her sensation novel *Ruth Hall* is read in women's-studies courses, presumably because it deals with *serious issues*. But her breezy columns were part of a revolution in American prose: the urbane style of Washington Irving was giving way to the seemingly artless colloquialism of Mark Twain. As the most successful journalist of her time, Fanny Fern probably did more than anyone else to push that revolution along. More to the point, her columns hold up to-day better than almost all the other ephemeral writing of the time. Though our manners have changed, our hearts and minds have not, and Fanny Fern still speaks directly to us in her sharp but friendly voice.

A HEAD-ACHE.

Now I AM in for it, with one of my unappeasable headaches. Don't talk to me of doctors; it is incurable as a love-fit; nothing on earth will stop it; you may put that down in your memorandum-book. Now, I suppose every body in the house to-day will put on their creakingest shoes; and every body will go up and down stairs humming all the tunes they ever heard, especially those I most dislike; and I suppose every thing that is cooked in the kitchen will boil and stew over, and the odor will come up to me; and I have such a nose! And I suppose all the little boys in the neighborhood, bless their little restless souls, will play duets on tin-pans and tin-kettles; and I suppose every body who comes into my room to ask me how I do, will squeak that horrid door, and keep squeaking it; and I suppose that un-happy dog confined over in that four-square-feet yard, will howl more deliriously than ever; and Mr. Jones's obnoxious blind will flap and bang till I am as crazy as an omnibus-driver who has a baulky horse, and whose passengers are hopping out behind without paying their fare; and I suppose some poor little child will be running under the window every now and then, screaming "Mother," and whenever I hear that, I think somebody wants me; and I've no doubt there will be "proof" to read to-day, and that that pertinacious and stentorian rag-man will lumber past on his crazy old cart, and insist on having some of my dry goods; and I feel it in my bones that oysters and oranges, and tape, and blacking, and brooms, and mats, and tin-ware, will settle and congregate on this side-walk, and assert their respective claims to my notice, till the sight of an undertaker would be a positive blessing.

Whack! how my head snaps! Don't tell me any living woman ever had such a headache before—because it will fill me with disgust. What o'clock is it? "Twelve." Merciful man! only twelve o'clock! I thought it was five. How am I to get through the day, I would like to know, for this headache won't let up till sundown; it never does. "Read to me." What'll you read? "Tom Moore!" as if I were not sick enough already! Moore! with his nightingales, and bulbuls, and jessamines; and loves and doves, and roses and poesies —till the introduction of an uneducated wildcat, or the tearingest kind of a hyena in his everlasting gardens, would be an untold relief. No—I hate Moore. Beside —he is the fellow who said, "When away from the lips that we love, we'll make love to the lips that are near." No wonder he was baptized *more*—carnivorous old profligate.

"Will I have a cup of tea?" No; of course I won't. I'm not an old maid. Tea! I'd like a dose of strychnine. There goes my head again—I should think a string of fire-crackers was fastened to each hair. Now the pain is in my left temple; now it is in my eyeballs; now—oh dear—it is everywhere. Sit down beside me, on the bed —don't jar it; now put your cold hand on my forehead —so—good gracious! There's a hand-organ! I knew it —the very one I moved here to get rid of. Playing the same old tune, too, composed of three notes: "tweedle —dum—tweedle—dee!" Now if that organ-man would pull each of my finger and toe-nails out by the roots, one by one, I wouldn't object, but that everlasting "tweedle—" oh dear!—Or if a cat's tail were to be ir-retrievably shut into yonder door—or a shirt-sleeve should be suddenly and unexpectedly thrown around an old maid's neck in this room, any thing—every thing but that eternal, die-away "tweedle." What's the use of a city government? What is the use of any thing? What is the use of *me?*

SUMMER TRAVEL.

TAKE A JOURNEY at this elevation of the thermometer! Not I. Think of the breakfastless start before daybreak —think of a twelve hours' ride on the sunny side of the cars, in the neighborhood of some persistent talker, rattling untranslatable jargon into your aching ears; think of a hurried repast, in some barbarous half-way house; amid a heterogeneous assortment of men, women, and children, beef, pork, and mutton; minus forks, minus spoons, minus castor, minus come-atable waiters, and four shillings and indigestion to pay. Think of a "collision"—disemboweled trunks, and a wooden leg; think of an arrival at a crowded hotel;

jammed, jaded, dusty, and dolorous; think of your closetless sentry-box of a room, infested by mosquitoes and Red Rovers; bed too narrow, window too small, candle too short, all the world and his wife a-bed, and the geography of the house an unexplained riddle. Think of your unrefreshing, vapor-bath sleep; think of the next morning, as seated on a dusty trunk, with your hair drooping about your ears, through which the whistle of the cars, and the jiggle-joggle of the brake-man, are still resounding; you try to remember, with your hand on your bewildered forehead, whether your breakfast robe is in the yellow trunk, or the black trunk, and if in either, whether it is at the top, bottom, or in the middle of the same, where your muslins and laces were deposited, what on earth you did with your dressing comb, and where amid your luggage, your toilet slippers may be possibly located. Think of a summons to breakfast at this interesting moment, the sun meanwhile streaming in through the blind chinks, with volcanic power. Think of all that, I say. Now, if I could travel incog, in masculine attire, no dresses to look after, no muslins to rumple, no bonnet to soil, no tresses to keep smooth, with only a hat and things, a neck-tie or two, a change of—of shirts—nothing but a moustache to twist into a horn when the dinner bell rings; just a dip into a wash-basin, a clean dicky, a jump into a pair of—trowsers, and above all, liberty to go where I liked, without being stared at or questioned; a seat in a chair on its hind-legs, on a breezy door-step, a seat on the stairs in a wide hall, "taking notes;" a peep everywhere I chose, by lordly right of my pantaloons; nobody nudging somebody, to inquire why Miss Spinks the authoress wore her hair in curls instead of plaits; or making the astounding discovery that it was hips, not hoops, that made her dress stand out—that now, would be worth talking about: I'll do it.

But stop—I should have to cut my hair short—I should have to shave every morning, or at any rate call for hot water and go through the motions; men would jostle rudely past me, just as if they never had said such pretty things to me in flounces; I should be obliged, just as I had secured a nice seat in the cars, to get up, and give it to some imperious woman, who would not even say "thank you;" I should have to look on with hungry eyes till "the ladies" were all served at table; I should have to pick up their fans, and reticules, and hand kerchiefs whenever they chose to drop them; I should have to give up the rocking-chairs, arm chairs, and sofas for their use, and be called "a brute" at that; I should have to rush out of the cars, with five minutes' grace, at some stopping place, to get a glass of milk, for some "crying baby," with a contracted swallowing apparatus, and be pursued for life by the curses of its owner, be cause the whistle sounded while his two shilling tumbler was yet in the voracious baby's tight grip. No—no—I'll stay a woman, and what's more, I'll stay at home.

SOLILOQUY OF A LITERARY HOUSEKEEPER.

"SPRING CLEANING!" Oh misery! Ceilings to be white-washed, walls to be cleaned, paint to be scoured, carpets to be taken up, shaken, and put down again; scrubbing women, painters, and whitewashers, all engaged for months ahead, or beginning on your house to secure the job, and then running off a day to somebody else's to secure another. Yes, spring cleaning to be done; closets, bags, and baskets to be disemboweled; furs and woolens to be packed away; children's last summer clothes to be inspected (not a garment that will fit—all grown up like Jack's bean-stalk); spring cleaning, sure enough. I might spring my feet off and not get all that done. When is that book of mine to get written, I'd like to know? It's Ma'am, will you have this? and Ma'am, will you have that? and Ma'am, will you have the other thing? May I be kissed if I hadn't more time to write when I lived in an attic on salt and potatoes, and scrubbed the floor myself. Must I turn my house topsy-turvy, and inside out, once a year, because my grandmother did, and send my MSS. flying to the four winds, for this traditionary "spring cleaning." Spring fiddlestick! Must I buy up all Broadway to be made into dresses, because all New York women go fashion-mad? What's the use of having a house, if you can't do as you like in it ? What's the use of being an authoress, if you can't indulge in the luxury of a shabby bonnet, or a comfortable old dress? What's the use of dressing when your cook can outshine you? What is the use of dragging brocade and velvet through ferry boats and omnibusses, to serve as mats for market-baskets and dirty boots? "There goes Lily Larkspur, the authoress, in that everlasting old black silk." Well—what's the use of being well off, if you can't wear old clothes. If I was poor, as I was once, I

couldn't afford it. Do you suppose I'm going to wrin-
kle up my face, scowling at unhappy little boys for
treading on a five-hundred-dollar silk? or fret myself
into a fever because some *gentleman* throws a cigar-
stump on its lustrous trailing folds? no, no; life is too
short for that, and much too earnest. Give me good
health—the morning for writing, and no interruptions,
plenty of fresh air afterwards, and an old gown to enjoy
it in, and you may mince along in your peacock dry-
goods till your soul is as shriveled as your body.

DINNER-PARTIES.

To FASTEN AS many drags as possible to the social ma-
chinery of to-day, seems to be the first idea of hospitality, which, there is every reason to fear, will gradually
be smothered in the process.

Perhaps the lady who gives the dinner-party would
really prefer a plain dinner with her friend Mrs. Jones,
than all the elaborate dinners she is in the habit of giving and attending; but her husband likes wines and
French cookery, and would consider anything else a
poor compliment to a guest; and so there's an end.

And now, what are these fine dinners? Just this: a
pleasant gleam of silver and china; a lovely disposition
of fruit and flowers; a great deal of dress, or undress,
on the part of the ladies; much swallow-tail, and an exquisite bit of cravat and kid-glove, on the part of the
gentlemen. Brains—as the gods please; but always a
procession of dishes, marched on and marshalled off,
for the requisite number of tedious hours, during which

you eat you know not what, because you must be ready with your answer for your elbow neighbor, or your *vis-a-vis*; during which, you taste much wine and nibble much confectionery, and finish up with coffee; and under the combined influence of all this you sink supinely into a soft chair or sofa, and the "feed" is over.

Everybody there feels just as you do. Everybody would like to creep into some quiet corner, and be let alone, till the process of digestion has had a chance.

Instead—they throw a too transparent enthusiasm into the inquiry, "How's your mother?" If the gods are kind, and there has been an inroad of measles or fever, the narrator may possibly give you ten minutes' reprieve from pumping up from beneath that dinner another query about "the baby." But if he—or she, too —is laboring, like yourself, with duck and quail, and paté and oyster, and wine and fruit and bon-bons, then may a good Providence put it into the distracted brain of the hostess to set some maiden a-foul of the piano!

Oh, but that is blessed! no matter what she plays, how hard she thumps, or how loud she screeches. Blessed—to lean back, and fold your kid gloves over your belt, and never move them till you applaud the performance, of which you know, nor care, any more than who struck Billy Patterson.

This over, you see a gentlemen coming towards you. You know by his looks, he too is suffering the pangs of repletion. Good heavens! how full of deceit is his smile, as he fastens on you, thinking *you* will talk! Mistaken man! you smile too, and both together agree that "the weather has been fine of late." This done, you look helplessly, with the untold pain of dumb animals, in each other's faces, and then glance furtively about to see if that piano-young-woman really means to leave your anguish unassuaged. She does. Hum!—you make an errand across the room to pick up a supposititious glove you dropped—and get rid of the parasite.

At last!—relief—there is your husband. *How* glad he is to see you! It's really worth going to the dinner-party to witness that man's affection for you at that moment. Now he can yawn behind his glove. Now he takes a seat *so* near, that no man or woman can interrupt his lazy heaven. He even smiles at you from very gladness of heart, and in thick utterance tells you, in order to keep you from going from his side, that "he don't see but you look as well as any woman in the room." You only needed that unwonted display of gallantry from the hypocritical wretch, to rise immediately and leave him to his fate, though you should, in doing it, rush madly on your own.

And this is "a dinner-party." For this men and women empty their purses, and fill their decanters and wardrobes, and merge their brains in their stomachs, and—are in the fashion!

Better is a leg of mutton and caper-sauce, and much lively talk, whensoever and wheresoever a friend, with or without an invitation, cares enough about you and yours with impromptu friendship to "drop in." Best clothes, best dishes, best wine, best parlors!—what are they, with rare exceptions, but extinguishers of wit and wisdom and digestion and geniality. Who will inaugurate us a little common-sense?

Queen Victoria—how glad I am she had such a good, loving husband, to compensate her for the misery of being a queen—tried her best to abolish the custom, prevalent in England at dinner, of the gentlemen remaining to guzzle wine after the ladies left. I am aware that guzzle is an unladylike word; but, as no other fits in there, I shall use it. Well—she succeeded only in shortening the guzzling period—not in abolishing it; so those consistent men remained, to drink toasts to "lovely women," whose backs they were so delighted to see retreating through the door.

What of it? Why, simply this, that Queen Victoria did what she could to civilize her own regal circle; and that she set a good precedent for American women of to-day to follow. I fail to see why, when a hostess has carefully watched the dishes and glasses come and go, at her husband's dinner-party, to the obstruction of all rational conversation, save by agonized spasms,—I fail to see why, when the gentlemen guests have eaten to satiety, and conversation might be supposed to be at last possible, why, at that precise, enjoyable period, the lady of the house should be obliged to accompany the empty plates to regions unknown and uncared for. This seems to me a question well worthy of consideration in this year of our Lord, 1868. It strikes me, rather an inglorious abdication for a woman of intelligence, who may be supposed to understand and take an interest in other things than the advance and retreat of salad, and ragouts, oysters, and chicken. I call it a relic of barbarism, of which men of intelligence should be ashamed. Then what advantage has the woman who cultivates her mental powers, over the veriest fool? It is

101

an insult to her. But you say, all women are not thoughtful or intelligent. Very true: and why should they be—save that they owe it to their own self-respect —when gentlemen thus offer premiums for insipidity? —why should they inform themselves upon any subjects but those of dressing well and feeding well?

It is a satisfaction to know that there are gentlemen, who endorse the other side of the question. There was lately a dinner given in New York to a literary gentleman of distinction. One of the gentlemen invited to attend it, said to his wife: "It is a shame that ladies should not attend this dinner. *You* ought to be there, and many other ladies who are authors." Acting upon this impulse, he suggested to the committee that ladies should be invited. The answer was: First—"It would be so awkward for the ladies. Secondly—there were very few literary ladies compared to the number of literary gentlemen." Now as to the question of "awkwardness," the boot, I think, was on the other foot; and if the ladies were awkward,—which was not a complimentary supposition,—why should the gentlemen be to blame for it? And if there were "few lady authoresses," why not ask the wives of the *editors* who were to be present?

No—this was not the reason.

What was it? *Tobacco*—yes, sir, tobacco! I don't add wine—but I might. In short, these men would be obliged to conduct themselves as gentlemen were ladies present; and they wanted a margin left for the reverse. They preferred a bar-room atmosphere to the refining presence of "lovely woman," about whom they wished to hiccup at a safe distance.

Perhaps, in justice, I should add, that it was suggested that they might perhaps see the animals feed
from the "musicians' balcony," or listen to the
speeches "through the crack of a door," with the servants, or in some such surreptitious and becoming and
complimentary manner, which a woman of spirit and
intelligence would, of course, be very likely to do.

To conclude, I trust those gentlemen who are in the
habit of bemoaning "the frivolity of our women, and
their sad addictedness to long milliner's bills," will
reckon up the cost of cigars and wine at these dinners,
from which ladies are excluded; and while they are on
the anxious seat, on the economy question, ask themselves whether, putting other reasons out of the question, the presence of ladies, on these occasions, would
not contribute greatly to *reduce their dinner expenses.*

THE HAPPY LOT OF A SEXTON.

NOT A BAD thing to be the sexton of a church. In the
first place, he gets a conspicuous start in life, by advertising on the outer wall of the church, his perfect willingness to bury all the parish in which he carries on his
cheerful business,—a business which can never be dull
with him, because somebody is always dying, and
somebody else is always being born for the same end.
Then Sunday comes regularly once a week, so that his
"shop" never closes, and consequently always wants
his broom of reform. Then the sexton has his little alle-
viations, when he has had enough of the sermon: he
can make an errand out in the vestibule, after imagi-

103

nary bad children, who might disturb the minister, or to see that the outer door don't creak or bang un-Sabbatically. When he gets tired of that, he can sit comfortably down on his stool near the door, which he can tilt back on its hind legs, out of view of all critical worshippers (except me), and then, and there, he can draw out that omnipresent and national jack-knife, which is his ever-present solace in every time of need. First—he can clean his nails, and pare them, varying the performance by biting off their refractory edges. Then he can commence scratching off any little spots on his trousers or coat with the point of the same. When this little exercise is concluded, and the sermon is not, he can draw from another pocket a case-comb, and put those fine touches to his hair which the early church-bell had interfered with. It is tiresome on him then for a few minutes, unless some impertinent sunbeam gilds the minister's sacerdotal nose, and gives him an excuse for going up in the gallery to lower a curtain, in that dexterous manner which only a professional can compass. By this time "seventeenthly" having been concluded by the minister, the sexton hurries to the church-door, doubling up with a dexterous twist any aisle-chairs which have done duty *pro tem.* and tucking them in their appropriate corner, and then takes his position in the porch, the most important personage present save the minister himself. To the questions, "Is it the clergymen of this church who has just preached?" addressed him by some stranger, and "Is there to be an afternoon or an evening service?" and "Can you tell me where is the clergyman's residence?" and "Will you hand this note to the clergyman?" etc., etc., he returns a prompt and proud answer. And, even when Miss Belinda Jones steps to his elbow, and requests that he will pay a little more attention to ventilating the church between the services, and in fact during the week, in order that she may escape the infliction of her usual Sunday headache; and when she expatiates touchingly on the blessing and healthfulness and cheapness of fresh air, and his Christian duty to apportion a sufficient quantity to each individual to sustain life, and that meek and quiet spirit that is enjoined; even then, he bows respectfully, nor mentions that, were ventilation thus insured by open windows, and the life of the audience prolonged, it might make him a little more trouble in dusting the cushions, which he could by no means permit. The polite sexton does not mention this, nor that he "hates fidgetty females," but he bows politely and affirmatively, locks up the bad air in the church all the same, and goes home to his roast-beef and his babies.

A BID FOR AN EDITORSHIP.

I THINK I should like to be an editor, if somebody would do all the disagreeable, hard work for me, and leave me only the fancy touches. I don't know how profound my political articles would be, but they would be *mine*. I think my book reviews would be pleasant reading, at least to everybody but some of the authors. I should have a high railing round my editorial desk, and "through the lattice" microscopically and leisurely regard the row of expectant men waiting outside for a hearing. I should not need a spittoon in my office. Nobody should contribute to my paper who smoked, or chewed, or snuffed tobacco; that would diminish my contributors' list about right. I should discard Webster and Walker, and inaugurate a dictionary of my own. I should allow anybody who felt inclined to send me samples of big strawberries and peaches, and bunches of flowers; and I should get a fine library, free gratis, out of the books sent me to review. As to grinding the axes of the givers in return, why that, of course, should always be left to the option of the editor. Before I commenced an editor's life, I should secure money enough in some way to be able to snap my fingers in the face of that grim ogre, "Stop my Paper!" I tell you I *wouldn't* stop it. It is a free country. I'd keep on sending it to him. I'd always have something in every number about him, so that he couldn't do without having it, how much soever he might want to.

Then you should see my desk. It should be dusted once a year, to show editors what a desk *might* be. My editorial chair shouldn't pivot; there should be no shadow of turning about that. Gibraltar should be a circumstance to it. The windows of my editorial den should be scraped with a sharp knife occasionally, to take off sufficient dirt to enable me to write legibly. I should keep my best bonnet in a bandbox under my desk, for any sudden dress emergency, as do editors their go-to-meetin' hat. Like them, too, I should have a small looking-glass for—visitors! also a bottle of —"medicine" for—visitors! I don't think I should need a safe, as the principles upon which my paper would be conducted would render it unnecessary. My object would be to amuse *myself*, and say just what came uppermost, not by any means to please or edify my species. Now, I have examined all the papers that cross my threshold, and I am very sure that I have hit on quite an original idea.

If it stormed badly on publication day, I wouldn't send the poor devils in my employ out with my paper, just because my subscribers fancied they wanted it. Let 'em wait. The first fair day they'd have it, of course. In the meantime, the printer's devil, and the compositors, and the rest of 'em, could play chequers till the sky cleared up.

If anybody sued me for libel, I'd—I'd whine out, "Aint you ashamed to annoy a female? Why don't you strike one of your own size?" I should insist on being treated with the deference due to a woman, though in all respects I should demand the untrammeled-seven-leagued-boots-freedom of a man. My object would be to hit everybody smack between the eyes, when I felt like it; and when I saw brutal retribution coming, to throw my silk apron over my head and whimper.

I have not yet decided upon the title of my paper. Children are not generally baptized until after they are born. Nor do I know who will stand sponsor. All that is in the misty future. As to the price, I should nail up a cash-box at the foot of the stairs, and people could drop in whatever they liked. I should, by that means, not only show my unshaken confidence in human na-ture, but also learn in what estimation the general pub-lic held my services. There's nothing so dear to my heart as spontaneity.

JAMES RUSSELL LOWELL.

Lowell is remembered, if seldom read, as a respected American poet, but he first leaped into the public eye with an audacious satire that has lost none of its ability either to amuse or to surprise us. *A Fable for Critics* is notable for its clever silliness, but also for its unusually perceptive criticisms of contemporary poets. One might not agree with every one of Lowell's opinions, but it would be hard to say any of them were not well thought out. Poe could not forgive what Lowell said about him (the *Fable for Critics* provoked one of Poe's famous hatchet reviews in his magazine, the *Southern Literary Messenger*), but a less prejudiced reader will probably agree that Lowell has painted a pretty fair portrait of Poe—"three fifths of him genius and two fifths sheer fudge"—in half a dozen lines.

Not content with producing the cleverest bit of poetical whimsy yet to come from America, Lowell added a preface set in prose, but actually written in the same meter as the poem. Then he topped it all off with a metrical title page, at which point we can only say that the joke has been carried to perfection.

READER! *walk up at once (it will soon be too late) and buy at a perfectly ruinous rate*

A

FABLE FOR CRITICS;

OR

Better—

I like, as a thing that the reader's first fancy may strike, an old fashioned title-page, such as presents a tabular view of the volume's contents—

A GLANCE
AT A FEW OF OUR LITERARY PROGENIES

(*Mrs. Malaprop's word*)

FROM

THE TUB OF DIOGENES;

THAT IS,

A SERIES OF JOKES

By A Wonderful Quiz,

who accompanies himself with a rub-a-dub-dub, full of spirit and grace on the top of the tub.

SET FORTH IN

October, the 21st day, in the year '48,

BY

G. P. PUTNAM, BROADWAY.

A FABLE FOR CRITICS.

IT BEING THE commonest mode of procedure, I premise a few candid remarks

TO THE READER:—

This trifle, begun to please only myself and my own private fancy, was laid on the shelf. But some friends, who had seen it, induced me, by dint of saying they liked it, to put it in print. That is, having come to that very conclusion, I asked their advice when 'twould make no confusion. For though (in the gentlest of ways) they had hinted it was scarce worth the while, I should doubtless have printed it.

I began it, intending a Fable, a frail, slender thing, rhyme-ywinged, with a sting in its tail. But, by addings and alterings not previously planned, digressions chance-hatched, like birds' eggs in the sand, and dawdlings to suit every whimsey's demand (always freeing the bird which I held in my hand, for the two perched, perhaps out of reach, in the tree),—it grew by degrees to the size which you see. I was like the old woman that carried the calf, and my neighbors, like hers, no doubt, wonder and laugh; and when, my strained arms with their grown burthen full, I call it my Fable, they call it a bull.

Having scrawled at full gallop (as far as that goes) in a style that is neither good verse nor bad prose, and being a person whom nobody knows, some people will

say I am rather more free with my readers than it is becoming to be, that I seem to expect them to wait on my leisure in following wherever I wander at pleasure, that, in short, I take more than a young author's lawful ease, and laugh in a queer way so like Mephistopheles, that the Public will doubt, as they grope through my rhythm, if in truth I am making fun *of* them or *with* them.

So the excellent Public is hereby assured that the sale of my book is already secured. For there is not a poet throughout the whole land but will purchase a copy or two out of hand, in the fond expectation of being amused in it, by seeing his betters cut up and abused in it. Now, I find, by a pretty exact calculation, there are something like ten thousand bards in the nation, of that special variety whom the Review and Magazine critics call *lofty* and *true*, and about thirty thousand (*this* tribe is increasing) of the kinds who are termed *full of promise* and *pleasing*. The Public will see by a glance at this schedule, that they cannot expect me to be over-sedulous about courting *them*, since it seems I have got enough fuel made sure of for boiling my pot.

As for such of our poets as find not their names mentioned once in my pages, with praises or blames, let them SEND IN THEIR CARDS, without further DELAY, to my friend G. P. PUTNAM, Esquire, in Broadway, where a LIST will be kept with the strictest regard to the day and the hour of receiving the card. Then, taking them up as I chance to have time (that is, if their names can be twisted in rhyme), I will honestly give each his PROPER POSITION, at the rate of ONE AUTHOR to each NEW

EDITION. Thus a PREMIUM is offered sufficiently HIGH (as
the magazines say when they tell their best lie) to induce bards to CLUB their resources and buy the balance
of every edition, until they have all of them fairly been
run through the mill.

One word to such readers (judicious and wise) as
read books with something behind the mere eyes, of
whom in the country, perhaps, there are two, including
myself, gentle reader, and you. All the characters
sketched in this slight *jeu d'esprit*, though, it may be,
they seem, here and there, rather free, and drawn from
a somewhat too cynical standpoint, are *meant* to be
faithful, for that is the grand point, and none but an
owl would feel sore at a rub from a jester who tells
you, without any subterfuge, that he sits in Diogenes'
tub.

A Preliminary Note to the Second Edition,

Though it well may be reckoned, of all composition,
the species at once most delightful and healthy, is a
thing which an author, unless he be wealthy and willing to pay for that kind of delight, is not, in all instances, called on to write, though there are, it is said,
who, their spirits to cheer, slip in a new title-page
three times a year, and in this way snuff up an imagi-
nary savor of that sweetest of dishes, the popular favor,
—much as if a starved painter should fall to and treat
the Ugolino inside to a picture of meat.

You remember (if not, pray turn, backward and
look) that, in writing the preface which ushered my

book, I treated you, excellent Public, not merely with a cool disregard, but downright cavalierly. Now I would not take back the least thing I then said, though I thereby could butter both sides of my bread, for I never could see that an author owed aught to the people he solaced, diverted, or taught; and, as for mere fame, I have long ago learned that the persons by whom it is finally earned are those with whom *your* verdict weighed not a pin, unsustained by the higher court sitting within.

But I wander from what I intended to say,—that you have, namely, shown such a liberal way of thinking, and so much æsthetic perception of anonymous worth in the handsome reception you gave to my book, spite of some private piques (having bought the first thousand in barely two weeks), that I think, past a doubt, if you measured the phiz of yours most devotedly, Wonderful Quiz, you would find that its vertical section was shorter, by an inch and two tenths, or 'twixt that and a quarter.

You have watched a child playing—in those wondrous years when belief is not bound to the eyes and the ears, and the vision divine is so clear and unmarred, that each baker of pies in the dirt is a bard? Give a knife and a shingle, he fits out a fleet, and, on that little mud-puddle over the street, his fancy, in purest good faith, will make sail round the globe with a puff of his breath for a gale, will visit, in barely ten minutes, all climes, and do the Columbus-feat hundreds of times. Or, suppose the young poet fresh stored with delights from that Bible of childhood, the Arabian Nights, he will turn to a crony and cry, "Jack, let's play that I am

113

a Genius!" Jacky straightway makes Aladdin's lamp
out of a stone, and, for hours, they enjoy each his own
supernatural powers. This is all very pretty and pleasant, but then suppose our two urchins, have grown
into men, and both have turned authors,—one says to
his brother, "Let's play we're the American some-
things or other,—say Homer or Sophocles, Goethe or
Scott (only let them be big enough, no matter what).
Come, you shall be Byron or Pope, which you choose:
I'll be Coleridge, and both shall write mutual reviews."
So they both (as mere strangers) before many days
send each other a cord of anonymous bays. Each piling
his epithets, smiles in his sleeve to see what his friend
can be made to believe; each, reading the other's unbi-
ased review, thinks—Here's pretty high praise, but no
more than my due. Well, we laugh at them both, and
yet make no great fuss when the same farce is acted to
benefit us. Even I, who, it asked, scarce a month since,
what Fudge meant, should have answered, the dear
Public's critical judgment, begin to think sharp-witted
Horace spoke sooth when he said that the Public *sometimes* hit the truth.

In reading these lines, you perhaps have a vision of a
person in pretty good health and condition; and yet,
since I put forth my primary edition, I have been
crushed, scorched, withered, used up and put down
(by Smith with the cordial assistance of Brown), in all,
if you put any faith in my rhymes, to the number of
ninety-five several times, and, while I am writing,—I
tremble to think of it, for I may at this moment be just
on the brink of it,—Molybdostom, angry at being
omitted, has begun a critique,—am I not to be pitied?

Now I shall not crush *them* since, indeed, for that matter, no pressure I know of could render them flatter; nor wither, nor scorch them,—no action of fire could make either them or their articles drier; nor waste time in putting them down—I am thinking not their own self-inflation will keep them from sinking; for there's this contradiction about the whole bevy,—though without the least weight, they are awfully heavy. No, my dear honest bore, *surdo fabulam narras*, they are no more to me than a rat in the arras. I can walk with the Doctor, get facts from the Don, or draw out the Lambish quintessence of John, and feel nothing more than a half-comic sorrow, to think that they all will be lying to-morrow tossed carelessly up on the waste-paper shelves, and forgotten by all but their half-dozen selves. Once snug in my attic, my fire in a roar, I leave the whole pack of them outside the door. With Hakluyt or Purchas I wander away to the black northern seas or barbaric Cathay; get *fou* with O'Shanter, and sober me then with that builder of brick-kilnish dramas, rare Ben; snuff Herbert, as holy as a flower on a grave; with Fletcher wax tender, o'er Chapman grow brave; with Marlowe or Kyd take a fine poet-rave; in Very, most Hebrew of Saxons, find peace; with Lycidas welter on vext Irish seas; with Webster grow wild, and climb earthward again, down by mystical Browne's Jacob's-ladder-like brain, to that spiritual Pepys (Cotton's version) Montaigne; find a new depth in Wordsworth, undreamed of before, that marvel, a poet divine who can bore. Or, out of my study, the scholar thrown off, Nature holds up her shield 'gainst the sneer and the scoff; the landscape, forever consol-

ing and kind, pours her wine and her oil on the smarts
of the mind. The waterfall, scattering its vanishing
gems; the tall grove of hemlocks, with moss on their
stems, like plashes of sunlight; the pond in the woods,
where no foot but mine and the bittern's intrudes,
where pitcher-plants purple and gentians hard by recall
to September the blue of June's sky; these are all my
kind neighbors, and leave me no wish to say aught to
you all, my poor critics, but—pish! I've buried the
hatchet: I'm twisting an allumette out of one of you
now, and relighting my calumet. In your private capac-
ities, come when you please, I will give you my hand
and a fresh pipe apiece.

As I ran through the leaves of my poor little book,
to take a fond author's first tremulous look, it was
quite an excitement to hunt the *errata*, sprawled in as
birds' tracks are in some kinds of strata (only these
made things crookeder). Fancy an heir that a father
had seen born well-featured and fair, turning suddenly
wry-nosed, club-footed, squint-eyed, hair-lipped, wap-
per-jawed, carrot-haired, from a pride become an aversion,—my case was yet worse. A club-foot (by way of
a change) in a verse, I might have forgiven, an *o*'s being wry, a limp in an *e*, or a cock in an *i*,—but to have
the sweet babe of my brain served in *pi!* I am not
queasy-stomached, but such a Thyestean banquet as
that was quite out of the question.

In the edition now issued no pains are neglected,
and my verses, as orators say, stand corrected. Yet
some blunders remain of the public's own make, which
I wish to correct for my personal sake. For instance, a
character drawn in pure fun and condensing the traits

of a dozen in one, has been, as I hear, by some persons applied to a good friend of mine, whom to stab in the side, as we walked along chatting and joking together, would not be *my* way. I can hardly tell whether a question will ever arise in which he and I should by any strange fortune agree, but meanwhile my esteem for him grows as I know him, and, though not the best judge on earth of a poem, he knows what it is he is saying and why, and is honest and fearless, two good points which I have not found so rife I can easily smother my love for them, whether on my side or t'other.

For my other *anonymi*, you may be sure that I know what is meant by a caricature, and what by a portrait. There *are* those who think it is capital fun to be spattering their ink on quiet, unquarrelsome folk, but the minute the game changes sides and the others begin it, they see something savage and horrible in it. As for me I respect neither women nor men for their gender, nor own any sex in a pen. I choose just to hint to some causeless unfriends that, as far as I know, there are always two ends (and one of them heaviest, too) to a staff, and two parties also to every good laugh.

On Cooper.

Here's Cooper, who's written six volumes to show
He's as good as a lord: well, let's grant that he's so;
If a person prefer that description of praise,
Why, a coronet's certainly cheaper than bays;
But he need take no pains to convince us he's not

117

(As his enemies say) the American Scott.
Choose any twelve men, and let C. read aloud
That one of his novels of which he's most proud,
And I'd lay any bet that, without ever quitting
Their box, they'd be all, to a man, for acquitting.
He has drawn you one character, though, that is new,
One wildflower he's plucked that is wet with the dew
Of this fresh Western world, and, the thing not to
    mince,
He has done naught but copy it ill ever since;
His Indians, with proper respect be it said,
Are just Natty Bumppo, daubed over with red,
And his very Long Toms are the same useful Nat,
Rigged up in duck pants and a sou'wester hat
(Though once in a Coffin, a good chance was found
To have slipped the old fellow away underground).
All his other men-figures are clothes upon sticks,
The *derniere chemise* of a man in a fix
(As a captain besieged, when his garrison small,
Sets up caps upon poles to be seen o'er the wall);
And the women he draws from one model don't vary.
All sappy as maples and flat as a prairie.
When a character's wanted, he goes to the task
As a cooper would do in composing a cask;
He picks out the staves, of their qualities heedful,
Just hoops them together as tight as is needful,
And, if the best fortune should crown the attempt, he
Has made at the most something wooden and empty.

    Don't suppose I would underrate Cooper's abilities;
If I thought you'd do that, I should feel very ill at ease;
The men who have given to *one* character life
And objective existence are not very rife;

118

You may number them all, both prose-writers and
    singers,
Without overrunning the bounds of your fingers,
And Natty won't go to oblivion quicker
Than Adams the parson or Primrose the vicar.
    "There is one thing in Cooper I like, too, and that is
That on manners he lectures his countrymen gratis;
Not precisely so either, because, for a rarity,
He is paid for his tickets in unpopularity.
Now he may overcharge his American pictures,
But you'll grant there's a good deal of truth in his
    strictures;
And I honor the man who is willing to sink
Half his present repute for the freedom to think,
And, when he has thought, be his cause strong or
    weak,
Will risk t'other half for the freedom to speak,
Caring naught for what vengeance the mob has in
    store,
Let that mob be the upper ten thousand or lower.

On Poe and Longfellow.

There comes Poe, with his raven, like Barnaby Rudge,
Three fifths of him genius and two fifths sheer fudge,
Who talks like a book of iambs and pentameters,
In a way to make people of common sense damn me-
    ters,
Who has written some things quite the best of their
    kind,

119

But the heart somehow seems all squeezed out by the
    mind,
Who—But hey-day! What's this? Messieurs Mathews
    and Poe,
You mustn't fling mud-balls at Longfellow so,
Does it make a man worse that his character's such
As to make his friends love him (as you think) too
    much?
Why, there is not a bard at this moment alive
More willing than he that his fellows should thrive;
While you are abusing him thus, even now
He would help either one of you out of a slough;
You may say that he's smooth and all that till you're
    hoarse,
But remember that elegance also is force;
After polishing granite as much as you will,
The heart keeps its tough old persistency still;
Deduct all you can, *that* still keeps you at bay;
Why, he'll live till men weary of Collins and Gray.
I'm not over-fond of Greek meters in English,
To me rhyme's a gain, so it be not too jinglish,
And your modern hexameter verses are no more
Like Greek ones than sleek Mr. Pope is like Homer;
As the roar of the sea to the coo of a pigeon is,
So, compared to your moderns, sounds old Melesi-
    genes;
I may be too partial, the reason, perhaps, o't is
That I've heard the old blind man recite his own rhap-
    sodies,
And my ear with that music impregnate may be,
Like the poor exiled shell with the soul of the sea,
Or as one can't bear Strauss when his nature is cloven

To its deeps within deeps by the stroke of Beethoven;
But, set that aside, and 'tis truth that I speak,
Had Theocritus written in English, not Greek,
I believe that his exquisite sense would scarce change a
    line
In that rare, tender, virgin-like pastoral Evangeline.
That's not ancient nor modern, its place is apart
Where time has no sway, in the realm of pure Art,
'Tis a shrine of retreat from Earth's hubbub and strife
As quiet and chaste as the author's own life.

On James Russell Lowell.

There is Lowell, who's striving Parnassus to climb
With a whole bale of isms tied together with rhyme,
He might get on alone, spite of brambles and boulders,
But he can't with that bundle he has on his shoulders,
The top of the hill he will ne'er come nigh reaching
Till he learns the distinction 'twixt singing and preach-
    ing;
His lyre has some chords that would ring pretty well,
But he'd rather by half make a drum of the shell,
And rattle away till he's old as Methusalem,
At the head of a march to the last new Jerusalem.

OLIVER WENDELL HOLMES

Few of our writers are equally well known for poetry and for prose, but Oliver Wendell Holmes has that distinction. His *Autocrat of the Breakfast Table* was something entirely new, not just in American letters but in the literature of the English language. The nearest predecessors are the rambling philosophical novels of Thomas Love Peacock; but there is something so sharp and distinct about the mind of Holmes that he never seems to ramble, even though it would be hard to say with any show of reason that there is anything but rambling in the book. The sample here shows off Holmes' prose at its best: intensely intellectual but unfailingly conversational.

"The Deacon's Masterpiece" applies the same virtues to comic verse. The tone is light, and it seems almost entirely natural—as if the poet's casual conversation simply happened to come out in rhyme and meter. Yet there is something sharp and distinct about the thought in this "logical tale"; nothing is fuzzy, nothing thought out only halfway.

It is probably superfluous to remind our readers that the son of Oliver Wendell Holmes—Oliver Wendell Holmes, Jr. —inherited his father's keen logical mind, and found work that suited his capacity sitting on the bench of the United States Supreme Court.

THE AUTOCRAT OF
THE BREAKFAST TABLE

—IF A FELLOW attacked my opinions in print would I reply? Not I. Do you think I don't understand what my friend, the Professor, long ago called *the hydrostatic paradox of controversy?*

Don't know what that means?—Well, I will tell you. You know, that, if you had a bent tube, one arm of which was of the size of a pipe-stem, and the other big enough to hold the ocean, water would stand at the same height in one as in the other. Controversy equalizes fools and wise men in the same way,—*and the fools know it.*

—No, but I often read what they say about other people. There are about a dozen phrases which all come tumbling along together, like the tongs, and the shovel, and the poker, and the brush, and the bellows, in one of those domestic avalanches that everybody knows. If you get one, you get the whole lot.

What are they?—Oh, that depends a good deal on latitude and longitude. Epithets follow the isothermal lines pretty accurately. Grouping them in two families, one finds himself a clever, genial, witty, wise, brilliant, sparkling, thoughtful, distinguished, celebrated, illustrious scholar and perfect gentleman, and first writer of the age; or a dull, foolish, wicked, pert, shallow, ignorant, insolent, traitorous, black-hearted outcast, and disgrace to civilization.

What do I think determines the set of phrases a man gets?—Well, I should say a set of influences something like these:—1st. Relationships, political, religious, social, domestic. 2d. Oyster, in the form of suppers given to gentlemen connected with criticism. I believe in the school, the college, and the clergy; but my sovereign logic, for regulating public opinion— which means commonly the opinion of half a dozen of

123

the critical gentry—is the following: *Major proposition.* Oysters *au naturel. Minor proposition.* The same "scalloped." *Conclusion.* That—(here insert entertainer's name) is clever, witty, wise, brilliant,—and the rest.

—No, it isn't exactly bribery. One man has oysters, and another epithets. It is an exchange of hospitalities; one gives a "spread" on linen, and the other on paper, —that is all. Don't you think you and I should be apt to do just so, if we were in the critical line? I am sure I couldn't resist the softening influences of hospitality. I don't like to dine out, you know,—I dine so well at our own table, [our landlady looked radiant,] and the company is so pleasant [a rustling movement of satisfaction among the boarders]; but if I did partake of a man's salt, with such additions as that article of food requires to make it palatable, I could never abuse him, and if I had to speak of him, I suppose I should hang my set of jingling epithets round him like a string of sleigh-bells. Good feeling helps society to make liars of most of us,—not absolute liars, but such careless handlers of truth that its sharp corners get terribly rounded. I love truth as chiefest among the virtues; I trust it runs in my blood; but I would never be a critic, because I know I could not always tell it. I might write a criticism of a book that happened to please me; that is another matter.

THE DEACON'S MASTERPIECE;
OR, THE WONDERFUL ONE-HOSS SHAY.

A Logical Story.

HAVE YOU HEARD of the wonderful one-hoss shay,
That was built in such a logical way
It ran a hundred years to a day,
And then, of a sudden, it—ah, but stay,
I'll tell you what happened without delay,
Scaring the parson into fits,
Frightening people out of their wits,—
Have you ever heard of that, I say?

Seventeen hundred and fifty-five,
Georgius Secundus was then alive,—
Snuffy old drone from the German hive;
That was the year when Lisbon-town
Saw the earth open and gulp her down,
And Braddock's army was done so brown,
Left without a scalp to its crown.
It was on the terrible earthquake-day
That the Deacon finished the one-hoss shay.

Now in building of chaises, I tell you what,
There is always *somewhere* a weakest spot,—
In hub, tire, felloe, in spring or thill,
In panel, or crossbar, or floor, or sill,
In screw, bolt, thoroughbrace,—lurking still,
Find it somewhere you must and will,—
Above or below, or within or without,—
And that's the reason, beyond a doubt,

125

A chaise *breaks down*, but doesn't *wear out*.

But the Deacon swore (as Deacons do,
With an "I dew vum," or an "I tell *yeou*,")
He would build one shay to beat the taown
'n' the keounty 'n' all the kentry raoun';
It should be so built that it *couldn'* break daown!
—"Fur," said the Deacon, "'t's mighty plain
Thut the weakes' place mus' stan' the strain;
'n' the way t' fix it, uz I maintain,
   Is only jest
T'' make that place uz strong uz the rest."

So the Deacon inquired of the village folk
Where he could find the strongest oak,
That couldn't be split nor bent nor broke,—
That was for spokes and floor and sills;
He sent for lancewood to make the thills;
The crossbars were ash, from the straightest trees,
The panels of whitewood, that cuts like cheese,
But lasts like iron for things like these;
The hubs of logs from the "Settler's ellum,"—
Last of its timber,—they couldn't sell 'em,
Never an axe had seen their chips,
And the wedges flew from between their lips,
Their blunt ends frizzled like celery-tips;
Step and prop-iron, bolt and screw,
Spring, tire, axle, and linchpin too,
Steel of the finest, bright and blue;
Thoroughbrace bison-skin, thick and wide;
Boot, top, dasher, from tough old hide
Found in the pit when the tanner died.

That was the way he "put her through."
"There!" said the Deacon, "naow she'll dew."

Do! I tell you, I rather guess
She was a wonder, and nothing less!

Colts grew horses, beards turned gray,
Deacon and deaconess dropped away,
Children and grandchildren—where were they?
But there stood the stout old one-hoss-shay
As fresh as on Lisbon-earthquake-day!

EIGHTEEN HUNDRED;—it came and found
The Deacon's Masterpiece strong and sound.
Eighteen hundred increased by ten;—
"Hahnsum kerridge" they called it then.
Eighteen hundred and twenty came;—
Running as usual; much the same.
Thirty and forty at last arrive,
And then come fifty, and FIFTY-FIVE.

Little of all we value here
Wakes on the morn of its hundredth year
Without both feeling and looking queer.
In fact, there's nothing that keeps its youth,
So far as I know, but a tree and truth.
(This is a moral that runs at large;
Take it.—You're welcome.—No extra charge.)

FIRST OF NOVEMBER,—the Earthquake-day.—
There are traces of age in the one-hoss-shay,
A general flavor of mild decay,

But nothing local, as one may say.
There couldn't be,—for the Deacon's art
Had made it so like in every part
That there wasn't a chance for one to start.
For the wheels were just as strong as the thills,
And the floor was just as strong as the sills,
And the panels just as strong as the floor,
And the whippletree neither less nor more,
And the back-crossbar as strong as the fore,
And spring and axle and hub encore,
And yet, as a whole, it is past a doubt
In another hour it will be worn out!

First of November, 'Fifty-five!
This morning the parson takes a drive.
Now, small boys, get out of the way!
Here comes the wonderful one-hoss-shay,
Drawn by a rat-tailed, ewe-necked bay.
"Huddup!" said the parson.—Off went they.

The parson was working his Sunday's text,—
Had got to *fifthly*, and stopped perplexed
At what the—Moses—was coming next.
All at once the horse stood still,
Close by the meet'n'-house on the hill.
—First a shiver, and then a thrill,
Then something decidedly like a spill,—

And the parson was sitting upon a rock,
At half-past nine by the meet'n'-house clock,—
Just the hour of the Earthquake shock!
—What do you think the parson found,

When he got up and stared around?
The poor old chaise in a heap or mound,
As if it had been to the mill and ground!
You see, of course, if you're not a dunce,
How it went to pieces all at once,—
All at once, and nothing first,—
Just as bubbles do when they burst.

End of the wonderful one-hoss-shay.
Logic is logic. That's all I say.

JOHN PHOENIX.

George Horatio Derby—alias Squibob or John Phoenix—is probably the first considerable writer to have come out of California. Although he is largely ignored by mainstream literary culture—whatever that is—today, he still has his rabid fans. And with good reason: he is very, very funny. His "New System of English Grammar" is earnestly recommended as a recitation piece; with practice, the example paragraphs (beginning with "As a 19 young and 76 beautiful lady...") may be rattled off at a breakneck pace, which cannot fail to reduce the audience to helpless giggles. Much of the humor comes from the fact that, superficially at least, this "new system" actually seems like a workable idea.

A NEW SYSTEM OF ENGLISH GRAMMAR.

I HAVE OFTEN thought that the adjectives of the English language were not sufficiently definite for the purposes of description. They have but three degrees of comparison—a very insufficient number, certainly, when we consider that they are to he applied to a thousand objects, which, though of the same general class or quality, differ from each other by a thousand different shades or degrees of the same peculiarity. Thus, though there are three hundred and sixty-five days in a year, all of which must, from the nature of things, differ from each other in the matter of climate,—we have but half a dozen expressions to convey to one another

130

our ideas of this inequality. We say—"It is a fine day;" "It is a *very* fine day;" "It is the *finest* day we have seen;" or, "It is an unpleasant day;" "A *very* unpleasant day;" "The *most* unpleasant day we ever saw." But it is plain, that none of these expressions give an *exact* idea of the nature of the day; and the two superlative expressions are generally untrue. I once heard a gentleman remark, on a rainy, snowy, windy and (in the ordinary English language) indescribable day, that it was "most preposterous weather." He came nearer to giving a correct idea of it, than he could have done by any ordinary mode of expression; but his description was not sufficiently definite.

Again:—we say of a lady—"She is beautiful;" "She is *very* beautiful," or "She is *perfectly* beautiful;"—descriptions, which, to one who never saw her, are no descriptions at all, for among thousands of women he has seen, probably no two are equally beautiful; and as to a *perfectly* beautiful woman, he knows that no such being was ever created—unless by G. P. R. James, for one of the two horsemen to fall in love with, and marry at the end of the second volume.

If I meet Smith in the street, and ask him—as I am pretty sure to do—"How he does?" he infallibly replies—"*Tolerable*, thank you"—which gives me no *exact* idea of Smith's health—for he has made the same reply to me on a hundred different occasions—on every one of which there *must* have been some slight shade of difference in his physical economy, and of course a corresponding change in his feelings.

To a man of a mathematical turn of mind—to a student and lover of the exact sciences these inaccuracies of expression—this inability to understand *exactly* how things are, must be a constant source of annoyance; and to one who like myself, unites this turn of mind to an ardent love of truth, for its own sake—the reflection that the English language does not enable us to speak the truth with exactness, is peculiarly painful. For this reason I have, with some trouble, made myself thoroughly acquainted with every ancient and modern language, in the hope that I might find some one of them that would enable me to express precisely my ideas; but the same insufficiency of adjectives exists in all except that of the Flathead Indians of Puget Sound, which consists of but forty-six words, mostly nouns; but to the constant use of which exists the objection, that nobody but that tribe can understand it. And as their literary and scientific advancement is not such as to make a residence among them, for a man of my disposition, desirable, I have abandoned the use of their language, in the belief that for me it is *hyas. cultus.*, or as the Spaniard hath it, *no me vale nada*.

Despairing, therefore, of making new discoveries in foreign languages, I have set myself seriously to work to reform our own; and have, I think, made an important discovery, which, when developed into a system and universally adopted, will give a precision of expression, and a consequent clearness of idea, that will leave little to be desired, and will, I modestly hope, immortalize my humble name as the promulgator of the truth and the benefactor of the human race.

Before entering upon my system I will give you an account of its discovery (which, perhaps I might with more modesty term an adaptation and enlargement of the idea of another), which will surprise you by its simplicity, and like the method of standing eggs on end, of Columbus, the inventions of printing, gunpowder and the mariner's compass— prove another exemplification of the truth of Hannah More's beautifully expressed sentiment:

"Large streams from little fountains flow,
Large aches from little toe-corns grow."

During the past week my attention was attracted by a large placard embellishing the corners of our streets, headed in mighty capitals, with the word "Phrenology," and illustrated by a map of a man's head, closely shaven, and laid off in lots, duly numbered from one to forty-seven. Beneath this edifying illustration appeared a legend, informing the inhabitants of San Diego and vicinity that Professor Dodge had arrived, and taken rooms (which was inaccurate, as he had but one room) at the Gyascutus House, where he would be happy to examine and furnish them with a chart of their heads, showing the moral and intellectual endowments, at the low price of three dollars each.

Always gratified with an opportunity of spending my money and making scientific researches, I immediately had my hair cut and carefully combed, and hastened to present myself and my head to the Professor's notice. I found him a tall and thin Professor, in a suit of rusty, not to say seedy black, with a closely buttoned vest, and no perceptible shirt-collar or wristbands. His nose was red, his spectacles were blue, and he wore a brown wig, beneath which, as I subsequently ascertained, his bald head was laid off in lots, marked and numbered with Indian ink, after the manner of the diagram upon his advertisement. Upon a small table lay many little books with yellow covers, several of the placards, pen and ink, a pair of iron calipers with brass knobs, and six dollars in silver. Having explained the object of my visit, and increased the pile of silver by six half-dollars from my pocket—whereat he smiled, and I observed he wore false teeth—(scientific men always do; they love to encourage art) the Professor placed me in a chair, and rapidly manipulating my head, after the manner of a *sham pooh* (I am not certain as to the orthography of this expression), said that my temperament was "lymphatic, nervous, bilious." I remarked that "I thought myself dyspeptic," but he made no reply. Then seizing on the callipers, he embraced with them my head in various places, and made notes upon a small card that lay near him on the table. He then stated that my "hair was getting very thin on the top," placed in my hand one of the yellow-covered books, which I found to be an almanac containing anecdotes about the virtues of Dodge's Hair Invigorator, and recommending it to my perusal, he remarked that he was agent for the sale of this wonderful fluid, and urged me to purchase a bottle—price two dollars. Stating my willingness to do so, the Professor produced it from a hair trunk that stood in a corner of the room, which he stated, by the way, was originally an ordinary pine box, on which the hair had grown since "the Invigorator" had been placed in it—(a singular fact) and recommended me to be cautious in wearing gloves while rubbing it upon my head, as unhappy accidents had occurred—the hair growing freely from the ends of the fingers, if used with the bare hand. He then seated himself at the table, and rapidly filling up what appeared to me a blank certificate, he soon handed over the following singular document.

"PHRENOLOGICAL CHART OF THE HEAD OF M. JOHN PHOENIX, by FLATBROKE B. DODGE, Professor of Phrenology, and inventor and proprietor of Dodge's celebrated Hair Invigorator, Stimulator of the Conscience, and Arouser of the Mental Faculties:

Temperament,—*Lymphatic*, *Nervous*, *Bilious*.

Size of Head, 11	Imitation, 11.
Amativeness, 11-1/2.	Self-Esteem, 1/2.
Caution, 3.	Benevolence, 12,
Combativeness, 2-1/2.	Mirth, 1.
Credulity, 1.	Language, 12.
Causality, 12.	Firmness, 2.
Conscientiousness, 12.	Veneration, 12.
Destructiveness, 9.	Philoprogenitiveness, 0.
Hope, 10."	

Having gazed on this for a few moments in mute astonishment—during which the Professor took a glass of brandy and water, and afterwards a mouthful of tobacco—I turned to him and requested an explanation.

"Why," said he, "it's very simple; the number 12 is the maximum, 1 the minimum; for instance, you are as benevolent as a man can be—therefore I mark you, Benevolence, 12. You have little or no self-esteem—hence I place you, Self-esteem, 1/2. You've scarcely any credulity—don't you see?"

I did see! This was my discovery. I saw at a flash how the English language was susceptible of improvement, and, fired with the glorious idea, I rushed from the room and the house; heedless of the Professor's request that I would buy more of his Invigorator; heedless of his alarmed cry that I would pay for the bottle I'd got; heedless that I tripped on the last step of the Gyascutus House, and smashed there the precious fluid (the step has now a growth of four inches of hair on it, and the people use it as a door-mat); I rushed home, and never grew calm till with pen, ink and paper before me, I commenced the development of my system.

This system—shall I say this great system—is exceedingly simple, and easily explained in a few words. In the first place, *"figures won't lie."* Let us then represent by the number 100, the maximum, the *ne plus ultra* of every human quality—grace, beauty, courage, strength, wisdom, learning—every thing. Let *perfection*, I say, be represented by 100, and an absolute minimum of all qualities by the number 1. Then by applying the numbers between, to the adjectives used in conversation, we shall be able to arrive at a very close approximation to the idea we wish to convey; in other words, we shall be enabled to speak the truth. Glorious, soul-inspiring idea! For instance, the most ordinary question asked of you is, "How do you do?" To this, instead of replying, "Pretty well," "Very well," "Quite well," or the like absurdities—after running through your mind that *perfection* of health is 100, no health at all, 1—you say, with a graceful bow, "Thank you, I'm 52 to day;" or, feeling poorly, "I'm 13, I'm obliged to you," or "I'm 68," or "75," or "87-1/2,"

136

as the case may be! Do you see how very close in this way you may approximate to the truth; and how clearly your questioner will understand what he so anxiously wishes to arrive at—your *exact* state of health?

Let this system be adopted into our elements of grammar, our conversation, our literature, and we become at once an exact, precise, mathematical, truth-telling people. It will apply to every thing but politics; there, truth being of no account, the system is useless. But in literature, how admirable! Take an example:

As a 19 young and 76 beautiful lady was 52 gaily tripping down the sidewalk of our 84 frequented street, she accidentally came in contact—100 (this shows that she came in close contact) with a 73 fat, but 87 good-humored looking gentleman, who was 93 (i.e. intently) gazing into the window of a toy-shop. Gracefully 56 extricating herself, she received the excuses of the 96 embarrassed Falstaff with a 68 bland smile, and continued on her way. But hardly—7—had she reached the corner of the block, ere she was overtaken by a 24 young man, 32 poorly dressed, but of an 85 expression of countenance; 91 hastily touching her 54 beautifully rounded arm, he said, to her 67 surprise—

"Madam, at the window of the toy-shop yonder, you dropped this bracelet, which I had the 71 good fortune to observe, and now have the 94 happiness to hand to you." (Of course the expression "94 happiness" is merely the young man's polite hyperbole.)

Blushing with 76 modesty, the lovely (76, as before, of course), lady took the bracelet—which was a 24 magnificent diamond clasp—(24 *magnificent*, playfully sarcastic; it was probably *not* one of Tucker's) from the young man's hand, and 84 hesitatingly drew from her beautifully 38 embroidered reticule a 67 port-monnaie. The young man noticed the action, and 73 proudly drawing back, added—

"Do not thank me; the pleasure of gazing for an instant at those 100 eyes (perhaps too exaggerated a compliment), has already more than compensated me for any trouble that I might have had."

She thanked him, however, and with a 67 deep blush and a 48 pensive air, turned from him, and pursued with a 33 slow step her promenade.

Of course you see that this is but the commencement of a pretty little tale, which I might throw off, if I had a mind to, showing in two volumes, or forty-eight chapters of thrilling interest, how the young man sought the girl's acquaintance, how the interest first excited, deepened into love, how they suffered much from the opposition of parents (her parents of course), and how, after much trouble, annoyance, and many perilous adventures, they were finally married—their happiness, of course, being represented by 100. But I trust that I have said enough to recommend my system to the good and truthful of the literary world; and besides, just at present I have something of more immediate importance to attend to.

You would hardly believe it, but that everlasting (100) scamp of a Professor has brought a suit against me for stealing a bottle of his disgusting Invigorator; and as the suit comes off before a Justice of the Peace, whose only principle of law is to find guilty and fine any accused person whom he thinks has any money— (because if he don't he has to take his costs in County

Scrip,) it behooves me to "take time by the fore-lock."
So, for the present, adieu. Should my system succeed
to the extent of my hopes and expectations, I shall
publish my new grammar early in the ensuing month,
with suitable dedication and preface; and should you,
with your well known liberality, publish my prospec-
tus, and give me a handsome literary notice, I shall be
pleased to furnish a presentation copy to each of the
little Pioneer children.

P. S. I regret to add that having just read this article
to Mrs. Phoenix, and asked her opinion thereon, she
replied, that "if a first-rate magazine article were represented by 100, she should judge this to be about 13;
or if the quintessence of stupidity were 100, she should
take this to be in the neighborhood of 96." This, as a
criticism, is perhaps a little discouraging, but as an exemplification of the merits of my system it is exceedingly flattering. How could she, I should like to know,
in ordinary language, have given so *exact* and truthful
an idea—how expressed so forcibly her opinion
(which, of course, differs from mine) on the subject?

As Dr. Samuel Johnson learnedly remarked to
James Boswell, Laird of Auchinleck, on a certain occasion—

"Sir, the proof of the pudding is in the eating
thereof."

ANTIDOTE FOR FLEAS.

THE FOLLOWING RECIPE from the writings of Miss Hannah More, may be found useful to your readers:

In a climate where the attacks of fleas are a constant source of annoyance, any method which will alleviate them becomes a *desideratum*. It is, therefore, with pleasure I make known the following recipe, which I am assured has been tried with efficacy.

Boil a quart of tar until it becomes quite thin. Remove the clothing, and before the tar becomes perfectly cool, with a broad at brush, apply a thin, smooth coating to the entire surface of the body and limbs. While the tar remains soft, the flea becomes entangled in its tenacious folds, and is rendered perfectly harmless; but it will soon form a hard, smooth coating, entirely impervious to his bite. Should the coating crack at the knee or elbow joints, it is merely necessary to retouch it slightly at those places. The whole coat should be renewed every three or four weeks. This remedy is sure, and having the advantage of simplicity and economy, should be generally known.

So much for Miss More. A still simpler method of preventing the attacks of these little pests, is one which I have lately discovered myself;—in theory only—I have not yet put it into practice. On feeling the bite of a flea, thrust the part bitten immediately into boiling water. The heat of the water destroys the insect and instantly removes the pain of the bite.

You have probably heard of old Parry Dox. I met him here a few days since, in a sadly seedy condition. He told me that he was still extravagantly fond of whisky, though he was constantly "running it down." I inquired after his wife. "She is dead, poor creature," said he, "and is probably far better off than ever she was here. She was a seamstress, and her greatest enjoyment of happiness in this world was only so, so."

FOR SALE. A valuable law library, lately the property of a distinguished legal gentleman of San Francisco, who has given up practice and removed to the Farralone Islands. It consists of one volume of "Hoyle's Games," complete, and may be seen at this office.

ORPHEUS C. KERR.

A favorite humorist of the Civil War era, Robert C. Newell took the name "Orpheus C. Kerr" as a pun on "Office Seeker," and his usual beat was the extravagances of government and the poor conduct of the war from the Northern side. Abraham Lincoln was a great admirer of his work, but it must be confessed that much of his humor is too topical to hold up well after a century and a half. This little poem, however, will never lose its power to amuse us as long as maps of the United States are filled with such colorful geographical names as these.

A DISTINCTIVELY AMERICAN POEM.

WHILE LOOKING OVER some old magazines in the *Lily* office one day, I found in an ancient British periodical a raking article upon American literature, wherein the critic affirmed that all our writers were but weak imitations of English authors, and that such a thing even as a Distinctively American Poem *sui generis*, had not yet been produced.

This radical sneer at the United States of America fired my Yankee blood and I vowed within myself to write a poem, not only distinctively American, but of such a character that only America could have produced it. In the solitude of my room, that night, I wooed the aboriginal muse, and two days thereafter the *Lily of the Valley* contained my distinctive American poem of

142

The American Traveller.

To Lake Aghmoogenegamook,
  All in the State of Maine,
A man from Wittequergauguam came
  One evening in the rain.

"I am a traveler," said he,
  "Just started on a tour,
And go to Nomjamskillicook
  To-morrow morn at four."

He took a tavern bed that night,
  And with the morrow's sun,
By way of Sekledobskus went,
  With carpet-bag and gun.

From thence he went to Absequoit,
  And there—quite tired of Maine—
He sought the mountains of Vermont,
  Upon a railroad train.

Dog Hollow, in the Green Mount State,
  Was his first stopping-place,
And then Skunk's Misery displayed
  Its sweetness and its grace.

Then, via Nine Holes and Goose Green,
  He traveled through the State,

143

And to Virginia, finally,
   Was guided by his fate.

Within the Old Dominion's bounds,
   He wandered up and down,
To-day, at Buzzard Roost ensconced,
   To-morrow, at Hell Town.

From thence, into Negationburg
   His route of travel lay.
Which having gained, he left the State
   And took a southward way.

North Carolina's friendly soil
   He trod at fall of night,
And, on a bed of softest down,
   He slept at Hell's Delight.

The country all about Pinch Gut
   So beautiful did seem,
That the beholder thought it like
   A picture in a dream.

At Tear Shirt too, the scenery
   Most charming did appear,
With Snatch It in the distance far,
   And Purgatory near.

But spite of all these pleasant scenes,
   The tourist stoutly swore,
That home is brightest, after all,
   And travel is a bore.

144

So back he went to Maine, straight way,
   A little wife he took;
And now is making nutmegs at
   Moosehicmagunticook.

In his note, introductory of this poem, the editor of the *Lily* affirmed (which is strictly true) that I had named none but veritable localities; and ventured the belief that the composition would remind his readers of Goldsmith. Upon which his scorpion contemporary in the next village observed, that there was rather more smith than gold about the poem. Genius is never appreciated until its possessor is dead; and even the useless praise it then obtains is chiefly due to the pleasure that is experienced in burying the poor wretch.

*Artemus Ward visits the Tomb of Shakespeare and makes
a slight mistake. (Illustration by J. H. Howard.)*

ARTEMUS WARD.

There was a school of American humorists, all but forgotten, whose main humor consisted in illiterate misspellings. Artemus Ward is not one of them.

It is easy to dismiss Artemus Ward as merely one of the misspellers, but his humor is of an altogether different sort. In fact, Charles Farrar Browne, the man behind the character of "Artemus Ward," used fewer and fewer unorthodox spellings as he became more and more famous and more and more confident in his technique.

The spellings suggest the ignorance of the supposed writer, of course; but the main purpose of the spellings was to make Artemus Ward's voice sound in our ears. They are phonetic spellings, and they represent very well a form of rural dialect that has all but disappeared in America. When we read the words the way they are written, we can hear the man as he must have sounded on stage in his extremely popular lectures.

The intellectual pretension of Artemus Ward is one of the sources of the fun: when he writes "seated be4 the fire," for example, he is not just displaying ignorance; he is showing a particular kind of ignorance, very common among us Americans, that is proud of its intellectual accomplishments. Yet the joke runs deeper than that, because Artemus Ward usually ends up showing himself the wiser man in any conversation involving a supposedly educated interlocutor.

It would not be too much to say, in fact, that Artemus Ward was the closest we came to producing Mark Twain before we produced Mark Twain. Mark Twain probably would have put himself below Artemus Ward; here, at any rate, is how Twain remembered him:

He was one of the kindest and gentlest of men, and the hold he took on the English people surpasses imagination. Artemus Ward once said to me gravely, almost sadly:

"Clemens, I have done too much fooling, too much trifling; I am going to write something that will live."

"Well, what for instance?"

In the same grave way, he said: "A lie."

It was an admirable surprise. I was just ready to cry; he was becoming pathetic.

Well into the twentieth century, there were many who still considered him superior to Mark Twain; and that we do not read him more today may be attributed to the fact that so few of us are taught to read phonetically.

"High-Handed Outrage at Utica," also known as "Outrage in Uticky," has a singular distinction as a footnote to some very momentous history. At one meeting, President Lincoln insisted on reading it to his cabinet before they got down to business, and those present recalled that there was uproarious laughter from the whole company except Stanton, the secretary of war, who didn't get it at all. Then, once the laughter had died down, it was time for the business of the day, and Lincoln read the first draft of his Emancipation Proclamation.

How it would have tickled Charles Farrar Browne to know that he was the opening act for the Emancipation Proclamation! Artemus Ward, on the other hand, might have accepted it as only his doo.

HIGH-HANDED OUTRAGE AT UTICA.

In the Faul of 1856, I showed my show in Uticky, a trooly grate sitty in the State of New York.

The people gave me a cordyal recepshun. The press was loud in her prases.

1 day as I was givin a descripshun of my Beests and Snaiks in my usual flowry stile what was my skorn & disgust to see a big burly feller walk up to the cage containin my wax figgers of the Lord's Last Supper, and cease Judas Iscarrot by the feet and drag him out on the ground. He then commenced fur to pound him as hard as he cood.

"What under the son are you abowt?" cried I.

Sez he, "What did you bring this pussylanermus cuss here fur?" and he hit the wax figger another tremenjis blow on the hed.

Sez I, "You egrejus ass, that air's a wax figger—a representashun of the false 'Postle."

Sez he, "That's all very well fur you to say, but I tell you, old man, that Judas Iscarrot can't show hisself in Utiky with impunerty by a darn site!" with which observashun he kaved in Judassis hed. The young man belonged to 1 of the first famerlies in Utiky. I sood him, and the Joory brawt in a verdick of Arson in the 3d degree.

149

THE CENSUS.

THE SENCES TAKER in our town being taken sick, he dep-pertised me to go out for him one day, and as he was too ill to give me information how to perceed, I was consekently compelled to go it blind. Sittin' down by the roadside I draw'd up the follerin' list of questions, which I proposed to ax the people I visited:

Wat's your age?

Whar' was you born?

Air you married, and if so, how do you like it?

How many children hav' you, and do they suff-ciently resemble you so as to proclood the possibility of their belongin' to any of your nabers?

Did you ever have the measles, and if so, how many?

Hav' you a twin brother several years older than yourself?

How many parents have you?

Do you read Watt's Hymns reg'lar?

Do you use bought'n tabacker?

Wat's your fitin' weight?

Air you troubled with biles?

How does your meresham culler?

State whether you air blind, deaf, idiotic, or got the heaves?

Do you know any Opry singers, and if so how much do they owe you?

What's the average of virtoo in the Ery canawl?

If four barrels of emtin's pored onto a barn floor will kiver it, how many plase can Dion Boucicault write in a year?

150

Is beans a reg'lar article of diet in your family?

How many chickens hav' you, on foot and in the shell?

Air you aware that Injiany whisky is used in New York shootin' galrys insted of pistols, and that it shoots furthest?

Was you ever at Niagry Falls?

Was you ever in the penitentiary?

State how much pork, impendin' crysis, Dutch cheese, poplar survinity, standard poetry, children's strainers, slave code, catnip, red flannel, ancient history, pickled tomatoes, old junk, perfoomery, coal ile, liberty, hoopskirts, etc., have you got on hand?

But it didn't work. I got into a row at the first house I stopt at, with some old maids. Disbelievin' the answers they give in regard to their ages I endeavored to open their mouths and look at their teeth, same as they do with horses, but they floo into a violent rage and tackled me with brooms and sich. Takin' the sences requires experience, like as any other bizness.

JOY IN THE HOUSE OF WARD

Dear Sirs,

I take my pen in hand to inform you that I am in a state of grate bliss, and trust these lines will find you injoyin the same blessins. I'm reguvinated. I've found the immortal waters of yooth, so to speak, and am as limber and frisky as a two-year-old steer, and in the futur them boys which sez to me "go up, old Bawld hed," will do so at the peril of their hazard, indivi-dooally. I'm very happy. My house is full of joy, and I have to git up nights and larf! Sumtimes I ax myself "is it not a dream?" & suthin withinto me sez "it air;" but when I look at them sweet little critters and hear 'em squawk, I know it is a reality—2 realitys, I may say—and I feel gay.

I returnd from the Summer Campane with my un-paraleld show of wax works and livin wild Beests of Pray in the early part of this munth. The peple of Baldinsville met me cordully and I immejitly commenst restin myself with my famerly. The other nite while I was down to the tavurn tostin my shins agin the bar room fire & amuzin the krowd with sum of my adven-turs, who shood cum in bare heded & terrible excited but Bill Stokes, who sez, sez he, "Old Ward, there's grate doing up to your house."

Sez I, "William, how so?"

Sez he, "Bust my gizzud, but its grate doins," & then larfed as if heed kill hisself.

Sez I, risin and puttin on a austeer look, "William, I woodnut be a fool if I had common cents."

But he kept on larfin till he was black in the face, when he fell over on the bunk where the hostler sleeps, and in a still small voice sed, "Twins!" I ashure you gents that the grass didn't grow under my feet on my way home, & I was followed by a enthoosiastic throng of my feller sitterzens, who hurrard for Old Ward at the top of their voises. I found the house chock full of peple. Thare was Mrs. Square Baxter and her three grown-up darters, lawyer Perkinses wife, Taberthy

Ripley, young Eben Parsuns, Deakun Simmuns folks, the Skoolmaster, Doctor Jordin, etsetterry, etsetterry. Mis Ward was in the west room, which jines the kitchin. Mis Square Baxter was mixin suthin in a dipper before the kitchin fire, & a small army of female wimin were rushin wildly round the house with bottles of camfire, peaces of flannil, &c. I never seed such a hubbub in my natral born dase. I cood not stay in the west room only a minit, so strong was my feelings, so I rusht out and ceased my dubbel barrild gun.

"What on airth ales the man?" sez Taberthy Ripley. "Sakes alive, what air you doin?" & she grabd me by the tales. "What's the matter with you?" she continnered.

"Twins, Marm," sez I, "twins!"

"I know it," sez she, coverin her pretty face with her aprun.

"Wall," sez I, "that's what's the matter with me!"

"Wall, put down that air gun, you pesky old fool," sed she.

"No, marm," sez I, "this is a Nashunal day. The glory of this here day isn't confined to Baldinsville by a darn site. On yonder woodshed," sed I, drawin myself up to my full hite and speakin in a show-actin voice, "will I fire a Nashunal saloot!" sayin whitch I tared myself from her grasp and rush to to the top of the shed whare I blazed away until Square Baxter's hired man and my son Artemus Juneyer cum and took me down by mane force.

On returnin to the Kitchin I found quite a lot of people seated be4 the fire, a talkin the event over. They made room for me & I sot down. "Quite a ep-

pisode," sed Docter Jordin, litin his pipe with a red-hot coal.

"Yes," sed I, "2 eppisodes, waying abowt 18 pounds jintly."

"A perfeck coop de tat," sed the skoolmaster.

"E pluribus unum, in proprietor persony," sed I, thinking I'd let him know I understood furrin lang-widges as well as he did, if I wasn't a skoolmaster.

"It is indeed a momentious event," sed young Eben Parsuns, who has been 2 quarters to the Akademy.

"I never heard twins called by that name afore," sed I, "but I spose it's all rite."

"We shall soon have Wards enuff," sed the editer of the Baldinsville *Bugle of Liberty*, who was lookin over a bundle of exchange papers in the corner, "to apply to the legislator for a City Charter."

"Good for you, old man!" sed I; "giv that air a con-spickius place in the next Bugle."

"How redicklus," sed pretty Susan Fletcher, coverin her face with her knittin work & larfin like all possest.

"Wall, for my part," sed Jane Maria Peasley, who is the crossest old made in the world, "I think you all act like a pack of fools."

Sez I, "Mis. Peasly, air you a parent?"

Sez she, "No, I aint."

Sez I, "Mis. Peasly, you never will be."

She left.

We sot there talkin & larfin until "the switchin hour of nite, when grave yards yawn & Josts troop 4th," as old Bill Shakespire aptlee obsarves in his dramy of John Sheppard, esq, or the Moral House Breaker, when we broke up & disbursed.

154

Muther & children is a doin well; & as Resolushuns is the order of the day I will feel obleeged if you'll insurt the follerin—

Whereas, two Eppisodes has happined up to the undersined's house, which is Twins; & Whereas I like this stile, sade twins bein of the male perswashun & both boys; there4 Be it

Resolved, That to them nabers who did the fare thing by sade Eppisodes my hart felt thanks is doo.

Resolved, That I do most hartily thank Engine Ko. No. 17, who, under the impreshun from the fuss at my house on that auspishus nite that thare was a konflagration goin on, kum galyiantly to the spot, but kindly refraned frum squirtin.

Resolved, That frum the Bottum of my Sole do I thank the Baldinsville brass band fur givin up the idea of Sarahnadin me, both on that great nite & sinse.

Resolved, That my thanks is doo several members of the Baldsinville meetin house who fur 3 whole dase hain't kalled me a sinful skoffer or intreeted me to mend my wicked wase and jine sade meetin house to onct.

Resolved, That my Boozum teams with meny kind emoshuns towards the follerin individoouls, to whit namelee—Mis. Square Baxter, who Jenerusly refoozed to take a sent for a bottle of camfire; lawyer Perkinses wife who rit sum versis on the Eppisodes; the Editer of the Baldinsville *Bugle of Liberty*, who nobly assisted me in wollupin my Kangeroo, which sagashus little cuss seriusly disturbed the Eppisodes by his outrajus screetchins & kickins up; Mis. Hirum Doolittle, who kindly furnisht sum cold vittles at a tryin time, when it wasunt konvenient to cook vittles at my hous; & the Peasleys, Parsunses & Watsunses fur there meny ax of kindness.

Trooly yures,
ARTEMUS WARD.

AT THE TOMB OF SHAKSPEARE.

MR. PUNCH, MY DEAR SIR,—I've been lingerin by the Tomb of the lamentid Shakspeare.

It is a success.

I do not hes'tate to pronounce it as such.

You may make any use of this opinion that you see fit. If you think its publication will subswerve the cause of litteratoor, you may publicate it.

I told my wife Betsy when I left home that I should go to the birthplace of the orthur of "Otheller" and other Plays. She said that as long as I kept out of Newgate she didn't care where I went. "But," I said, "don't you know he was the greatest Poit that ever lived? Not one of these common poits, like that young idyit who writes verses to our daughter, about the Roses as growses, and the Breezes as blowses—but a Boss Poit—also a philosopher, also a man who knew a great deal about everything."

She was packing my things at the time, and the only answer she made was to ask me if I was goin to carry both of my red flannel night-caps.

Yes. I've been to Stratford onto the Avon, the Birthplace of Shakspeare. Mr. S. is now no more. He's been dead over three hundred (300) years. The peple of his native town are justly proud of him. They cherish his mem'ry, and them as sell pictures of his birthplace, &c., make it prof'tible cherishin it. Almost everybody buys a pictur to put into their Albiom.

As I stood gazing on the spot where Shakspeare is s'posed to have fell down on the ice and hurt hisself when a boy, (this spot cannot be bought—the town authorities say it shall never be taken from Stratford), I wondered if three hundred years hence picturs of *my* birthplace will be in demand? Will the peple of my native town be proud of me in three hundred years? I guess they won't short of that time because they say the fat man weighing 1000 pounds which I exhibited there was stuffed out with pillers and cushions, which he said one very hot day in July, "Oh bother, I can't stand this," and commenced pullin the pillers out from under his weskit, and heavin 'em at the audience. I never saw a man lose flesh so fast in my life. The audience said I was a pretty man to come chiselin my own townsmen in that way. I said, "Do not be angry, fellercitizens. I exhibited him simply as a work of art. I simply wished to show you that a man could grow fat without the aid of cod-liver oil." But they wouldn't listen to me. They are a low and grovelin set of peple, who excite a feelin of loathin in every brest where lorfty emotions and original idees have a bidin place.

I stopped at Leamington a few minits on my way to Stratford onto the Avon, and a very beautiful town it is. I went into a shoe shop to make a purchis, and as I entered I saw over the door those dear familiar words, "By Appintment: H. R. H.;" and I said to the man, "Squire, excuse me, but this is too much. I have seen in London four hundred boot and shoe shops by Appintment: H. R. H.; and now *you're* at it. It is simply onpossible that the Prince can wear 400 pairs of boots. Don't tell me," I said, in a voice choked with emotion —"Oh, do not tell me that you also make boots for him. Say slippers—say that you mend a boot now and then for him; but do not tell me that you make 'em reg'lar for him."

The man smilt, and said I didn't understand these things. He said I perhaps had not noticed in London that dealers in all sorts of articles was By Appintment. I said, "Oh, *hadn't* I?" Then a sudden thought flasht over me. "I have it!" I said. "When the Prince walks through a street, he no doubt looks at the shop windows."

The man said, "No doubt."

"And the enterprisin tradesman," I continnerd, "the moment the Prince gets out of sight, rushes frantically and has a tin sign painted, By Appintment, H. R. H.! It is a beautiful, a great idee!"

I then bought a pair of shoe strings, and wringin the shopman's honest hand, I started for the Tomb of Shakspeare in a hired fly. It look't however more like a spider.

"And this," I said, as I stood in the old church-yard at Stratford, beside a Tombstone, "this marks the spot where lies William W. Shakspeare. Alars! and this is the spot where—"

"You've got the wrong grave," said a man—a worthy villager: "Shakspeare is buried inside the church."

"Oh," I said, "a boy told me this was it." The boy larfed and put the shillin I'd given him onto his left eye in a inglorious manner, and commenced moving backwards towards the street.

I pursood and captered him, and after talking to him a spell in a skarcastic stile, I let him went.

The old church was damp and chill. It was rainin. The only persons there when I entered was a fine bluff old gentleman who was talking in a excited manner to a fashnibly dressed young man.

"No, Earnest Montresser," the old gentleman said, "it is idle to pursoo this subjeck no further. You can never marry my daughter. You were seen last Monday in Piccadilly without a umbreller! I said then, as I say now, any young man as venturs out in a uncertain climit like this without a umbreller, lacks foresight, caution, strength of mind and stability; and he is not a proper person to intrust a daughter's happiness to."

I slapt the old gentleman on the shoulder, and I said: "You're right! You're one of those kind of men, you are—"

He wheeled suddenly round, and in a indignant voice, said, "Go way—go way! This is a privit intervoo."

I didn't stop to enrich the old gentleman's mind with my conversation. I sort of inferred that he wasn't inclined to listen to me, and so I went on. But he was right about the umbreller. I'm really delighted with this grand old country, *Mr. Punch*, but you must admit that it does rain rayther numerously here. Whether this is owing to a monerkal form of gov'ment or not I leave all candid and onprejudiced persons to say.

William Shakspeare was born in Stratford in 1564. All the commentaters, Shaksperian scholars, etsetry, are agreed on this, which is about the only thing they are agreed on in regard to him, except that his mantle hasn't fallen onto any poet or dramatist hard enough to hurt said poet or dramatist *much*. And there is no doubt if these commentaters and persons continner investigating Shakspeare's career, we shall not, in doo time, know anything about it at all.

When a mere lad little William attended the Grammar School, because, as he said, the Grammar School wouldn't attend him. This remarkable remark, comin from one so young and inexperunced, set peple to thinkin there might be somethin in this lad. He subsequently wrote *Hamlet* and *George Barnwell*. When his kind teacher went to London to accept a position in the offices of the Metropolitan Railway, little William was chosen by his fellow pupils to deliver a farewell address.

"Go on, Sir," he said, "in a glorus career. Be like a eagle, and soar, and the soarer you get the more we shall all be gratified! That's so."

My young readers, who wish to know about Shakspeare, better get these vallyable remarks framed.

I returned to the hotel. Meetin a young married couple, they asked me if I could direct them to the hotel which Washington Irving used to keep?

"I've understood that he was onsuccessful as a lan'lord," said the lady.

"We've understood," said the young man, "that he busted up."

I told 'em I was a stranger, and hurried away. They were from my country, and ondoubtedly represented a thrifty Ile well somewhere in Pennsylvany. It's a common thing, by the way, for a old farmer in Pennsylvany to wake up some mornin' and find Ile squirtin all around his back yard. He sells out for a 'normous price, and his children put on gorgeous harness and start on a tower to astonish people. They succeed in doin it. Meantime the Ile squirts and squirts, and Time rolls on. Let it roll.

A very nice old town is Stratford, and a capital inn is the Red Horse. Every admirer of the great S. must go there once certinly; and to say one isn't a admirer of him, is equv'lent to sayin one has jest about brains enough to become a efficient tinker.

Some kind person has sent me Chawcer's *poems*. Mr. C. had talent, but he couldn't spel. No man has a right to be a lit'rary man onless he knows how to spel. It is a pity that Chawcer, who had geneyus, was so unedicated. He's the wuss speller I know of.

I guess I'm through, and so I lay down the pen, which is more mightier than the sword, but which I'm fraid would stand a rayther slim chance beside the needle gun.

Adoo! Adoo!

Artemus Ward.

A VISIT TO THE BRITISH MUSEUM.

Mr. Punch, My dear Sir,—You didn't get a instructiv article from my pen last week on account of my nervus sistim havin underwent a dreffle shock. I got caught in a brief shine of sun, and it utterly upsot me. I was walkin in Regent Street one day last week, enjoyin your rich black fog and bracing rains, when all at once the Sun bust out and actooally shone for nearly half an hour steady. I acted promptly. I called a cab and told the driver to run his hoss at a friteful rate of speed to my lodgins, but it wasn't of no avale. I had orful cramps, and my appytite left me, and my pults went down to 10 degrees below zero. But by careful nussin I shall no doubt recover speedy, if the present sparklin and exileratin weather continners.

[All of the foregoin is sarcasum.]

It's a sing'lar fack, but I never sot eyes on your ex-cellent British Mooseum till the other day. I've sent a great many peple there, as also to your genial Tower of London, however. It happened thusly: When one of my excellent countrymen jest arrived in London would come and see me, and display a inclination to cling to me too lengthy, thus showing a respect for me which I feel I do not deserve, I would sugjest a visit to the Mooseum and Tower. The Mooseum would ockepy him a day at leest, and the Tower another. Thus I've derived considerable peace and comfort from them no-ble edifisses, and I hope they will long continner to grace your metroplis. There's my fren Col. Larkins, from Wisconsin, who I regret to say understands the Jamaica question, and wants to talk with me about it; I sent him to the Tower four days ago, and he hasn't got throogh with it yit. He likes it very much, and he writes me that he can't never thank me sufficient for directin him to so interestin a bildin. I writ him not to mention it. The Col. says it is fortnit we live in a intel-lectooal age which wouldn't countenance such infamus things as occurd in this Tower. I'm aware that it is fashin'ble to compliment this age, but I ain't so clear that the Col. is altogether right. This is a very re-spectable age, but it's pretty easily riled; and consid-erin upon how slight a provycation we who live in it go to cuttin each other's throats, it may perhaps be doubted whether our intellecks is so much massiver than our ancestors' intellecks was, after all.

I allus ride outside with the cabman. I am of humble parentage, but I have (if you will permit me to say so) the spirit of the eagle, which chafes when shut up in a four-wheeler, and I feel much eagler when I'm in the open air. So on the mornin on which I went to the Mooseum I lit a pipe, and callin a cab, I told the driver to take me there as quick as his Arabian charger could go. The driver was under the inflooence of beer and narrerly escaped runnin over a aged female in the match trade, whereupon I remonstratid with him. I said, "That poor old woman may be the only mother of a young man like you." Then throwing considerable pathos into my voice, I said: "You have a mother?"

He said, "You lie!" I got down and called another cab, but said nothin to this driver about his parents.

The British Mooseum is a magnificent free show for the people. It is kept open for the benefit of all.

The humble costymonger, who traverses the busy streets with a cart containin all kinds of vegetables, such as carrots, turnips, etc, and drawn by a spirited jackass—he can go to the Mooseum and reap benefits therefrom as well as the lord of high degree.

"And this," I said, "is the British Mooseum! These noble walls," I continnerd, punching them with my umbreller to see if the masonry was all right—but I wasn't allowd to finish my enthoosiastic remarks, for a man with a gold band on his hat said, in a hash voice, that I must stop pokin the walls. I told him I would do so by all means. "You see," I said, taking hold of the tassel which waved from the man's belt, and drawin him close to me in a confidential way, "You see, I'm lookin round this Mooseum, and if I like it I shall buy it."

Instid of larfin hartily at these remarks, which was made in a goakin spirit, the man frowned darkly and walked away.

I first visited the stuffed animals, of which the gorillers interested me most. These simple-minded monsters live in Afriky, and are believed to be human beins to a slight extent, altho' they are not allowed to vote. In this department is one or two superior giraffes. I never woulded I were a bird, but I've sometimes wished I was a giraffe, on account of the long distance from his mouth to his stummuck. Hence, if he loved beer, one mugful would give him as much enjoyment while goin down, as forty mugfuls would ordinary persons. And he wouldn't get intoxicated, which is a beastly way of amusin oneself, I must say. I like a little beer now and then, and when the teetotallers inform us, as they frekently do, that it is vile stuff, and that even the swine shrink from it, I say it only shows that the swine is a ass who don't know what's good; but to pour gin and brandy down one's throat as freely as though it were fresh milk, is the most idiotic way of goin' to the devil that I know of.

I enjoyed myself very much lookin at the Egyptian mummays, the Greek vasis, etc, but it occurd to me there was rayther too many "Roman antiquitys of a uncertin date." Now, I like the British Mooseum, as I said afore, but when I see a lot of erthen jugs and pots stuck up on shelves, and all "of a uncertin date," I'm at a loss to 'zackly determin whether they are a thousand years old or was bought recent. I can cry like a child over a jug one thousand years of age, especially if it is a Roman jug; but a jug of a uncertin date doesn't overwhelm me with emotions. Jugs and pots of a uncertin age is doubtles vallyable property, but, like the debentures of the London, Chatham, and Dover Railway, a man doesn't want too many of them.

I was debarred out of the great readin-room. A man told me I must apply by letter for admission, and that I must get somebody to testify that I was respectable. I'm a little 'fraid I shan't get in there. Seein a elderly gentleman, with a beneverlent-lookin face near by, I venturd to ask him if he would certify that I was respectable. He said he certainly would not, but he would put me in charge of a policeman, if that would do me any good. A thought struck me. "I refer you to 'Mr. Punch'," I said.

"Well," said a man, who had listened to my application, "you *have* done it now! You stood some chance before."

I will get this infamus wretch's name before you go to press, so you can denounce him in the present number of your excellent journal.

The statute of Apollo is a pretty slick statute. A young yeoman seemed deeply imprest with it. He viewd it with silent admiration. At home, in the beautiful rural districks where the daisy sweetly blooms, he would be swearin in a horrible manner at his bullocks, and whacking 'em over the head with a hayfork; but here, in the presence of Art, he is a changed bein.

I told the attendant that if the British nation would stand the expens of a marble bust of myself, I would willingly sit to some talented sculpist.

"I feel," I said, "that this is a dooty I owe to posterity."

He said it was hily prob'l, but he was inclined to think that the British nation wouldn't care to enrich the Mooseum with a bust of me, altho' he venturd to think that if I paid for one myself it would be accepted cheerfully by Madam Tussaud, who would give it a prom'nent position in her Chamber of Horrers. The young man was very polite, and I thankt him kindly.

After visitin the Refreshment room and partakin of half a chicken "of a uncertin age," like the Roman antiquitys I have previsly spoken of, I prepared to leave. As I passed through the animal room I observed with pane that a benevolint person was urgin the stufft elephant to accept a cold muffin, but I did not feel called on to remostrate with him, any more than I did with two

young persons of diff'rent sexes who had retired behind the Rynosserhoss to squeeze each other's hands.
In fack, I rayther approved of the latter proceedin, for
it carrid me back to the sunny spring-time of *my* life.
I'm in the shear and yeller leaf now, but I don't forgit
the time when to squeeze my Betsy's hand sent a thrill
through me like fellin off the roof of a two-story house;
and I never squozed that gentle hand without wantin to
do so some more, and feelin that it did me good.

Trooly Yours,
Artemus Ward.

ABRAHAM LINCOLN.

Of President Lincoln's place in history we have nothing to say here; but with little hesitation we declare that he was our funniest president. He loved to tell old jokes, but his humor really shone when he was confronted with a desperate situation. There was nothing too serious to laugh at; and thus, in the face of national catastrophe and almost unbearable personal grief, Lincoln kept his sanity.

One of his private secretaries wrote a book of Lincoln's "table talk," and from that we take these representative samples.

Mr. Alexander H. Stephens relates that during the famous "peace conference," on a steamer in Hampton Roads, between President Lincoln and the three Confederate Commissioners, one of them, Mr. Hunter, insisted that the recognition of the power of President Jefferson Davis to make a treaty was the first and indispensable step to peace. He referred to the correspondence between Charles I. and his Parliament as a trustworthy precedent of a constitutional ruler dealing with rebels. Mr. Lincoln put on an expression of grim, sarcastic humor as he replied: "Upon questions of history, I must refer you to Mr. Seward, for he is posted in such things, and I don't pretend to be bright. My only distinct recollection of the matter is that Charles lost his head."

Mr. Lincoln was one day asked: "How many men do you suppose the Confederates have now in the field?"

"Twelve hundred thousand, according to the best authority," was the prompt reply.

"Good Heavens!" exclaimed the inquirer.

"Yes, sir, twelve hundred thousand. No doubt of it. You see, all our generals, when they get whipped, say the enemy outnumbers them from three or five to one, and I must believe them. We have four hundred thousand in the field and three times four makes twelve. Don't you see it?"

Concerning the probable political strength of one of the presidential candidates, in 1864, Mr. Lincoln gravely read to a friend the account in 1 Samuel, of David's forces at the Cave of Adulam: "And every one that was in distress, and every one that was in debt, and every one that was discontented, gathered themselves unto him, and he became a captain over them, and there were with him about four hundred men."

After listening to a plea on behalf of a soldier condemned to death: "Well!—I don't believe shooting will do him any good.—Give me that pen."

To a man who had applied for a pardon for his son, condemned to be shot. A direct pardon could not be given, under the circumstances, but the president had written:

"Job Smith is not to be shot until further orders from me,"—and the anxious father had begged for something more definite.

169

Said Mr. Lincoln, "Well, my old friend, I see you are not very well acquainted with me. If your son never looks on death till further orders come from me, to shoot him, he will live to be a great deal older than Methusaleh."

WHILE GENERAL GRANT'S ability as a commander was yet in doubt, a storm of criticisms assailed him. At one time during the siege of Vicksburg, a delegation of his critics waited upon the President and vigorously demanded the substitution of some other general.

"Well, well," responded Mr. Lincoln, "but why should Grant be removed?"

"Why? Why, he drinks too much whiskey."

That particular accusation had been withheld until that moment, but now the President's face put on its most caustic expression as he responded: "Ah! that's it! By the way, gentlemen, can either of you tell me where General Grant gets his whiskey? I think I'd better send a barrel of that whiskey to every general in the field."

JOSH BILLINGS.

Josh Billings was enormously popular in his time, but his reputation has suffered perhaps even more than Artemus Ward's from his unorthodox spelling. It must be confessed that his spellings are not used as skillfully as Artemus Ward's; there they conveyed the sound of the showman's voice; here they convey only the presumed ignorance of the writer. (Henry Wheeler Shaw, the real writer behind Josh Billings, supposedly began his practice of deliberate misspelling because he was not at all sure that he could actually spell correctly.) It is quite probable that our educational theories and our solitary habits have doomed the misspelling humorists to obscurity; when most readers were reading by the sounds of the letters, and when much reading was done aloud, writers like Josh Billings had a much broader appeal. Perhaps the real problem is that they use the wrong misspellings: Josh Billings might be a success all over again if we transliterated his work into texting jargon.

Nevertheless, once one grows accustomed to the spelling, there is a great deal of fun in some of Josh Billings. The spellings were not what made him popular, of course: what made him popular was his ability to articulate exactly what his wide readership of ordinary Americans *would* have said on any given subject if only they had been a little more clever.

NATRAL HISTORY.

It is not the moste deliteful task, tew write the natral history ov the *Louse*, thare iz enny quantity of thorobred folks, who would konsidder it a kontaminashun,

171

az black az pattent leather, to *say* louse, or even *think* louse, but a louse is a fackt, and aul fackts are never more at home, nor more unwilling to move, than when they git into the head. The *louse* is one ov the gems ov antiquity. They are worn in the hair, and are more ornamental than useful.

Not having enny encyclopedia from which tew sponge mi informashun, and then pass it oph for mi own creashun, i shall be forced, while talking about the louse, "tew fight it out on the line" ov observashun, and when mi knowledge, and experience gives out, i shall tap mi imaginashun, ov which i hav a crude supply.

Book edukashun iz a phatting thing, it makes a man stick out with other folks opinyuns, and iz a good thing tu make the vulgar rool up the white ov their eyes, and wonder how enny man could ever kno so mutch wisdum.

Schooling, when I waz a colt, didn't lie around so loose az it duz now, and learning waz picked up oftner by running yure head aginst a stun wall, than by enny other kind ov mineralogy.

I have studied botany all day, in a flat meadow, pulling cowslops for greens, and then classified them, by picking them over and gitting them reddy for the pot.

All the astronomy i ever got i larnt in spearing suckers bi moonlite, and mi geoligy culminated at the further end of a woodchucks hole, espeshily if i got the woodchuck.

Az for moral philosophy and rhetorick, if it iz the science ov hooking green apples and water-mellons 30 years ago, and being auful sorry for it now, i am up head in that class.

But all this iz remote from the louse.

The louse iz a familiar animal, very sedentary in hiz habits, not apt tew git lost. They kan be cultivated without the aid ov a guide book, and with half a chance will multiply and thicken az much az pimples on the goose.

Thare iz no ground so fruitful for the full develop- ment ov this little domestick collateral, az a districkt school hous, and while the yung idea iz breaking its shell, and playing hide and go seek on the inside ov the dear urchins skull, the louse iz playing tag on the out- side, and quite often gets on to the school mom.

I hav alwus had a hi venerashun for the louse, not bekause i consider them az enny evidence of genius, or even neatness, but becauze they remind me ov my boy- hood innocence, the days away back in the alpahabet ov memory, when i sot on the flatt side ov a slab bench, and spelt out old Webster with one hand, and stirred the top ov my head with the other.

Philosophikally handled, the louse are gregarious, and were a complete suckcess at one time in Egypt, bible historians don't hesitate tew say, that they were aul the rage at that time, the whole crust ov the earth simmered and biled with them, like a pot ov steaming flax seed, they were a drug in the market.

But this waz more louse than waz necessary, or pleasant, and waz a punishment for sum sin, and ain't spoke ov, az a matter tew brag on.

The louse are all well enuff in their place, and for the sake ov variety, perhaps a few ov them are just az good az more would be.

They were desighned for sum wize purpose, and for that very reason, are respektabel.

When, (in the lapse of time,) it cums tew be revealed to us, that a single louse, chewing away on the summit ov Daniel Webster's head, when he waz a little schoolboy, waz the telegraphick tutch tew the wire that bust the fust idee in hiz brain, we shall see wisdom in the louse, and shant stick up our noze, untill we turn a back summersett, at these venerable soldjers, in the grand army ov progression.

After we hav reached years ov discretion, and have got our edukashun, and our karakters have got done developing, and we begin tew hold offiss, and are elekted justiss ov the peace, for instance, and don't seem tew need enny more louse tew stir us up, it iz time enuff then tew be sassy to them.

Az for me, thare iz only one piece (thus far) ov vital creation, that i aktually *hate*, and that iz a bed-bugg. I simply *dispize* snaiks, *fear* musketoze, *avoid* fleas, don't *associate* with the cockroach, *go around* toads, *back out* square for a hornet.

Nevertheless, moreover, to wit, i must say, even at this day of refinement, and bell letters, i do aktually luv to stand on tip-toe, and see a romping, red-cheeked, blew-eyed boy, chased up stairs and then down stair, and then out in the garden, and finally caught and throwed, and held firmly between hiz mother's kneeze, and see an old, warped, fine-toothed horn comb go and come, half buried through a flood ov lawless hair, and drag each trip to the light, a fat and lively louse—and, in conclusion, to hear him pop as mother pins him with her thumnail fast tew the center ov the comb, fills me chuck up to the brim with something, i don't know what the feeling iz; perhaps sumboddy out ov a job can tell me.

Mark Twain.

MARK TWAIN.

Mark Twain (Samuel Clemens) stands at the peak of American humor, and probably of American literature; it is for that very reason that he occupies a relatively small space in this Anthology. Our aim in this book is to introduce new readers to delightful companions they have never met before; but everyone knows Mark Twain, and almost everyone loves him.

Instead of picking the very most famous works of Mark Twain, therefore, we have included this one literary essay that, while it is well known, is not as often read as his novels and stories. It shows us everything that was best in Mark Twain. He is an absolutely natural writer; the words on the page seem to come straight from the mouth of the man himself. He manages to make his own prodigious intellect accessible to the most ordinary reader: watch how effortlessly he runs through his deep knowledge of alluvial geology, applies some sophisticated mathematical calculations, and rips apart a formerly thrilling episode in Cooper in such a way that it all feels as effortless to us as it was to Twain. And finally, he can make us laugh so hard that tears roll down our cheeks.

This little essay, in fact, is probably the single worst thing that ever happened to Cooper's reputation. More people today have read it than have read the novels that fall under its scalpel. Mark Twain was a towering intellectual giant who wrote in the ordinary language that everybody speaks; Cooper was a man of average powers who tried to write as if he were a towering intellectual giant. The collision of the two is one of the funniest moments in nineteenth-century literature, and it left Cooper mortally wounded. If we could make one request of our readers, therefore, it would be that they give Cooper a little more credit than Twain gives him. Mark Twain is ten times the writer that Cooper ever was; but

Mark Twain is ten times the writer that almost *anybody* else ever was. Cooper's pretentiousness rubbed him the wrong way, and deserved the drubbing he gave it; but after all that, Cooper is still worth reading.

FENIMORE COOPER'S LITERARY OFFENSES.

The Pathfinder and *The Deerslayer* stand at the head of Cooper's novels as artistic creations. There are others of his works which contain parts as perfect as are to be found in these, and scenes even more thrilling. Not one can be compared with either of them as a finished whole.

The defects in both of these tales are comparatively slight. They were pure works of art.—*Prof. Lounsbury.*

The five tales reveal an extraordinary fulness of invention...One of the very greatest characters in fiction, Natty Bumppo....

The craft of the woodsman, the tricks of the trapper, all the delicate art of the forest, were familiar to Cooper from his youth up.—*Prof. Brander Matthews.*

Cooper is the greatest artist in the domain of romantic fiction yet produced by America.— *Wilkie Collins.*

It seems to me that it was far from right for the Professor of English Literature in Yale, the Professor of English Literature in Columbia, and Wilkie Collins to deliver opinions on Cooper's literature without having read some of it. It would have been much more deco-rous to keep silent and let persons talk who have read Cooper.

Cooper's art has some defects. In one place in *Deer-slayer*, and in the restricted space of two-thirds of a page, Cooper has scored 114 offenses against literary art out of a possible 115. It breaks the record.

There are nineteen rules governing literary art in the domain of romantic fiction—some say twenty-two. In *Deerslayer* Cooper violated eighteen of them. These eighteen require:

1. That a tale shall accomplish something and arrive somewhere. But the Deerslayer tale accomplishes noth-ing and arrives in the air.

2. They require that the episodes of a tale shall be necessary parts of the tale, and shall help to develop it. But as the Deerslayer tale is not a tale, and accom-plishes nothing and arrives nowhere, the episodes have no rightful place in the work, since there was nothing for them to develop.

3. They require that the personages in a tale shall be alive, except in the case of corpses, and that always the reader shall be able to tell the corpses from the others. But this detail has often been overlooked in the Deer-slayer tale.

4. They require that the personages in a tale, both dead and alive, shall exhibit a sufficient excuse for be-ing there. But this detail also has been overlooked in the Deerslayer tale.

5. They require that when the personages of a tale deal in conversation, the talk shall sound like human talk, and be talk such as human beings would be likely

to talk in the given circumstances, and have a discoverable meaning, also a discoverable purpose, and a show
of relevancy, and remain in the neighborhood of the
subject in hand, and be interesting to the reader, and
help out the tale, and stop when the people cannot
think of anything more to say. But this requirement
has been ignored from the beginning of the Deerslayer
tale to the end of it.

6. They require that when the author describes the
character of a personage in his tale, the conduct and
conversation of that personage shall justify said description. But this law gets little or no attention in the
Deerslayer tale, as Natty Bumppo's case will amply
prove.

7. They require that when a personage talks like an
illustrated, gilt-edged, tree-calf, hand-tooled, seven-
dollar Friendship's Offering in the beginning of a paragraph, he shall not talk like a negro minstrel in the end
of it. But this rule is flung down and danced upon in
the Deerslayer tale.

8. They require that crass stupidities shall not be
played upon the reader as "the craft of the woodsman,
the delicate art of the forest," by either the author or
the people in the tale. But this rule is persistently violated in the Deerslayer tale.

9. They require that the personages of a tale shall
confine themselves to possibilities and let miracles
alone; or, if they venture a miracle, the author must so
plausibly set it forth as to make it look possible and
reasonable. But these rules are not respected in the
Deerslayer tale.

10. They require that the author shall make the reader feel a deep interest in the personages of his tale and in their fate; and that he shall make the reader love the good people in the tale and hate the bad ones. But the reader of the Deerslayer tale dislikes the good people in it, is indifferent to the others, and wishes they would all get drowned together.

11. They require that the characters in a tale shall be so clearly defined that the reader can tell beforehand what each will do in a given emergency. But in the Deerslayer tale this rule is vacated.

In addition to these large rules there are some little ones. These require that the author shall:

12. Say what he is proposing to say, not merely come near it.

13. Use the right word, not its second cousin.

14. Eschew surplusage.

15. Not omit necessary details.

16. Avoid slovenliness of form.

17. Use good grammar.

18. Employ a simple and straightforward style.

Even these seven are coldly and persistently violated in the Deerslayer tale.

Cooper's gift in the way of invention was not a rich endowment; but such as it was he liked to work it, he was pleased with the effects, and indeed he did some quite sweet things with it. In his little box of stage properties he kept six or eight cunning devices, tricks, artifices for his savages and woodsmen to deceive and circumvent each other with, and he was never so happy as when he was working these innocent things and seeing them go. A favorite one was to make a moccasined person tread in the tracks of the moccasined enemy, and thus hide his own trail. Cooper wore out barrels and barrels of moccasins in working that trick. Another stage-property that he pulled out of his box pretty frequently was his broken twig. He prized his broken twig above all the rest of his effects, and worked it the hardest. It is a restful chapter in any book of his when somebody doesn't step on a dry twig and alarm all the reds and whites for two hundred yards around. Every time a Cooper person is in peril, and absolute silence is worth four dollars a minute, he is sure to step on a dry twig. There may be a hundred handier things to step on, but that wouldn't satisfy Cooper. Cooper requires him to turn out and find a dry twig; and if he can't do it, go and borrow one. In fact, the Leather Stocking Series ought to have been called the Broken Twig Series.

I am sorry there is not room to put in a few dozen instances of the delicate art of the forest, as practised by Natty Bumppo and some of the other Cooperian experts. Perhaps we may venture two or three samples. Cooper was a sailor—a naval officer; yet he gravely tells us how a vessel, driving towards a lee shore in a gale, is steered for a particular spot by her skipper because he knows of an undertow there which will hold her back against the gale and save her. For just pure woodcraft, or sailorcraft, or whatever it is, isn't that neat? For several years Cooper was daily in the society of artillery, and he ought to have noticed that when a cannon-ball strikes the ground it either buries itself or skips a hundred feet or so; skips again a hundred feet or so—and so on, till finally it gets tired and rolls.

Now in one place he loses some "females"—as he always calls women—in the edge of a wood near a plain at night in a fog, on purpose to give Bumppo a chance to show off the delicate art of the forest before the reader. These mislaid people are hunting for a fort. They hear a cannonblast, and a cannon-ball presently comes rolling into the wood and stops at their feet. To the females this suggests nothing. The case is very different with the admirable Bumppo. I wish I may never know peace again if he doesn't strike out promptly and follow the track of that cannon-ball across the plain through the dense fog and find the fort. Isn't it a daisy? If Cooper had any real knowledge of Nature's ways of doing things, he had a most delicate art in concealing the fact. For instance: one of his acute Indian experts, Chingachgook (pronounced Chicago, I think), has lost the trail of a person he is tracking through the forest. Apparently that trail is hopelessly lost. Neither you nor I could ever have guessed out the way to find it. It was very different with Chicago. Chicago was not stumped for long. He turned a running stream out of its course, and there, in the slush in its old bed, were that person's moccasin-tracks. The current did not wash them away, as it would have done in all other like cases—no, even the eternal laws of Nature have to vacate when Cooper wants to put up a delicate job of woodcraft on the reader.

We must be a little wary when Brander Matthews tells us that Cooper's books "reveal an extraordinary fulness of invention." As a rule, I am quite willing to accept Brander Matthews's literary judgments and applaud his lucid and graceful phrasing of them; but that particular statement needs to be taken with a few tons of salt. Bless your heart, Cooper hadn't any more invention than a horse; and I don't mean a high-class horse, either; I mean a clothes-horse. It would be very difficult to find a really clever "situation" in Cooper's books, and still more difficult to find one of any kind which he has failed to render absurd by his handling of it. Look at the episodes of "the caves"; and at the celebrated scuffle between Maqua and those others on the table-land a few days later; and at Hurry Harry's queer water-transit from the castle to the ark; and at Deerslayer's half-hour with his first corpse; and at the quarrel between Hurry Harry and Deerslayer later; and at —but choose for yourself; you can't go amiss.

If Cooper had been an observer his inventive faculty would have worked better; not more interestingly, but more rationally, more plausibly. Cooper's proudest creations in the way of "situations" suffer noticeably from the absence of the observer's protecting gift. Cooper's eye was splendidly inaccurate. Cooper seldom saw anything correctly. He saw nearly all things as through a glass eye, darkly. Of course a man who cannot see the commonest little every-day matters accurately is working at a disadvantage when he is constructing a "situation." In the Deerslayer tale Cooper has a stream which is fifty feet wide where it flows out of a lake; it presently narrows to twenty as it meanders along for no given reason; and yet when a stream acts like that it ought to be required to explain itself. Fourteen pages later the width of the brook's outlet from the lake has suddenly shrunk thirty feet, and become "the narrowest part of the stream." This shrinkage is not ac-

counted for. The stream has bends in it, a sure indication that it has alluvial banks and cuts them; yet these bends are only thirty and fifty feet long. If Cooper had been a nice and punctilious observer he would have noticed that the bends were oftener nine hundred feet long than short of it.

Cooper made the exit of that stream fifty feet wide, in the first place, for no particular reason; in the second place, he narrowed it to less than twenty to accommodate some Indians. He bends a "sapling" to the form of an arch over this narrow passage, and conceals six Indians in its foliage. They are "laying" for a settler's scow or ark which is coming up the stream on its way to the lake; it is being hauled against the stiff current by a rope whose stationary end is anchored in the lake; its rate of progress cannot be more than a mile an hour. Cooper describes the ark, but pretty obscurely. In the matter of dimensions "it was little more than a modern canal-boat." Let us guess, then, that it was about one hundred and forty feet long. It was of "greater breadth than common." Let us guess, then, that it was about sixteen feet wide. This leviathan had been prowling down bends which were but a third as long as itself, and scraping between banks where it had only two feet of space to spare on each side. We cannot too much admire this miracle. A low-roofed log dwelling occupies "two-thirds of the ark's length"—a dwelling ninety feet long and sixteen feet wide, let us say a kind of vestibule train. The dwelling has two rooms—each forty-five feet long and sixteen feet wide, let us guess. One of them is the bedroom of the Hutter girls, Judith and Hetty; the other is the parlor in the daytime, at night it is papa's bedchamber. The ark is arriving at the stream's exit now, whose width has been reduced to less than twenty feet to accommodate the Indians—say to eighteen. There is a foot to spare on each side of the boat. Did the Indians notice that there was going to be a tight squeeze there? Did they notice that they could make money by climbing down out of that arched sapling and just stepping aboard when the ark scraped by? No, other Indians would have noticed these things, but Cooper's Indians never notice anything. Cooper thinks they are marvelous creatures for noticing, but he was almost always in error about his Indians. There was seldom a sane one among them.

The ark is one hundred and forty feet long; the dwelling is ninety feet long. The idea of the Indians is to drop softly and secretly from the arched sapling to the dwelling as the ark creeps along under it at the rate of a mile an hour, and butcher the family. It will take the ark a minute and a half to pass under. It will take the ninety foot dwelling a minute to pass under. Now, then, what did the six Indians do? It would take you thirty years to guess, and even then you would have to give it up, I believe. Therefore, I will tell you what the Indians did. Their chief, a person of quite extraordinary intellect for a Cooper Indian, warily watched the canal-boat as it squeezed along under him, and when he had got his calculations fined down to exactly the right shade, as he judged, he let go and dropped. And missed the house! That is actually what he did. He missed the house, and landed in the stern of the scow. It was not much of a fall, yet it knocked him silly. He lay there unconscious. If the house had been ninety-seven feet long he would have made the trip. The fault was Cooper's, not his. The error lay in the construction of the house. Cooper was no architect.

There still remained in the roost five Indians.

The boat has passed under and is now out of their reach. Let me explain what the five did—you would not be able to reason it out for yourself. No. 1 jumped for the boat, but fell in the water astern of it. Then No. 2 jumped for the boat, but fell in the water still farther astern of it. Then No. 3 jumped for the boat, and fell a good way astern of it. Then No. 4 jumped for the boat, and fell in the water away astern. Then even No. 5 made a jump for the boat—for he was a Cooper Indian. In the matter of intellect, the difference between a Cooper Indian and the Indian that stands in front of the cigar-shop is not spacious. The scow episode is really a sublime burst of invention; but it does not thrill, because the inaccuracy of the details throws a sort of air of fictitiousness and general improbability over it. This comes of Cooper's inadequacy as an observer.

The reader will find some examples of Cooper's high talent for inaccurate observation in the account of the shooting-match in *The Pathfinder*.

> "A common wrought nail was driven lightly into the target, its head having been first touched with paint."

The color of the paint is not stated—an important omission, but Cooper deals freely in important omissions. No, after all, it was not an important omission;

for this nail-head is a hundred yards from the marks-men, and could not be seen by them at that distance, no matter what its color might be.

How far can the best eyes see a common house-fly? A hundred yards? It is quite impossible. Very well; eyes that cannot see a house-fly that is a hundred yards away cannot see an ordinary nailhead at that distance, for the size of the two objects is the same. It takes a keen eye to see a fly or a nailhead at fifty yards—one hundred and fifty feet. Can the reader do it?

The nail was lightly driven, its head painted, and game called. Then the Cooper miracles began. The bullet of the first marksman chipped an edge off the nail-head; the next man's bullet drove the nail a little way into the target—and removed all the paint. Haven't the miracles gone far enough now? Not to suit Cooper; for the purpose of this whole scheme is to show off his prodigy, Deerslayer Hawkeye—Long-Rifle—Leather-Stocking—Pathfinder—Bumppo before the ladies.

> " 'Be all ready to clench it, boys!' cried out Pathfinder, stepping into his friend's tracks the instant they were vacant. 'Never mind a new nail; I can see that, though the paint is gone, and what I can see I can hit at a hundred yards, though it were only a mosquito's eye. Be ready to clench!'
>
> "The rifle cracked, the bullet sped its way, and the head of the nail was buried in the wood, covered by the piece of flattened lead."

188

There, you see, is a man who could hunt flies with a rifle, and command a ducal salary in a Wild West show to-day if we had him back with us.

The recorded feat is certainly surprising just as it stands; but it is not surprising enough for Cooper. Cooper adds a touch. He has made Pathfinder do this miracle with another man's rifle; and not only that, but Pathfinder did not have even the advantage of loading it himself. He had everything against him, and yet he made that impossible shot; and not only made it, but did it with absolute confidence, saying, "Be ready to clench." Now a person like that would have undertaken that same feat with a brickbat, and with Cooper to help he would have achieved it, too.

Pathfinder showed off handsomely that day before the ladies. His very first feat was a thing which no Wild West show can touch. He was standing with the group of marksmen, observing—a hundred yards from the target, mind; one Jasper raised his rifle and drove the centre of the bull's-eye. Then the Quartermaster fired. The target exhibited no result this time. There was a laugh. "It's a dead miss," said Major Lundie. Pathfinder waited an impressive moment or two; then said, in that calm, indifferent, know-it-all way of his, "No, Major, he has covered Jasper's bullet, as will be seen if any one will take the trouble to examine the target."

Wasn't it remarkable! How could he see that little pellet fly through the air and enter that distant bullet-hole? Yet that is what he did; for nothing is impossible to a Cooper person. Did any of those people have any deep-seated doubts about this thing? No; for that would imply sanity, and these were all Cooper people.

> "The respect for Pathfinder's skill and for his *quickness and accuracy of sight*" (the italics are mine) "was so profound and general, that the instant he made this declaration the spectators began to distrust their own opinions, and a dozen rushed to the target in order to ascertain the fact. There, sure enough, it was found that the Quartermaster's bullet had gone through the hole made by Jasper's, and that, too, so accurately as to require a minute examination to be certain of the circumstance, which, however, was soon clearly established by discovering one bullet over the other in the stump against which the target was placed."

They made a "minute" examination; but never mind, how could they know that there were two bullets in that hole without digging the latest one out? for neither probe nor eyesight could prove the presence of any more than one bullet. Did they dig? No; as we shall see. It is the Pathfinder's turn now; he steps out before the ladies, takes aim, and fires.

But, alas! here is a disappointment; an incredible, an unimaginable disappointment—for the target's aspect is unchanged; there is nothing there but that same old bullet-hole!

> " 'If one dared to hint at such a thing,' cried Major Duncan, 'I should say that the Pathfinder has also missed the target!' "

As nobody had missed it yet, the "also" was not necessary; but never mind about that, for the Pathfinder is going to speak.

> " 'No, no, Major,' said he, confidently, 'that would be a risky declaration. I didn't load the piece, and can't say what was in it; but if it was lead, you will find the bullet driving down those of the Quartermaster and Jasper, else is not my name Pathfinder.'
>
> "A shout from the target announced the truth of this assertion."

Is the miracle sufficient as it stands? Not for Cooper. The Pathfinder speaks again, as he "now slowly advances towards the stage occupied by the females":

> " 'That's not all, boys, that's not all; if you find the target touched at all, I'll own to a miss. The Quartermaster cut the wood, but you'll find no wood cut by that last messenger."

The miracle is at last complete. He knew—doubtless saw—at the distance of a hundred yards—that his bullet had passed into the hole without fraying the edges. There were now three bullets in that one hole—three bullets embedded processionally in the body of the stump back of the target. Everybody knew this—somehow or other—and yet nobody had dug any of them out to make sure. Cooper is not a close observer, but he is interesting. He is certainly always that, no matter what happens. And he is more interesting when

191

he is not noticing what he is about than when he is. This is a considerable merit.

The conversations in the Cooper books have a curious sound in our modern ears. To believe that such talk really ever came out of people's mouths would be to believe that there was a time when time was of no value to a person who thought he had something to say; when it was the custom to spread a two-minute remark out to ten; when a man's mouth was a rolling-mill, and busied itself all day long in turning four-foot pigs of thought into thirty-foot bars of conversational railroad iron by attenuation; when subjects were seldom faithfully stuck to, but the talk wandered all around and arrived nowhere; when conversations consisted mainly of irrelevancies, with here and there a relevancy, a relevancy with an embarrassed look, as not being able to explain how it got there.

Cooper was certainly not a master in the construction of dialogue. Inaccurate observation defeated him here as it defeated him in so many other enterprises of his. He even failed to notice that the man who talks corrupt English six days in the week must and will talk it on the seventh, and can't help himself. In the Deerslayer story he lets Deerslayer talk the showiest kind of book-talk sometimes, and at other times the basest of base dialects. For instance, when some one asks him if he has a sweetheart, and if so, where she abides, this is his majestic answer:

> " 'She's in the forest—hanging from the boughs of the trees, in a soft rain—in the dew on the open grass—the clouds that float about in the

blue heavens—the birds that sing in the woods—
the sweet springs where I slake my thirst—and in
all the other glorious gifts that come from God's
Providence!' "

And he preceded that, a little before, with this:

" 'It consarns me as all things that touches a
fri'nd consarns a fri'nd.' "

And this is another of his remarks:

" 'If I was Injin born, now, I might tell of this, or
carry in the scalp and boast of the expl'ite afore the
whole tribe; or if my inimy had only been a bear' "—
and so on.

We cannot imagine such a thing as a veteran Scotch
Commander-in-Chief comporting himself in the field
like a windy melodramatic actor, but Cooper could. On
one occasion Alice and Cora were being chased by the
French through a fog in the neighborhood of their father's fort:

" 'Point de quartier aux coquins!' cried an eager pursuer, who seemed to direct the operations
of the enemy.

" 'Stand firm and be ready, my gallant 60ths!'
suddenly exclaimed a voice above them; 'wait to
see the enemy; fire low, and sweep the glacis.'

" 'Father? father!' exclaimed a piercing cry
from out the mist; 'it is I! Alice! thy own Elsie!
spare, O! save your daughters!'

" 'Hold!' shouted the former speaker, in the
awful tones of parental agony, the sound reaching
even to the woods, and rolling back in solemn

193

echo. "'Tis she! God has restored me my children! Throw open the sally-port; to the field,
60ths, to the field! pull not a trigger, lest ye kill
my lambs! Drive off these dogs of France with
your steel!' "

Cooper's word-sense was singularly dull. When a
person has a poor ear for music he will flat and sharp
right along without knowing it. He keeps near the
tune, but it is not the tune. When a person has a poor
ear for words, the result is a literary flatting and sharp-
ing; you perceive what he is intending to say, but you
also perceive that he doesn't say it. This is Cooper. He
was not a word-musician. His ear was satisfied with the
approximate word. I will furnish some circumstantial
evidence in support of this charge. My instances are
gathered from half a dozen pages of the tale called
Deerslayer. He uses "verbal," for "oral"; "precision,"
for "facility"; "phenomena," for "marvels"; "necessary," for "predetermined"; "unsophisticated," for
"primitive"; "preparation," for "expectancy"; "re-
buked," for "subdued"; "dependent on," for "resulting from"; "fact," for "condition"; "fact," for "conjecture"; "precaution," for "caution"; "explain," for "de-
termine"; "mortified," for "disappointed"; "meretri-
cious," for "factitious"; "materially," for "considerably"; "decreasing," for "deepening"; "increasing,"
for "disappearing"; "embedded," for "enclosed";
"treacherous," for "hostile"; "stood," for "stooped";
"softened," for "replaced"; "rejoined," for "remarked"; "situation," for "condition"; "different," for
"differing"; "insensible," for "unsentient"; "brevity,"
for "celerity"; "distrusted," for "suspicious"; "mental

194

imbecility," for "imbecility"; "eyes," for "sight"; "counteracting," for "opposing"; "funeral obsequies," for "obsequies."

There have been daring people in the world who claimed that Cooper could write English, but they are all dead now—all dead but Lounsbury. I don't remember that Lounsbury makes the claim in so many words, still he makes it, for he says that Deerslayer is a "pure work of art." Pure, in that connection, means faultless —faultless in all details—and language is a detail. If Mr. Lounsbury had only compared Cooper's English with the English which he writes himself—but it is plain that he didn't; and so it is likely that he imagines until this day that Cooper's is as clean and compact as his own. Now I feel sure, deep down in my heart, that Cooper wrote about the poorest English that exists in our language, and that the English of Deerslayer is the very worst that even Cooper ever wrote.

I may be mistaken, but it does seem to me that Deerslayer is not a work of art in any sense; it does seem to me that it is destitute of every detail that goes to the making of a work of art; in truth, it seems to me that Deerslayer is just simply a literary delirium tremens.

A work of art? It has no invention; it has no order, system, sequence, or result; it has no lifelikeness, no thrill, no stir, no seeming of reality; its characters are confusedly drawn, and by their acts and words they prove that they are not the sort of people the author claims that they are; its humor is pathetic; its pathos is funny; its conversations are—oh! indescribable; its love-scenes odious; its English a crime against the language.

Counting these out, what is left is Art. I think we must all admit that.

JULIA A. MOORE.

We feel a little shame in laughing at the sincere attempts of a would-be poet; but the shame passes, and the laughter remains. Julia A. Moore, the Sweet Singer of Michigan, became a celebrity of a sort, and her Sentimental Song Book a surprise bestseller, on the strength of her reputation as one of the worst poets in American history. Her poems are better parodies than the best intentional parodies of driveling sentimental poetry, and she still has a small cult of fanatical admirers today.

"This little book is composed of truthful pieces," she wrote in her preface. "All those which speak of being killed, died or drowned, are truthful songs; others are 'more truth than poetry.' "

We have chosen "Ashtabula Disaster" as representative of this unusual poet's talent. As you read it, keep in mind the author's own words from another one of her poems:

> And now kind friends, what I have wrote,
>   I hope you will pass o'er,
> And not criticize as some have done,
>   Hitherto herebefore.

197

ASHTABULA DISASTER.

Air—"*Gently Down the Stream of Time.*"

Have you heard of the dreadful fate
  Of Mr. P. P. Bliss and wife?
Of their death I will relate,
  And also others lost their life;
Ashtabula Bridge disaster,
  Where so many people died
Without a thought that destruction
  Would plunge them 'neath the wheel of tide.

Chorus:
Swiftly passed the engine's call,
  Hastening souls on to death,
Warning not one of them all;
  It brought despair right and left.

Among the ruins are many friends,
  Crushed to death amidst the roar;
On one thread all may depend,
  And hope they've reached the other shore.
P. P. Bliss showed great devotion
  To his faithful wife, his pride,
When he saw that she must perish,
  He died a martyr by her side.

P. P. Bliss went home above—
   Left all friends, earth and fame,
To rest in God's holy love;
   Left on earth his work and name.
The people love his work by numbers,
   It is read by great and small,
He by it will be remembered,
   He has left it for us all.

His good name from time to time
   Will rise on land and sea;
It is known in distant climes,
   Let it echo wide and free.
One good man among the number,
   Found sweet rest in a short time,
His weary soul may sweetly slumber
   Within the vale, heaven sublime.

Destruction lay on every side,
   Confusion, fire and despair;
No help, no hope, so they died,
   Two hundred people over there.
Many ties was there broken,
   Many a heart was filled with pain,
Each one left a little token,
   For above they live again.

MAX ADELER.

Charles Heber Clark, who wrote under the name Max
Adeler, was one of those blessed souls who wrote for the joy
of it rather than for the money. He was in the newspaper
business, but as a proprietor—he was one of the owners of
the *Bulletin* in Philadelphia, which nearly everybody read until the early 1980s. His book *Elbow Room* was a big seller in
Europe as well as America, and we cannot think why he is
not mentioned more often these days. These two little selections are fair samples of his work.

IMPROVED CONGRESSIONAL RECORD.

IF CONGRESS RESOLVE to act upon the suggestion of Sen-
ator Miller that the Congressional Record be issued as
a weekly and sent to every family in the country, some
modification ought to be made in the contents of the
Record. The paper is much too heavy and dismal in its
present condition to be welcomed in the ordinary
American household. Perhaps it might have a puzzle
department, and if so one of the first puzzles could take
the shape of an inquiry how it happens that so many
Congressmen get rich on a salary of five thousand a
year. The department of answers to correspondents
could be enriched with references to letters from office
seekers, and the department of Household Economy
could contain explanations of how the members frank
their shirts home through the post-office so as to get
them in the family wash. As for the general contents,

describing the business proceedings in the Senate and the House, we recommend that these should be put in the form of verse. We should treat them, say, something in this fashion:

> Mr. Hill
> Introduced a bill
> To give John Smith a pension.
> Mr. Bayard
> Talked himself tired,
> But said nothing worthy of mention.

This would be succinct, musical, and to a degree impressive. The youngest reader could grasp the meaning of it, and it could be easily committed to memory. Or a scene in the House might be depicted in such terms as these:

> A very able speech was made by Cox, of
>   Minnesota,
> Respecting the necessity of protecting the black
>   voter,
> 'Twas indignantly responded to by Smith, of
>   Alabama,
> Whose abominable talk was silenced by the
>   Speaker's hammer.
> Then Atkinson, of Kansas, rose to make an
>   explanation,
> But was pulled down by a colleague in a state of
>   indignation.
> And Mr. Alexander, in a speech about insurance,
> Taxed the patience of his hearers pretty nearly
>   past endurance.

> After which Judge Whittaker denounced the
>   reciprocity
> Treaty with Hawaii as a scandalous monstrosity...

Of course versification of the Congressional Record
would require the services of a poet laureate of rather
unusual powers. If Congress shall accept seriously the
suggestions which we make with an earnest desire to
promote the public interest, we shall venture to recommend the selection of the Sweet Singer of Michigan as
the first occupant of the laureate's office.

THE EDITOR OF THE *PATRIOT*.

MAJOR SLOTT, LIKE most other editors, is continually
persecuted by bores, but recently he was the victim of
a peculiarly dastardly attack from a person of this class.
While he was sitting in the office of the *Patriot*, writing
an editorial about "Our Grinding Monopolies," he
suddenly became conscious of the presence of a fearful
smell. He stopped, snuffed the air two or three times,
and at last lighted a cigar to fumigate the room. Then
he heard footsteps upon the stairs, and as they drew
nearer the smell grew stronger. When it had reached a
degree of intensity that caused the major to fear that it
might break some of the furniture, there was a knock
at the door. Then a man entered with a bundle under
his arm, and as he did so the major thought that he
had never smelt such a fiendish smell in the whole
course of his life. He held his nose; and when the man

202

saw the gesture, he said, "I thought so; the usual effect. You hold it tight while I explain."

"What hab you god id that buddle?" asked the major.

"That, sir," said the man, "is Barker's Carbolic Disinfecting Door-mat. I am Barker, and this is the mat. I invented it, and it's a big thing."

"Is id thad thad smells so thudderig bad?" asked the major, with his nostrils tightly shut.

"Yes, sir; smells very strong, but it's a healthy smell. It's invigorating. It braces the system. I'll tell you—"

"Gid oud with the blabed thig!" exclaimed the major.

"I must tell you all about it first. I called to explain it to you. You see I've been investigating the causes of epidemic diseases. Some scientists think they are spread by molecules in the air; others attribute them to gases generated in the sewers; others hold that they are conveyed by contagion; but I—"

"Aid you goig to tague thad idferdal thig away frob here?" asked the major.

"But I have discovered that these diseases are spread by the agency of door-mats. Do you understand? Door-mats! And I'll explain to you how it's done. Here's a man who's been in a house where there's disease. He gets it on his boots. The leather is porous, and it becomes saturated. He goes to another house and wipes his boots on the mat. Now, every man who uses that mat must get some of the stuff on his boots, and he spreads it over every other door-mat that he wipes them on. Now, don't he?"

203

"Why dode you tague thad sbell frob udder by dose?"

"Well, then, my idea is to construct a door-mat that will disinfect those boots. I do it by saturating the mat with carbolic acid and drying it gradually. I have one here prepared by my process. Shall I unroll it?"

"If you do, I'll blow your braids out!" shouted the major.

"Oh, very well, then. Now, the objection to this beautiful invention is that it possesses a very strong and positive odor."

"I'll bed it does," said the major.

"And as this is offensive to many persons, I give to each purchaser a 'nose-guard,' which is to be worn upon the nose while in a house where the carbolic mat is placed. This nose-guard is filled with a substance which completely neutralizes the smell, and it has only one disadvantage. Now, what is that?"

"Are you goig to quid and led me breathe, or are you goig to stay here all day log?"

"Have patience, now; I'm coming to the point. I say, what is that? It is that the neutralizing substance in the nose-guard evaporates too quickly. And how do I remedy that? I give to every man who buys a mat and a nose-guard two bottles of 'neutralizer.' What it is composed of is a secret. But the bottles are to be carried in the pocket, so as to be ready for every emergency. The disadvantage of this plan consists of the fact that the neutralizer is highly explosive, and if a man should happen to sit down on a bottle of it in his coat-tail pocket suddenly it might hist him through the roof. But see how beautiful my scheme is."

"Oh, thudder add lightnig! aid you ever goig to quid?"

"See how complete it is! By paying twenty dollars additional, every man who takes a mat has his life protected in the Hopelessly Mutual Accident Insurance Company, so that it really makes no great difference whether he is busted through the shingles or not. Now, does it?"

"Oh, dode ask me. I dode care a ced about id, adyway."

"Well, then, what I want you to do is to give me a first-rate notice in your paper, describing the invention, giving the public some general notion of its merits and recommending its adoption into general use. You give me a half-column puff, and I'll make the thing square by leaving you one of the mats, with a couple of bottles of the neutralizer and a nose-guard. I'll leave them now."

"Whad d'you say?"

"I say I'll just leave you a mat and the other fixings for you to look over at your leisure."

"You biserable scoundrel, if you lay wod ob those blasted thigs dowd here, I'll burder you od the spod! I wod stad such foolishness."

"Won't you notice it, either?"

"Certaidly nod. I woulded do id for ten thousad dollars a lide."

"Well, then, let it alone; and I hope one of those epidemic diseases will get you and lay you up for life."

As Mr. Barker withdrew, Major Slott threw up the windows, and after catching his breath, he called down stairs to a reporter, "Perkins, follow that man and hear what he's got to say, and then blast him in a column of the awfulest vituperation you know how to write."

Perkins obeyed orders, and now Barker has a libel suit pending against *The Patriot*, while the carbolic mat has not yet been introduced to this market.

WILL W. CLARK.

Mr. Clark is probably the most thoroughly forgotten of all the writers in this collection. In fact, we were unable to find any of his writings at all, with the exception of this little autobiography he produced for a book about American humorists published in 1882. Under the names "Gilhooley" and "Frisbee" he wrote humorous columns for the *Leader* in Pittsburgh—a paper whose owner later married Lillian Russell, so it was a success as far as that goes. As for the rest, we shall simply let Mr. Clark speak for himself.

My BIOGRAPHY IS not a particularly interesting chapter, and is in fact the romance of a poor young man. Still I think I am a humorist. Away down in the innermost recesses of my system I feel I am a humorist, but by some unfortunate combination of circumstances the public has never tumbled to the fact, with the proper precision and accuracy; the public wouldn't tumble if a marble front would fall on it. That is probably the reason I am on the ragged edge of genteel poverty at the present time instead of rolling in luxury.

I was born in the classic precincts of Hardscrabble, of poor and presumably honest parents. I took a fancy to literature from my mother, who was a Scotch-Irish woman, a great reader, and knew Burns by heart.

The old man was an Englishman with a bald head and side whiskers, and had a faculty of accumulating money, a faculty, I regret to say, which is not hereditary in our family. He used to remark, with some of that fine humor which I possess to such an intense degree, that he came from Derbyshire, where they were strong in the arm and weak in the head.

The most striking evidence of weakness on his part was his presenting me with a watch, in consideration of which I was not to enter the army.

On this occasion I became apprised, for the first time, that I was a humorist, as I had no notion of going to the front. I think it is much better to be a miserable poltroon during a war than a one-legged organ-grinder after it.

It is singular that as a boy I was a good deal like other boys. At school I was the teacher's pet. She liked me because I was pretty, and she noticed that budding genius which has developed so grandly since, but of which the public has failed to take proper cognizance. When I had reached decimals in arithmetic and could declaim "Rolla's Address to the Peruvians," the old man considered that my education was complete, and put me to work.

He was a rough carpenter, and I became a rough carpenter. I think I was the roughest carpenter in the United States. I built a shed once that was constructed in a manner so diametrically opposite to all the rules of carpentry, that it caved in three days after its completion and killed two coal heavers. On another occasion my employer noticed that I put a lock on upside down and hung a door the wrong way. He kindly but firmly suggested that I should quit. After revolving the question in my own mind I did quit; I thought the employer would be angry if I didn't.

When my father died he left me some money and I was pretty well fixed, but in a moment of aberration of

mind I yielded to the advice of some of my friends and joined a building and loan association. That settled it; in a short time the association gobbled my property and was loaning my money to some one else. If I had a hundred sons I would advise them all to be solicitors for or presidents of building and loan associations. There's money in it.

After that I made the most gigantic mistake of my life. I got a job on a newspaper as a reporter, and, after stoving my legs up running a route, I bloomed out as a humorist writer. As I said before, the people don't know I'm a humorist, but that is due to their lack of appreciation, and is no fault of mine. I have written some of the most exquisitely all-but funny things I ever saw, and I am now engaged on a series of important jokes for an almanac. I have a wife, three children, and an occasional dose of dyspepsia.

I do not intend to retire from business for some time. The newspaper business is easy, and especially easy is the task of running the funny end of it. A fellow has merely to be funny when he feels sad, and to grind out humorous items every day in the year. Then the salary of newspaper men is so enormous that college graduates would rather take a situation on a newspaper than get a job driving a street car. I am still grinding out mental pabulum for the public, and still waiting for some appreciative newspaper publisher to offer me a situation at $5,000 per annum.

BILL NYE.

Bill Nye (whose full name was Edgar Wilson Nye, but if he wanted to be called "Bill" that was his business) founded a paper in Laramie, Wyoming, that is still going today, and from there managed the considerable feat of gaining a national reputation. His specialty was presenting more or less true information—he wrote a history of the United States, for example—in a way that brought out all the natural absurdities of the subject.

BILL NYE'S ARCTIC-LE.

THE EXCITEMENT CONSEQUENT upon the anticipated departure of Mr. Gilder for the north pole has recently awakened in the bosom of the American people a new interest in what I may term that great *terra incognita*, if I may be pardoned for using a phrase from my own mother tongue.

Let us for a moment look back across the bleak waste of years and see what wonderful progress has been made in the discovery of the pole. We may then ask ourselves, who will be first to tack his location notice on the gnawed and season-cracked surface of the pole itself, and what will he do with it after he has so filed upon it?

Iceland, I presume, was discovered about 860 A. D., or 1,026 years ago, but the stampede to Iceland has always been under control, and you can get corner lots in the most desirable cities of Iceland, and wear a long rickety name with links in it like a rosewood sausage, to-day at a low price. Naddodr, a Norwegian viking, discovered Iceland A. D. 860, but he did not live to meet Lieutenant Greely or any of our most cele- brated northern tourists. Why Naddodr yearned to go north and[discover a colder country than his own, why he should seek to wet his feet and get icicles down his back in order to bring to light more snow-banks and chilblains, I cannot at this time understand. Why should a robust and prosperous viking roam around in the cold trying to nose out more frost-bitten Es- quimaux, when he could remain at home and vike?

But I leave this to the thinking mind. Let the think- ing mind grapple with it. It has no charms for me. Moreover, I haven't that kind of a mind.

Octher, another Norwegian gentleman, sailed around North cape and crossed the arctic circle in 890 A. D., but he crossed it in the night, and didn't notice it at the time.

Two or three years later, Erik the Red took a large snow-shovel and discovered the east coast of Green- land. Erik the Red was a Northman, and he flourished about the ninth century, and before the war. He sailed around in that country for several years, drinking bay rum and bear's oil and having a good time. He wore fur underclothes all the time, winter and summer, and evaded the poll-tax for a long time. Erik also estab- lished a settlement on the south-east coast of Green- land in about latitude 60 degrees north. These people remained here for some time, subsisting on shrimp salad, sea-moss farina, and neat's-foot oil. But finally they became so bored with the quiet country life and the backward springs that they removed from there to a land that is fairer than day, to use the words of another. They removed during the holidays, leaving their axle grease and all they held dear, including their remains.

From that on down to 1380 we hear or read varying and disconnected accounts of people who have been up that way, acquired a large red chilblain, made an observation, and died. Representatives from almost every quarter of the globe have been to the far north, eaten their little hunch of jerked polar-bear, and then the polar-bear has eaten his little hunch of jerked explorer, and so the good work went on.

The polar bear, with his wonderful retentive faculties, has succeeded in retaining his great secret regarding the pole, together with the man who came out there to find out about it. So up to 1380 a large number of nameless explorers went to this celebrated watering-place, shot a few pemmican, ate a jerked whale, shuddered a couple of times, and died. It has been the history of arctic exploration from the earliest ages. Men have taken their lives and a few doughnuts in their hands, wandered away into the uncertain light of the frozen north, made a few observations—to each other regarding the backward spring—and then cached their skeletons forever.

In 1380 two Italians named Lem took a load of sun-kissed bananas and made a voyage to the extreme north, but the historian says that the accounts are so conflicting, and as the stories told by the two brothers did not agree and neither ever told it the same on two separate occasions, the history of their voyage is not used very much.

Years rolled on, boys continued to go to school and see in their geographies enticing pictures of men in expensive fur clothing running sharp iron spears and long dangerous stab knives into ferocious white bears and snorting around on large cakes of cold ice and having a good time. These inspired the growing youth to rise up and do likewise. So every nation 'neath the sun has contributed its assortments of choice, white skeletons and second hand clothes to the remorseless maw of the hungry and ravenous north.

And still the great pole continued to squeak on through days that were six months long and nights that made breakfast seem almost useless.

In 1477 Columbus went up that way, but did not succeed in starving to death. He got a bird's-eye view of a large deposit of dark-blue ice, got hungry and came home.

During the fifteenth and sixteenth centuries the northern nations of Europe, and especially the Dutch, kept the discovery business red-hot, but they did not get any fragments of the true pole. The maritime nations of Europe, together with other foreign powers, dynasties, and human beings, for some time had spells of visiting the polar seas and neglecting to come back. It was the custom then as it is now, to go twenty rods farther than any other man had ever been, eat a deviled bootleg, curl up, and perish. Thousands of the best and brightest minds of all ages have yielded to this wild desire to live on sperm oil, pain-killer and jerked walrus, keep a little blue diary for thirteen weeks, and then feed it to a tall white bear with red gums.

That is not all. Millions of gallons of whiskey are sent to these frozen countries and used by the explorer in treating the untutored Esquimaux, who are not, and never will be, voters. It seems to me utterly ill-advised and shamefully idiotic.

BILL NYE ATTENDS BOOTH'S "HAMLET."

LAST EVENING I went to hear Mr. Edwin Booth in "Hamlet." I had read the play before, but it was better as he gave it, I think.

The play of "Hamlet" is not catchy, and there is a noticeable lack of local gags in it. A gentleman who stood up behind me and leaned against his breath all the evening said that he thought Ophelia's singing was too disconnected. He is a keen observer and has seen a great many plays. He went out frequently between the acts, and always came back in better spirits. He noticed that I wept a little in one or two places, and said that if I thought that was affecting I ought to see "Only a Farmer's Daughter." He drives a 'bus for the Hollenden Hotel here and has seen a great deal of life. Still, he talked freely with me through the evening, and told me what was coming next. He is a great admirer of the drama, and night after night he may be seen in the foyer, accompanied only by his breath.

There is considerable discussion among critics as to whether Hamlet was really insane or not, but I think that he assumed it in order to throw the prosecution off the track, for he was a very smart man, and when his uncle tried to work off some of his Danish prevarications on him I fully expected him to pull a card out of his pocket and present it to his royal tallness, on which might be seen the legend:

I AM SOMETHING OF A LIAR MYSELF!

But I am glad he did not, for it would have seemed out of character in a play like that.

Mr. Booth wore a dark, water-proof cloak all the evening and a sword with which he frequently killed people. He was dressed in black throughout, with hair of the same shade. He is using the same hair in "Hamlet" that he did twenty years ago, though he uses less of it. He wears black knickerbockers and long, black, crockless stockings.

Mr. Booth is doing well in the acting business, frequently getting as high as $2 apiece for tickets to his performances. He was encored by the audience several times last night, but refrained from repeating the play, fearing that it would make it late for those who had to go back to Belladonna, O., after the close of the entertainment.

Toward the end of the play a little rough on rats gets into the elderberry wine and the royal family drink it, after which there is considerable excitement, and a man with a good, reliable stomach-pump would have all he could do. Several of the royal family curl up and perish.

They do not die in the house.

During an interview between Hamlet and his mother an old gentleman who has the honor to be Ophelia's father hides behind a picket fence, so as to overhear the conversation. He gets excited and says something in a low, gutteral tone of voice, whereupon Hamlet runs his sword through the picket fence in such a way as to bore a large hole into the old man, who then dies.

I have heard a great many people speak the piece beginning—

To be or not to be,

but Mr. Booth does it better than any one I have ever heard. I once heard an elocutionist—kind of a smart Alickutionist as my friend The Hoosier Poet would say. This man recited "To be or not to be" in a manner which, he said, had frequently brought tears to eyes unused to weep. He recited it with his right hand socked into his bosom up to the elbow and his fair hair tossed about over his brow. His teeming brain, which claimed to be kind of a four-horse teaming brain, as it were, seemed to be on fire, and to all appearances he was indeed mad. So were the people who listened to him. He hissed it through his clinched teeth and snorted it through his ripe, red nose, wailed it up into the ceiling, and bleated it down the aisles, rolled it over and over against the rafters of his reverberating mouth, handed it out in big capsules, or hissed it through his puckered atomizer of a mouth, wailed and bellowed like a wild and maddened tailless steer in fly-time, darted across the stage like a headless hen, ripped the gentle atmosphere into shreds with his guinea-hen voluntary, bowed to us, and teetered off the stage.

Mr. Booth does not hoist his shoulders and settle back on his "pastern jints" like a man who is about to set a refractory brake on a coal car, neither does he immerse his right arm in his bosom up to the second joint. He seems to have the idea that Hamlet spoke these lines mostly because he felt like saying something instead of doing it to introduce a set of health-lift gestures and a hoarse, baritone snort.

A head of dank hair, a low, mellow, union-depot tone of voice, and a dark-blue, three sheet poster will not make a successful Hamlet, and blessed be the man who knows this without experimenting on the people till he has bunions on his immortal soul. I have sent a note to Mr. Booth this morning asking him to call at my room, No. 6-5/8, and saying that I would give him my idea about the drama from a purely unpartisan standpoint, but it is raining so fast now that I fear he will not be able to come.

THE GRAMMATICAL BOY.

McGuffey's readers were staples of the one-room schoolhouse of the nineteenth century. Their reputation has endured among homeschoolers and in some private religious schools, where they are still used today in facsimile reprints from the originals. Their fans (among whom you may count Dr. Boli) believe that young readers gain much from their wide vocabulary, and from their early introduction of readings from Shakespeare and other English classics. Neverthe-

217

less, Bill Nye gets right at the heart of what might sometimes make McGuffey's readers laughable to children of today.

SOMETIMES A SAD homesick feeling comes over me when I compare the prevailing style of anecdote and school literature with the old McGuffey brand, so well known thirty years ago. To-day our juvenile literature, it seems to me, is so transparent, so easy to understand that I am not surprised to learn that the rising genera-tion shows signs of lawlessness.

Boys to-day do not use the respectful language and large, luxuriant words that they did when Mr. McGuf-fey used to stand around and report their conversations for his justly celebrated school reader. It is disagreeable to think of, but it is none the less true, and for one I think we should face the facts.

I ask the careful student of school literature to com-pare the following selection, which I have written my-self with great care, and arranged with special refer-ence to the matter of choice and difficult words, with the flippant and commonplace terms used in the aver-age school book of to-day.

One day as George Pillgarlic was going to his tasks, and while passing through the wood, he spied a tall man approaching in an opposite direction along the highway.

"Ah!" thought George, in a low, mellow tone of voice, "whom have we here?"

"Good morning, my fine fellow," exclaimed the stranger, pleasantly. "Do you reside in this locality?"

"Indeed I do," retorted George, cheerily, doffing his cap. "In yonder cottage, near the glen, my widowed mother and her thirteen children dwell with me."

"And is your father dead?" exclaimed the man, with a rising inflection.

"Extremely so," murmured the lad, "and, oh, sir, that is why my poor mother is a widow."

"And how did your papa die?" asked the man, as he thoughtfully stood on the other foot awhile.

"Alas! sir," said George, as a large hot tear stole down his pale cheek, and fell with a loud report on the warty surface of his bare foot, "he was lost at sea in a bitter gale. The good ship foundered two years ago last Christmastide, and father was foundered at the same time. No one knew of the loss of the ship and that the crew was drowned until the next spring, and it was then too late."

"And what is your age, my fine fellow?" quoth the stranger.

"If I live till next October," said the boy, in a declamatory tone of voice suitable for a Second Reader. "I will be seven years of age."

"And who provides for your mother and her large family of children?" queried the man.

"Indeed, I do, sir," replied George, in a shrill tone. "I toil, oh, so hard, sir, for we are very, very poor, and since my elder sister, Ann, was married and brought her husband home to live with us, I have to toil more assiduously than heretofore."

"And by what means do you obtain a livelihood?" exclaimed the man, in slowly measured and grammatical words.

"By digging wells, kind sir," replied George, picking up a tired ant as he spoke and stroking it on the back. "I have a good education, and so I am able to dig wells as well as a man. I do this day-times and take in washing at night. In this way I am enabled barely to maintain our family in a precarious manner; but, oh, sir, should my other sisters marry, I fear that some of my brothers-in-law would have to suffer."

"And do you not fear the deadly fire-damp?" asked the stranger in an earnest tone.

"Not by a damp sight," answered George, with a low gurgling laugh, for he was a great wag.

"You are indeed a brave lad," exclaimed the stranger, as he repressed a smile. "And do you not at times become very weary and wish for other ways of passing your time?"

"Indeed, I do, sir," said the lad. "I would fain run and romp and be gay like other boys, but I must engage in constant manual exercise, or we will have no bread to eat, and I have not seen a pie since papa perished in the moist and moaning sea."

"And what if I were to tell you that your papa did not perish at sea, but was saved from a humid grave?" asked the stranger in pleasing tones.

"Ah, sir," exclaimed George, in a genteel manner, again doffing his cap, "I am too polite to tell you what I would say, and beside, sir, you are much larger than I am."

"But, my brave lad," said the man in low musical tones, "do you not know me, Georgie? Oh, George!"

"I must say," replied George, "that you have the advantage of me. Whilst I may have met you before, I cannot at this moment place you, sir."

"My son! oh, my son!" murmured the man, at the same time taking a large strawberry mark out of his valise and showing it to the lad. "Do you not recognize your parent on your father's side? When our good ship went to the bottom, all perished save me. I swam several miles through the billows, and at last utterly exhausted, gave up all hope of life. Suddenly I stepped on something hard. It was the United States.

"And now, my brave boy," exclaimed the man with great glee, "see what I have brought for you." It was but the work of a moment to unclasp from a shawl-strap which he held in his hand and present to George's astonished gaze a large 40-cent water-melon, which until now had been concealed by the shawl-strap.

EUGENE FIELD.

Eugene Field was a journalist who wrote clever and funny columns, with a sideline in pleasant children's verses. Early in his career, however, he spent two years editing the *Tribune* in Denver, and from that experience came the immortally cranky *Tribune Primer*. It is a mean-spirited parody of New England school primers, so prodigally mean-spirited that the mean-spiritedness becomes a source of delirious joy. It also gives us a twisted but probably far too accurate caricature of the office of a typical American daily newspaper in the early 1880s.

FROM THE TRIBUNE PRIMER.

The Bad Man.

Here is a Man who has just Stopped his Paper. What a Miserable looking Creature he is. He looks as if he had been stealing Sheep. How will he Know what is going on, now that he has Stopped his Paper? He will Borrow his Neighbor's Paper. One of these Days he will Break his leg, or be a Candidate for Office, and then the Paper will Say Nothing about it. That will be treating him just Right, will it not, little Children?

The Editor's Knife.

Here we have a Knife. It looks like a Saw, but it is a knife. It belongs to an Editor, and is used for Sharpening Pencils, killing Roaches, opening Champagne Bottles, and Cutting the Hearts out of Bad men who Come into the office to Whale the Reporters. There is Blood on the Blade of the Knife, but the Editor will Calmly Lick it off, and then the Blade will be as clean and Bright as ever. The Knife cost seventy Cents, and was Imported from London, Connecticut. If you are Good, perhaps the Editor will Give it to you to Cut off the Cat's Tail.

The Nasty Oil.

Do not take the Castor Oil. It is very Nasty and will Make you sick. Mamma wants you to Take it so you Will be Sick and can't go Out and Play with the other Boys and Girls. If Mamma will give you a Velocipede and a Goat and a Top and a Doll, then you may Take the Castor Oil and it will not Hurt you.

Generous Richard.

This is good Little Richard. His Mamma has Taught him to be Generous. See, he has the Measles, and he is going over to Give them to his Neighbors. Is he not a Nice Boy? When you get the Measles, you must give them to all the little Boys and Girls you can.

If you Do, maybe your Mamma will Give you Something. I guess she will Give you a Licking.

The Bad Mamma.

Why is this little Girl crying? Because her Mamma will not let her put Molasses and Feathers on the Baby's face. What a bad Mamma! The little Girl who never had any Mamma must enjoy herself. Papas are Nicer than Mammas. No little girl ever Marries a Mamma, and perhaps that is Why Mammas are so Bad to little Girls. Never mind; when Mamma goes out of the Room, Slap the horrid Baby, and if it Cries, you can tell your Mamma it Has the Colic.

The Contribution Plate.

This is a Contribution Plate. It has just been Handed around. What is there upon it? Now Count very Slow or you will Make a Mistake. Four Buttons, one Nickel, a Blue Chip, and one Spectacle glass. Yes, that is Right. What will be Done with all these Nice things? They will be sent to foreign Countries for the good of the Poor Heathens. How the Poor Heathens will Rejoice.

The Proof-Reader.

See the Proof-Reader. He has been reading the Proof of a Medical Convention. He is not Swearing. He is reading the Bible. You cannot See the Bible. It is Locked up in an Iron Box in the Editor's Room. The Proof-Reader is Saying something about Damming Something. Perhaps it is the Creek.

The Mud.

The Mud is in the Street. The Lady has on a pair of Red Stockings. She is Trying to Cross the Street. Let us all give Three cheers for the Mud.

Mamma's Scissors.

These are Mamma's Scissors. They do not Seem to be in good Health. Well, they are a little Aged. They have considerable Work to Do. Mamma uses them to Chop Kindling, cut Stove Pipe, pull Tacks, drive Nails, cut the children's Hair, punch new Holes in the Calendar, slice Bar soap, pound beef Steak, open tomato Cans, Shear the New Foundland dog, and cut out her New silk Dress. Why doesn't Papa get Mamma a new Pair of Scissors? You should not Ask such a Naughty question. Papa cannot Afford to Play Billiards and Indulge his Extravagant Family in the Luxuries of Life.

The Poet

Who is this Creature with Long Hair and a Wild Eye? He is a poet. He writes Poems on Spring and Women's Eyes and Strange, unreal Things of that Kind. He is always Wishing he was Dead, but he wouldn't Let anybody Kill him if he could Get away. A mighty good Sausage Stuffer was Spoiled when the Man became a Poet. He would Look well Standing under a Descending Pile Driver.

The Business Manager.

Here we Have a Business Manager. He is Blowing about the Circulation of the Paper. He is Saying the Paper has Entered upon an Era of Unprecedented Prosperity. In a Minute he will Go up Stairs and Chide the Editor for leaving his Gas Burning while he Went out for a Drink of Water, and he will dock a Reporter Four Dollars because a Subscriber has Licked him and he cannot Work. Little Children, if we Believed Business Managers went to Heaven, we would Give up our Pew in Church.

BEN KING.

There is not all that much to know about Ben King. He was a poet from St. Joseph, Michigan, who succeeded in building up a strong local reputation. Some of his poems were of the popular sentimental sort; but he had a slightly twisted sense of humor that often came out in his verse, as we see in these two examples.

IF I SHOULD DIE.

If I SHOULD die to-night
And you should come to my cold corpse and say,
Weeping and heartsick, o'er my lifeless clay—
    If I should die tonight,
And you should come in deepest grief and woe—
And say: "Here's that ten dollars that I owe,"
    I might arise in my large white cravat
    And say, "What's that?"

    If I should die to-night
And you should come to my cold corpse and kneel,
Clasping my bier to show the grief you feel,
    I say, if I should die to-night
And you should come to me, and there and then
Just even hint 'bout paying me that ten,
    I might arise the while,
    But I'd drop dead again.

LOVEY-LOVES.

OH, LOVE! let us love with a love that loves,
  Loving on with a love forever;
For a love that loves not the love it should love—
  I wot such a love will sever.
But, when two loves love this lovable love,
  Love loves with a love that is best;
And this love-loving, lovable, love-lasting love
  Loves on in pure love's loveliness.

Oh, chide not the love when its lovey-love loves
  With lovable, loving caresses;
For one feels that the lovingest love love can love,
  Love on in love's own lovelinesses.
And love, when it does love, in secret should love—
  'Tis there where love most is admired;
But the two lovey-loves that don't care where they love
  Make the public most mightily tired.

ROBERT J. BURDETTE.

Robert J. Burdette wrote for the *Hawkeye* in Burlington, Iowa. He married a woman who was at death's door, but her marriage to him rallied her enough that she lived for years as an invalid. Invalid or not, though, it was she who suggested to him that he ought to write down some of the funny things he said; and for years he wrote his funniest stuff while sitting by her bed. She also insisted that he would be a success as a lecturer, and so he was, in spite of his own misgivings.

In this story, Burdette mentions Bancroft's *History of the United States*, which is a remarkable work that deserves to be lifted out of its current obscurity; but it is true that Bancroft seemed to have an infinite number of fat volumes in him. Contrary to the prediction in this little story, however, the production of supplementary volumes ceased with Bancroft's death in 1891.

ROLLO LEARNING TO READ.

When Rollo was five years young, his father said to him one evening:

"Rollo, put away your roller skates and bicycle, carry that rowing machine out into the hall, and come to me. It is time for you to learn to read."

Then Rollo's father opened the book which he had sent home on a truck and talked to the little boy about it. It was Bancroft's History of the United States, half complete in twenty-three volumes. Rollo's father explained to Rollo and Mary his system of education, with special reference to Rollo's learning to read. His plan was that Mary should teach Rollo fifteen hours a day for ten years, and by that time Rollo would be half through the beginning of the first volume, and would like it very much indeed.

Rollo was delighted at the prospect. He cried aloud:

"Oh, papa! thank you very much. When I read this book clear through, all the way to the end of the last volume, may I have another little book to read ?"

"No," replied his father, "that may not be; because you will never get to the last volume of this one. For as fast as you read one volume, the author of this history, or his heirs, executors, administrators, or assigns, will write another as an appendix. So even though you should live to be a very old man, like the boy preacher, this history will always be twenty-three volumes ahead of you. Now, Mary and Rollo, this will be a hard task (pronounced tawsk) for both of you, and Mary must remember that Rollo is a very little boy, and must be very patient and gentle."

The next morning after the one preceding it, Mary began the first lesson. In the beginning she was so gentle and patient that her mother went away and cried, because she feared her dear little daughter was becoming too good for this sinful world, and might soon spread her wings and fly away and be an angel.

But in the space of a short time, the novelty of the expedition wore off, and Mary resumed running her temper—which was of the old-fashioned, low-pressure kind, just forward of the fire-box—on its old schedule. When she pointed to "A" for the seventh time, and Rollo said "W," she tore the page out by the roots, hit her little brother such a whack over the head with the big book that it set his birthday back six weeks, slapped him twice, and was just going to bite him, when her mother came in. Mary told her that Rollo had fallen down stairs and torn his book and raised that dreadful lump on his head. This time Mary's mother restrained her emotion, and Mary cried. But it was not because she feared her mother was pining away. Oh, no; it was her mother's rugged health and virile strength that grieved Mary, as long as the seance lasted, which was during the entire performance.

That evening Rollo's father taught Rollo his lesson and made Mary sit by and observe his methods, because, he said, that would be normal instruction for her. He said:

"Mary, you must learn to control your temper and curb your impatience if you want to wear low-neck dresses, and teach school. You must be sweet and patient, or you will never succeed as a teacher. Now, Rollo, what is this letter?"

"I dunno," said Rollo, resolutely.

"That is A," said his father, sweetly.

"Huh," replied Rollo, "I knowed that."

"Then why did you not say so?" replied his father, so sweetly that Jonas, the hired boy, sitting in the corner, licked his chops.

Rollo's father went on with the lesson:

"What is this, Rollo ?"

"I dunno," said Rollo, hesitatingly.

"Sure?" asked his father. "You do not know what it is?"

"Nuck," said Rollo.

"It is A," said his father.

"A what?" asked Rollo.

"A nothing," replied his father, "it is just A. Now, what is it?"

"Just A," said Rollo.

"Do not be flip, my son," said Mr. Holliday, "but attend to your lesson. What letter is this?"

"I dunno," said Rollo.

"Don't fib to me," said his father, gently, "you said a minute ago that you knew. That is N."

"Yes, sir," replied Rollo, meekly. Rollo, although he was a little boy, was no slouch, if he did wear bibs; he knew where he lived without looking at the door-plate. When it came time to be meek, there was no boy this side of the planet Mars who could be meeker, on shorter notice. So he said, "Yes, sir," with that subdued and well pleased alacrity of a boy who has just been asked to guess the answer to the conundrum, "Will you have another piece of pie?"

"Well," said his father, rather suddenly, "what is it?"

"M," said Rollo, confidently.

"N!" yelled his father, in three-line Gothic.

"N," echoed Rollo, in lower case nonpareil.

"B-a-n," said his father, "what does that spell?"

"Cat?" suggested Rollo, a trifle uncertainly.

"Cat?" snapped his father, with a sarcastic inflection, "b-a-n, cat! Where were you raised? Ban! B-a-n —Ban! Say it! Say it, or I'll get at you with a skate-strap!"

"B-a-m, band," said Rollo, who was beginning to wish that he had a rain-check and could come back and see the remaining innings some other day.

"Ba-a-a-an!" shouted his father, "B-a-n, Ban, Ban, Ban! Now say Ban!"

"Ban," said Rollo, with a little gasp.

"That's right," his father said, in an encouraging tone; "you will learn to read one of these years if you give your mind to it. All he needs, you see, Mary, is a teacher who doesn't lose patience with him the first time he makes a mistake. Now, Rollo, how do you spell, B-a-n—Ban ?"

Rollo started out timidly on c-a—then changed to d-o,—and finally compromised on h-e-n.

Mr. Holiday made a pass at him with Volume I, but Rollo saw it coming and got out of the way.

"B-a-n!" his father shouted, "B-a-n, Ban! Ban! Ban! Ban! Ban! Now go on, if you think you know how to spell that! What comes next? Oh, you're enough to tire the patience of Job! I've a good mind to make you learn by the Pollard system, and begin where you leave off! Go ahead, why don't you? Whatta you waiting for? Read on! What comes next? Why, croft, of course; anybody ought to know that—c-r-o-f-t, croft, Bancroft! What does that apostrophe mean? I mean, what does that punctuation mark between t and s stand for? You don't know? Take that, then! (whack). What comes after Bancroft? Spell it! Spell it, I tell you, and don't be all night about it! Can't, eh? Well, read it then; if you can't spell it, read it. H-i-s-t-o-r-y-ry, history; Bancroft's History of the United States! Now what does that spell? I mean, spell that!

Spell it! Oh, go away! Go to bed! Stupid, stupid child," he added as the little boy went weeping out of the room, "he'll never learn anything so long as he lives. I declare he has tired me all out, and I used to teach school in Trivoli township, too. Taught one whole winter in district number three when Nick Worthington was county superintendent, and had my salary look here, Mary, what do you find in that English grammar to giggle about? You go to bed, too, and listen to me—if Rollo can't read that whole book clear through without making a mistake to-morrow night, you'll wish you had been born without a back, that's all."

The following morning, when Rollo's father drove away to business, he paused a moment as Rollo stood at the gate for a final good-by kiss—for Rollo's daily good byes began at the door and lasted as long as his father was in sight—Mr. Holliday said:

"Some day, Rollo, you will thank me for teaching you to read."

"Yes, sir," replied Rollo, respectfully, and then added, "but not this day."

Rollo's head, though it had here and there transient bumps consequent upon foot-ball practice, was not naturally or permanently hilly. On the contrary, it was quite level.

SPELL AND DEFINE:
Tact
Imperturbability
Ebullition
Exasperation

234

Red-hot
Knout
Lamb
Philosopher
Terrier

Which end of a rattan hurts the more ?—Why does read-ing make a full man?—Is an occasional whipping good for a boy?—At precisely what age does corporal punishment cease to be effective?—And why?—State, in exact terms, how much better are grown up people without the rod, than little people with it.—And why?—When would a series of good sound whippings have been of the greatest benefit to Solomon, when he was a godly young man, or an idolatrous old one?—In order to reform this world thoroughly, then, whom should we thrash, the children or the grown-up peo-ple?—And why?—If, then, the whipping post should be abolished in Delaware, why should it be retained in the nurs-ery and the school room?—Write on the board, in large let-ters, the following sentence:

If a boy ten years old should be whipped for breaking a window, what should be done to a man thirty-five years old for breaking the third commandment?

GEORGE ADE.

"Fables in Slang" made the reputation of George Ade, whose long and successful career as a Chicago columnist gave him ample opportunities to observe the worst in human nature. Like many another satirist, he turned to the forms of children's literature to point out how little the moral certainties we absorbed in childhood have to do with the realities of adult life.

THE FABLE OF A STATESMAN WHO COULDN'T MAKE GOOD.

ONCE THERE WAS a Bluff whose Long Suit was Glittering Generalities.

He hated to Work and it hurt his Eyes to read Law, but on a Clear Day he could be heard a Mile, so he became a Statesman.

Whenever the Foresters had a Picnic they invited him to make the Principal Address, because he was the only Orator who could beat out the Merry-Go-Round.

The Habit of Dignity enveloped him.

Upon his Brow Deliberation sat. He wore a Fireman's moustache and a White Lawn Tie, and he loved to Talk about the Flag.

At a Clam-Bake in 1884 he hurled Defiance at all the Princes and Potentates of Europe, and the Sovereign Voters, caught up by his Matchless Eloquence and Unswerving Courage, elected him to the Legislature.

236

While he was in the Legislature he discovered that these United States were an Asylum for the Down-Trodden and oppressed of the Whole World, and frequently called Attention to the Fact. When some one asked him if he was cutting up any Easy Money or would it be safe for a Man with a Watch to go to Sleep in the same Room with him, he would take a Drink of Water and begin to plead for Cuba.

Once an Investigating Committee got after him and he was about to be Shown Up for Dallying with Corporations, but he put on a fresh White Tie and made a Speech about our Heroic Dead on a Hundred Battle-Fields, and Most People said it was simply Impossible for such a Thunderous Patriot to be a Crook. So he played the Glittering Generality stronger than ever.

In Due Time he Married a Widow of the Bantam Division. The Reason she married him was that he looked to her to be a Coming Congressman and she wanted to get a Whack at Washington Society. Besides, she lived in a Flat and the Janitor would not permit her to keep a Dog.

About Ten Days after they were Married he came Home at 4 A.M. in a Sea-Going Hack and he was Saturated. Next Morning she had him up on the Carpet and wanted to know How About It.

He arose and put his Right Hand inside of his Prince Albert Coat and began.

"Madam," he said, "During a Long, and, I trust, a not altogether fruitless Career as a Servant of the Peepul, I have always stood in the Fierce Light of Publicity, and my Record is an Open Book which he who runs may——"

"Nix! Nix!" she said, rapping for order with a Tea-Cup. "Let go of the Flying Rings. Get back to the Green Earth!"

He dilated his Nostrils and said: "From the Rock-Bound Hills of Maine in the North to the Everglades of Florida——"

"Forget the Everglades," she said, rapping again. "That Superheated Atmosphere may have a certain Tonic Effect on the Hydrocephalous Voter, but if you want to adjust yourself with Wifey, you come down to Cases."

So he went out after Breakfast and bought a $22 Hat in order to Square himself.

MORAL: *Some Women should be given the Right to Vote.*

THE FABLE OF SISTER MAE, WHO DID AS WELL AS COULD BE EXPECTED.

Two SISTERS LIVED in Chicago, the Home of Opportunity.

Luella was a Good Girl, who had taken Prizes at the Mission Sunday School, but she was Plain, much. Her Features did not seem to know the value of Team Work. Her Clothes fit her Intermittently, as it were. She was what would be called a Lumpy Dresser. But she had a good Heart.

Luella found Employment at a Hat Factory. All she had to do was to put Red Linings in Hats for the Country Trade; and every Saturday Evening, when

Work was called on account of Darkness, the Boss met her as she went out and crowded three Dollars on her.

The other Sister was Different.

She began as Mary, then changed to Marie, and her Finish was Mae.

From earliest Youth she had lacked Industry and Application.

She was short on Intellect but long on Shape.

The Vain Pleasures of the World attracted her. By skipping the Long Words she could read how Rupert Bansiford led Sibyl Gray into the Conservatory and made Love that scorched the Begonias. Sometimes she just Ached to light out with an Opera Company.

When she couldn't stand up Luella for any more Car Fare she went out looking for Work, and hoping she wouldn't find it. The sagacious Proprietor of a Lunch Room employed her as Cashier. In a little While she learned to count Money, and could hold down the Job.

Marie was a Strong Card. The Male Patrons of the Establishment hovered around the Desk long after paying their Checks. Within a Month the Receipts of the Place had doubled.

It was often remarked that Marie was a Pippin. Her Date Book had to be kept on the Double Entry System.

Although her Grammar was Sad, it made no Odds. Her Picture was on many a Button.

A Credit Man from the Wholesale House across the Street told her that any time she wanted to see the Telegraph Poles rush past, she could tear Transportation out of his Book. But Marie turned him down for a

Bucket Shop Man, who was not Handsome, but was awful Generous.

They were Married, and went to live in a Flat with a Quarter-Sawed Oak Chiffonier and Pink Rugs. She was Mae at this Stage of the Game.

Shortly after this, Wheat jumped twenty-two points, and the Husband didn't do a Thing.

Mae bought a Thumb Ring and a Pug Dog, and began to speak of the Swede Help as "The Maid."

Then she decided that she wanted to live in a House, because, in a Flat, One could never be sure of One's Neighbors. So they moved into a Sarcophagus on the Boulevard, right in between two Old Families, who had made their Money soon after the Fire, and Ice began to form on the hottest Days.

Mae bought an Automobile, and blew her Allowance against Beauty Doctors. The Smell of Cooking made her Faint, and she couldn't see where the Working Classes came in at all.

When she attended the theater a Box was none too good. Husband went along, in evening clothes and a Yachting Cap, and he had two large Diamonds in his Shirt Front.

Sometimes she went to a Vogner Concert, and sat through it, and she wouldn't Admit any more that the Russell Brothers, as the Irish Chambermaids, hit her just about Right.

She was determined to break into Society if she had to use an Ax.

At last she Got There; but it cost her many a Reed Bird and several Gross of Cold Quarts.

In the Hey-Day of Prosperity did Mae forget Luella? No, indeed.

She took Luella away from the Hat Factory, where the Pay was three Dollars a Week, and gave her a Position as Assistant Cook at five Dollars.

MORAL: *Industry and Perseverance bring a sure Reward.*

"Say, waiter, please look as pleasant as possible."

BILLY BAXTER.

William H. Kountz, Jr., never considered himself a writer; he was a businessman. But good advertising calls for a certain cleverness, and he was certainly up to the task of advertising a liver tonic.

The Duquesne Distributing Company of Pittsburg (the spelling was not yet standardized, and the Post Office spelled it without the H) was a bottler of what we should call soda pop today; but in those days soda pop was medicinal, and it was a favorite remedy for a hangover.

Kountz hit on the idea of humorous letters from one Billy Baxter, a typical young man about Pittsburgh, the first one describing the events that led to the hangover. The little pamphlet did its job: it was a huge success, and the author gained an instant reputation as a promising humorist. He followed up with a few more letters in a similar vein, and perhaps he might have been persuaded eventually to think of himself as a literary man; but he died unexpectedly at not quite thirty-two. *Billy Baxter's Letters* were published posthumously in a little book that seems to have been remarkably popular; copies of it still turn up all over, in bookstores and libraries and attics. The letters were also frequently anthologized in books of American humor over the next few years. We may regret that the author did not live long enough to develop the character of "Billy Baxter" further, but we can be grateful for these few breezy glimpses of Pittsburgh life at the end of the nineteenth century.

We have retained the advertising content, because it is written in the same amusing style by the same hand. The whole performance is a museum of the breezy slang of the 1890s.

243

ONE NIGHT.

A Kind of a Preface.

THE BAXTER LETTERS are written in the up-to-date slang of the day, by one who has seen several of the sides of life, and who has also come in contact with a few of the corners.

We will mail "One Night" to any address in North America upon receipt of four cents' in postage. Do not lick stamps and attach to letter of request, as at some future date we may wish to use same, and the Government foolishly requires a whole stamp.

As there are several people in the United States with whom we are not personally acquainted, and not being mind-readers, we ask that all signatures be written plainly.

Admiral Dewey's Letter.

In November, 1898, we sent Admiral Dewey a copy of "One Night." The appended letter is photographed from the original reply addressed to the president of our company, which was received March 9, 1899.

Flagship Olympia, Manila, Jan'y 28/99

Dear Sir,
Accept my best thanks for the book (One Night) which you were good enough to send me.

Very truly, George Dewey

We also sent a copy to His Royal Highness, Albert, Prince of Wales, and, having heard nothing from him, it now looks as though Al were going to snub us. Under the circumstances, when he runs for King we can't be for him.

One Night.

Pittsburg, Pa., August, 189-.
Dear Jim:

You remember I wrote you about a sack suit I ordered last week. Well, it came yesterday, and you know the finish. Why can't a fellow put on a new suit, make a few calls, and go home like a gentleman? The minute I got into that suit, I fell off the water wagon with an awful bump, although I hadn't touched a drink for thirty-seven days. Oh! But I got a lovely bun on. That's the last. No more for me. There's nothing in it. If anybody says, "Have something, Billy," you'll see your Uncle Bill take to the trees.

Yesterday at 2:30 I had a hundred and ten dollars; this morning I'm there with a dollar eighty, and that's the draw out of a two-dollar touch. If there is any truth in the old saying that money talks, I am certainly deaf and dumb to-day. Besides I have a card in my pocket which says I've opened up a running account of thirty-two forty at George's place. I wonder if this George is on the level, because I'll swear I don't think I was in there at all. I'll bet he stuck the forty on anyway. You know me, Jim; I am one of those bright people who tries to keep up with a lot of guys who have nothing to do but blow their coin. I stood around yesterday and looked wise, and licked up about four high-balls; then I kind of stretched. Whenever I give one of those little stretches and swell up a bit that's a sign I am commencing to get wealthy. I switched over and took a couple of gin fizzes, and then it hit me I was richer than Jay Gould ever was; I had the Rothschilds backed clear off the board; and I made William H. Vanderbilt look like a hundred-to-one shot. You understand, Jim, this was yesterday. I got a little red spot in each cheek, and then I leaned over the bar and whispered, "Mr. Bartender, break a bottle of that Pommery." Ordinarily I call the booze clerk by his first name, but when you are cutting into the grape at four dollars per, you always want to say Mr. Bartender, and you should always whisper, or just nod your head each time you open a new bottle, as it makes it appear as though you were accustomed to ordering wine. You see, Jim, that's where I go off my dip. That wine affair is an awful stunt for a fellow who makes not over two thousand a year, carries ten thousand life, and rooms in a flat that's fifteen a month stronger than he can stand. But to continue, I lost the push I started out with, and got mixed up with a fellow named Thorne, or Thorpe, or something like that, and we got along great for a while. He knew a lot of fellows in Boston that I did, and every time we struck a new mutual friend we opened another bottle. I don't know just what the total population of Boston is, but we must have known everybody there. Finally Thorne got to crying because his mother had died. You know I am a good fellow, so I cried, too. I always cry some time during a bat, and there was an opening for your life. I cried so hard that the bartender had to ask me to stop three different times. I made Niobe look like a two spot. Between sobs I asked him about the sad affair, and found that his mother had died when he was born. I guess it had just struck him. Then there were doings.

I had wasted a wad of cries that would float the Maine, and I was sore for fair. A fat fellow cut into the argument, and some one soaked him in the eye, and then, as they say in Texas, "there was three minutes rough house." In the general bustle a seedy looking man pinched the Fresh Air Fund, box and all. You know I'm not much for the bat cave, and to avoid such after-complications as patrol wagons and things, I blew the bunch and started up street. I guess the wind must have been against me, as I was tacking.

I met Johnny Black, and he was going to keep a date with a couple of swell heiresses at one of the hotel dining-rooms. I saw them on the street to-day, and they won't do. One of them wore an amethyst ring that weighed about sixty carats, and the other had on white slippers covered with little beads.

I don't know anything about them, but I'll gamble that they are the kind of people that have pictures of the family and wreaths in the parlor. They looked fine and daisy last night, though. Probably the grape. My girl's name was Estelle. Wouldn't that scald you? Estelle handed me a lot of talk about having seen me on the street for the last two years, and how she had always been dying to meet me, and I got swelled up and bought wine like a horse owner. Johnny was shaking his head and motioning for me to chop, but what cared

I? Estelle was saying, "He done it," "I seen it," and "Usen't you?" right along, but the grape stood for everything.

Estelle's friend was talking about her piano, and how hard it was to get good servants nowadays, and say, Jim, I've heard knockers in my time, but Estelle is the original leader of the anvil chorus. She just put everybody in town on the pan and roasted them to a whisper. She could build the best battleship Dewey ever saw with her little hammer. Estelle's friend, after much urging, then sang a pathetic ballad entitled, "She Should Be Scolded, but Not Turned Adrift," and I sat there with one eye shut, so that I could see single, and kept saying, "Per'fly beauf'ful."

About this time I commenced to forget. I remember getting an awful rise out of Estelle by remarking that her switch didn't match her hair. She came up like a human yeast cake. Johnny sided with the dame, and said I might at least try to act like a gentleman, even if I weren't one. Perhaps the grape wasn't getting to Johnny by this time. He was nobby and boss. He was dropping his r's like a Southerner, and you know how much of a Southerner Johnny is—Johnstown, Pa.; and he was hollering around about his little three-year-old, standard-bred, and registered bay mare out of Highland Belle, by Homer Wilkes, with a mark of twenty-one, that could out-trot any thing of her age that ever champed a bit. Did you get that, Jim? That ever champed a bit; and still he said at noon to-day that he had had two, possibly three, glasses of wine, but no more. The only way that mare of Johnny's can go a mile in twenty-one is "In the Baggage Coach Ahead."

Say, Jim, I've never said much about it, but you let any of these fellows who own horses get a soak on, and they get to be a kind of a village pest, with their talk about blowing up in the stretch, shoe blisters on the left forearm, etc. Now, since when did a horse get an arm? They have got me winging. I can't follow them at all.

But to return to last night. When Johnny threw that thing at me about champing the bit, it was all off to Buffalo with little Will. I went out of business right there.

When I got up this morning I had to ask the bell-boy what hotel I was in. I'll see the fellows to-night, and they'll all tell me how dirty my face was, and what I called so and so, and make me feel as bad as they possibly can. It's a wonder a fellow doesn't get used to that, but I never do; I feel meaner each time. Guess I'll take the veil.

Don't fail to come down Saturday. Several of us are going yachting on the Ohio River. It will be lovely billiards.

Yours as ever,
Billy.

P. S.—Do you know anything about that George's place?

Horse Sense.

Sometimes you eat too much, sometimes you drink too much, and sometimes you do both. In any event, you feel like the very old scratch the next morning. Too much liquor overheats the blood. Too much food, and the liver goes on a strike. The first remedy which should suggest itself is a purgative which will act on the liver, and cleanse the system of all the indigestible junk with which it has been overtaxed. This is positively the foundation for permanent relief. The next thing is to cool the blood. Now, isn't it common horse sense?

Think it over.

The R—R— is the only water which acts on the liver. Its base is sodium phosphate.

The R—R— is the only water which cools the blood, Overheated blood is what causes the pressure on the head.

The R—R— is the only pleasant-tasting aperient water of any strength on the market to-day.

We have stumbled onto a good thing, and we've got the money to push it.

You remember the man who at breakfast said: "Waiter, bring me about ten grains of oatmeal, and put stickers on it so that it will stay down; and say, waiter, please look as pleasant as possible, for I feel like h—l."

Well, that's how a person's stomach gets some mornings.

If you are going to drink an aperient, why try to force down a water that is warm, and tastes like a lot of bad eggs, doesn't touch your liver, and won't cool your blood, when you can get the R—R—, cold and sparkling and pleasant, which will do all these things?

If you are annoyed with constipation, stomach or liver trouble, use as your system dictates, and see bow much better you feel. It can't hurt you. Best before breakfast.

WALLACE IRWIN.

Wallace Irwin is probably best known today, and that only in academic circles of a particular sort, for his somewhat hysterical views on the "yellow peril." In his early career, however, he showed a gift for clever verse. This little poem about the chivalrous shark taps into one of the deep fountains of humor: taking an object of unmitigated dread and making it silly. The poem was popular enough to be set to music, and Burl Ives made a famous recording of the resulting song.

THE RHYME OF THE CHIVALROUS SHARK.

Most chivalrous fish of the ocean,
    To ladies forbearing and mild,
Though his record be dark, is the man-eating shark
    Who will eat neither woman nor child.

He dines upon seamen and skippers,
    And tourists his hunger assuage,
And a fresh cabin boy will inspire him with joy
    If he's past the maturity age.

A doctor, a lawyer, a preacher,
    He'll gobble one any fine day,
But the ladies, God bless 'em, he'll only address 'em
    Politely and go on his way.

I can readily cite you an instance
    Where a lovely young lady of Breem,

Who was tender and sweet and delicious to eat,
   Fell into the bay with a scream.

She struggled and flounced in the water
   And signaled in vain for her bark,
And she'd surely been drowned if she hadn't been found
   By a chivalrous man-eating shark.

He bowed in a manner most polished,
   Thus soothing her impulses wild;
"Don't be frightened," he said, "I've been properly bred
   And will eat neither woman nor child."

Then he proffered his fin and she took it—
   Such a gallantry none can dispute—
While the passengers cheered as the vessel they neared
   And a broadside was fired in salute.

And they soon stood alongside the vessel,
   When a life-saving dingey was lowered
With the pick of the crew, and her relatives, too,
   And the mate and the skipper aboard.

So they took her aboard in a jiffy,
   And the shark stood attention the while,
Then he raised on his flipper and ate up the skipper
   And went on his way with a smile.

And this shows that the prince of the ocean,
   To ladies forbearing and mild,
Though his record be dark, is the man-eating shark
   Who will eat neither woman nor child.

FRANKLIN PIERCE ADAMS.

Franklin Pierce Adams lived to a good old age, and in that time contributed many humorous essays that place him near the top of the heap of twentieth-century humorists. In his youth, however, he accomplished something rather more extraordinary than that: he translated Horace and Catullus into modern vernacular English, making the old Romans sing ragtime songs that were at once absolutely up to date and quite faithful to their original meaning. His translations make the classical poets live in our minds as the Ira Gershwin and Lorenz Hart of their day.

Here we present two of the translations from Horace, and a number of short items from F. P. A.'s "Overset" column.

IN CHLORIN.

Horace: Book III, Ode 15.
"Uxor pauperis Ibyci—"

Your conduct, naughty Chloris, is
  Not just exactly Horace's
   Ideal of a lady
   At the shady
    Time of life;
  You mustn't throw your soul away
  On foolishness, like Pholoe—
   Her days are folly-laden—
   She's a maiden,
    You're a wife.

Your daughter, with propriety,
  May look for male society,
   Do one thing and another
   In which mother
    Shouldn't mix;
  But revels Bacchanalian
  Are—or should be—quite alien
   To you a married person,
   Something worse'n
    Forty-six!

Yes, Chloris, you cut up too much,
  You love the dance and cup too much,
   Your years are quickly flitting—
   To your knitting,
    Right about!
  Forget the incidental things
  That keep you from parental things—
   The World, the Flesh, the Devil,
   On the level,
    Cut 'em out!

AD LYDIAM.

Horace: Book I., Ode 13.
"Quem tu, Lydia, Telephi Cervicem roseam,
cerea Telephi—"

What time thou yearnest for the arms
  Of Telephus, I fain would twist 'em;

When thou dost praise his other charms
   It just upsets my well-known system;
     My brain is like a three-ring circus,
     In short, it gets my *capra hircus*.

My reason reels, my cheeks grow pale,
   My heart becomes unduly spiteful,
My verses in the *Evening Mail*
   Are far from snappy and delightful.
     I put a civil question, Lyddy:
     Is that a way to treat one's stiddy?

What mean those marks upon thee, girl?
   Those prints of brutal osculation?
Great grief! that lowlife and that churl!
   That Telephus abomination!
     Can him, O votary of Venus,
     Else everything is off between us.

O triply beatific those
   Whose state is classified as married,
Untroubled by the green-eyed woes,
   By such upheavals never harried.
     Ay, three times happy are the wed ones,
     Who cleave together till they're dead ones.

OVERSET.

Every time we tell anybody to cheer up, things might be worse, we run away for fear we might be asked to specify how.

Watching an aeroplane race, some of the spectators tell us, is more fun than watching a yacht race. The boredom endures less than an hour.

Our notion of an optimist is a man who, knowing that each year was worse than the preceding, thinks next year will be better.
And a pessimist is a man who knows the next year can't be any worse than the last one.

If Mr. Shaw or the successor of Sir William S. Gilbert would like a theme, there is the riot at the munition factory the day universal disarmament goes into effect.

War may be prohibited some day, but probably you'll always be able to get one on a doctor's prescription.

"Yes," is our reply to an advertisement we read over a man's shoulder in the Subway last night—"Are you afraid of your banker?" Also of the assistant receiving teller, the bank policeman, and the assistant paying teller.
Once, summoning all our assurance, we asked the paying teller to let us have the money in clean fives or

tens. "Are you willing to take these?" he asked, counting out soiled bills. "Yes," was our reply; and, although we give the bank, unhesitatingly, all our money, we never shall ask another favor of them.

What worried us the first day of school was how everybody but us in the room appeared to know the words and music of these songs. Was the world, we thought, frightened to dizziness, like that? Was everybody to know more than we? And that, Dr. Freud, is a fear we never have been able to overwhelm....The other children, we learned later, knew these songs because their older brothers and sisters had sung them.

And yet it wasn't long after that first day that a youth named Hosmer Dorland and we were kept in after school for having sung too loud.

It is a malicious pleasure to think, riding up in the cool Subway, of the motorists driving home through traffic jams; and it is a malicious pleasure to muse, driving home through the fresh air, of the thousands standing up in the hot and sticky Subway.

Ours is a sincere doubt as to whether the question "And what did *you* do during the Great War?" might not embarrass, among others, God.

Our favorite way of wasting time is trying to say something in praise of paper towels.

Whether any studies are to be jettisoned in order to shorten the West Point course one year is not evident.

258

Greek, Latin, and English, three obsolescent languages, are generally the first to go. We hate to see Greek and Latin dropped from various curricula, but the chucking of English is unimportant. The use of it is purely academic and the study of it does the graduate no good in his terrific struggle to pay for a five-room apartment. At best, it gives him a taste for reading, and reading cuts into evenings that might be spent meeting people who will advance him in a business way.

Yesterday's *American* carried an essay on comedy, whose last paragraph read: "And the fun-makers have their place in the world." Like most essays on this theme, it is patronizing and condescending. It seems to us that the writers of these essays are saying to themselves, "If I didn't have more important stuff to do, I'd take an afternoon off and write a lot of funny stuff myself." Now, the essayist can't get any information about the subject, because he is resistant and unyielding; and when he interviews somebody who has a reputation for spoken or written comedy, he doesn't quite trust him. "Good morning," says the interviewer. "Good morning," says the comedian. "That isn't so funny," the interviewer thinks to himself, "but there is probably some hidden meaning there, or a slap at me, or at somebody else. I wonder what he really meant by 'Good morning.' I must be careful what I say to this man."

Autobiographical stuff, you say. In a measure. Slight as our reputation is, and founded as it is on the sandy soil of contributions, whenever we say "Yes" to the query "Busy?" it precipitates a storm of merriment that our elaborate and spontaneous jests do not unleash.

As to the fun-makers having their place in the world, we are old and gray and full of sleep, and we are leaning to the opinion that nobody but the fun-makers has any place in the world.

Which, we hasten to add, is at once a more tolerant and a more superior attitude than it seems. We cannot speak for other planets, but the resident members of the human race haven't done much in their brief history to take them out of the fun-loving class.

When Mr. Will Hays becomes head of the film producers, he will be endowed, we hope, with tyrannical powers. In which event he should make it a misdemeanor for a scenarist to use the inverted predicate in simple declarative sentences. "Comes to this peaceful valley a human jackal" we can endure, but the other night at "Orphans of the Storm," when the words appeared "Pass the little years," all we could whisper was "Pass the prussic acid."

GELETT BURGESS.

To say that he has crafted one immortal piece of nonsense is to say enough to justify any man's life, and if Gelett Burgess had given us nothing else, he gave us the famous (though unseen) Purple Cow.

He was considerably more versatile than that, however, and if you have ever read anything that was overwritten to a ghastly extent, you will thank him for "The Oval Moon."

THE PURPLE COW'S *Projected Feast:*
Reflections on a Mythic Beast,
Who's quite Remarkable, at Least.

I never saw a Purple Cow;
  I never hope to See One;
But I can Tell you, Anyhow,
  I'd rather See than Be One.

THE PURPIL COWE: *Perilla* Says *she Wrote it.*
The Last Four lines are Mine, and So I Quote it.

A Mayde there was, semely and meke enow,
She sate a-milken of a purpil Cowe:
Rosy hire Cheke as in the Month of Maye,
And sikerly her merry Songe was gay
As of the Larke vprift, washen in Dewe;
Like Shene of Sterres, sperkled hire Eyen two.
Now came ther by that Way a hendy Knight

261

The Mayde espien in morwening Light.
A faire Person he was—of Corage trewe
With lusty Berd and Chekes of rody Hewe:
Dere Ladye (quod he) far and wide I've straied
Vncouthe Aventure in straunge Contrie made
Fro Berwicke vnto Ware. Pardé I vowe
Erewhiles I never faw a purpil Cowe!
Fayn wold I knowe how Catel thus can be?
Tel me I pray you, of yore Courtesie!
The Mayde hire Milken stent—Goode Sir she saide,
The Master's Mandement on vs ylaid
Decrees that in these yclept gilden Houres
Hys Kyne shall ete of nought but Vylet Floures!

THE OVAL MOON: *Poorly Translated.*
The Author was Intoxicated?

THERE WAS AN astonishing oval blue moon a-bubble amongst the clouds, striking a sidewise chord of wild, blatant reluctance athwart the bowl of curds with which I stroked her.

O Love!—dead, and all your adjectives still in you.

A harsh and brittle whisper of a dream—a rough, red shadow-ghost of awful prominence welled out and up through all the inharmonious phases of the night. A frog bleated, and turned his toe to slumber. The fringe of despair hung round about my agony; the stars went mad, the moon—that blurred, blue, bleeding moon— the very toadstools on the lawn, the close-clipped crust of foamy fire-lit hedge, balked, choking, grey, upon the ring of flame-spent turf.

O Heaven and Happy Bard! O freighted moors, conducive to my ecstasy! Each unto each was there, all yet was vain!

Now, in this hushed and turbid clime, the rancid relics of the mist are not so gog with hume and spray, as in the rest. Did not the viper hurl his macrocosmic integer in time? In such wise, I marvelled, might the whole world, peeled thin and narrow in the spectres of the night's reply, go wild and leer in many efforts to be insincere.

But, Gosh! What agony!

The avalanche of superinsistent medroles—the pink of pure, prismatic diaphrams, spoldrum and whood—all Hell was there, and, weeping, lured me on.

So time went out, and came again, and disappeared. I was too proud, too anxious to rehearse my sentiment for this, the dishevelled, procrastinating fear that might have held me. The hotbed of palpitating remorse that drew me (and She, too, with Her heavy hopes ajar) the very thomes of past prognostications speeding to sub-ject shams of wide and whooping fantasies—

Oh! oh! oh! It was too terrible!

There was no nothing there—only the semblance of sharp moist scalding epochs, ah, too long unfelt! The little whining birds that She had known, the windy abyss above us, the Northern Paradox—these indeed She had; but where were sign of the three new-joined Mysteries—the things that all applaud forsooth?

I began so slowly, too; so secretly gaunt in that old world where She had been! There was a fair old teem-ing thought, an echo-shape on my horizon, that reeked, and, tempering to its fresh-found tone, bewil-

dered the ashes of the miasmic Past. Yet I belted on
new moods, and, as I say, the hurtling phantom broke.
How could She know what awful riot each red cone
awoke?

How could She know?
How could She know?
What?

THE TOWEL AND THE DOOR, *Ah, Well,*
The Moral I'd not Dare to Tell!

The Towel Hangs Upon the Wall,
And Somehow, I don't Care, at All!
The Door is Open; I Must Say,
I Rather Fancy it That Way!

PSYCHOLOPHON: *Supposed to Be*
Translated from the Old Parsee.

Twine then the rays
  Round her soft Theban tissues!
All will be as She says,
  When that dead Past reissues.
Matters not what nor where,
  Hark, to the moon's dim cluster!
How was her heavy hair
  Lithe as a feather duster!

Matters not when nor whence;
  Flittertigibbet!
Sounds make the song, not sense,
  Thus I inhibit!

CONFESSION: *and a Portrait Too,*
    Upon a Background that I Rue

Ah, yes, I wrote the "Purple Cow"—
  I'm Sorry, now, I wrote it;
But I can tell you Anyhow
  I'll Kill you if you Quote it!

CAROLYN WELLS.

Carolyn Wells gained her greatest popularity as the prolific author of many popular mystery novels;—"prolific" is rather an understatement, since at her peak she was turning out several a year. Before she entered the detective business, however, she was known to connoisseurs as one of our most promising humorists. Her humor is at once gentle and surprisingly pointed, and if it reminds us a bit of Gelett Burgess, Carolyn Wells herself would be very pleased: she considered Burgess her preceptor in the art of nonsense.

THE TWO YOUNG MEN.

ONCE ON A TIME there were Two Young Men of Promising Capabilities.

One pursued no Especial Branch of Education, but Contented himself with a Smattering of many different Arts and Sciences, exhibiting a Moderate Proficiency in Each. When he Came to Make a Choice of some means of Earning a Livelihood, he found he was Unsuccessful, for he had no Specialty, and Every Employer seemed to Require an Expert in his Line.

The Other, from his Earliest Youth, bent all his Energies toward Learning to play the Piano. He studied at Home and Abroad with Greatest Masters, and he Achieved Wonderful Success. But as he was about to Begin his Triumphant and Profitable Career, he had the Misfortune to lose both Thumbs in a Railway Accident. Thus he was Deprived of his Intended Means of Earning a Living, and as he had no other Accomplishment he was Forced to Subsist on Charity.

Morals

This Fable teaches that a Jack of all Trades is Master of None, and that It Is Not Well to put All our Eggs in One Basket.

THE TWO AUTOMOBILISTS.

ONCE ON A TIME there were Two Young Men, each of whom Bought an Automobile.

One Young Man, being of a Bold and Audacious nature, said: "I will make my Machine go so Fast that I will break all Previous Records."

Accordingly, he did So, and he Flew through the Small Town like a Red Dragon Pursuing his Prey.

Unheeding all Obstacles in his Mad Career, his Automobile ran into a Wall of Rock, and was dashed to Pieces. Also, the young Man was killed.

The Other Young Man, being of a Timorous and Careful Disposition, started off with great Caution and Rode at a Slow Pace, pausing now and then, Lest he might Run into Something.

The Result was, that Two Automobiles and an Ice Wagon ran into him from behind, spoiling his Car and Killing the Cautious Young Man.

Morals

This Fable teaches Us, The More Haste The Less Speed, and Delays Are Dangerous.

THE POSTER-GIRL.

The blessed Poster-girl leaned out
  From a pinky-purple heaven;
One eye was red and one was green;
  Her bang was cut uneven;
She had three fingers on her hand,
  And the hairs on her head were seven.

Her robe, ungirt from clasp to hem,
  No sunflowers did adorn;
But a heavy Turkish portiere
  Was very neatly worn;
And the hair that lay along her back
  Was yellow like canned corn.

It was a kind of wobbly wave
  That she was standing on,
And high aloft she flung a scarf
  That must have weighed a ton;
And she was rather tall—at least
  She reached up to the sun.

She curved and writhed, and then she said,
   Less green of speech than blue:
"Perhaps I *am* absurd—perhaps
   I *don't* appeal to you;
But my artistic worth depends
   Upon the point of view."

I saw her smile, although her eyes
   Were only smudgy smears;
And then she swished her swirling arms,
   And wagged her gorgeous ears,
She sobbed a blue-and-green-checked sob,
   And wept some purple tears.

ELBERT HUBBARD.

We could call him the American William Morris, but he was more American than he was William Morris. Elbert Hubbard founded the Roycrofters, an arts-and-crafts community in East Aurora, New York, and set up a printing press there in imitation of Morris' Kelmscott Press. For most of his life, he shared Morris' socialist ideals, though he later turned against socialism in favor of free competition. But where Morris specialized in the medieval, and himself wrote in a quasi-medieval style, Hubbard produced beautifully printed books and magazines full of his own homespun American philosophy. The stream that runs through Artemus Ward and Mark Twain flows right into Elbert Hubbard; no one would mistake him for anything but an American writer.

Hubbard died in the sinking of the *Lusitania* in 1915. He and his wife, knowing that there was a very real risk that one of them would die and the other survive, refused to join the melée for the lifeboats. Instead, they walked calmly, arm in arm, into an open stateroom, and locked the door behind them.

Elbert Hubbard's most characteristic work was a magazine, printed on his own press and bound as a book, which he called *The Philistine*. Every issue is full of Hubbard's own essays on whatever he happened to be thinking of at the time, and where there was any space on a page he filled it with a little homespun aphorism. Many of these essays have no titles; they simply begin in the middle of a page and keep going until Hubbard runs out of things to say on the subject.

FOOTBALL OCCUPIES THE same relation to education that a bull fight does to farming.

IT IS BEAUTIFUL what a bunch there is of us in the United States Senate—Bob Taylor of Tennessee, Bob LaFollette of Wisconsin, Ben Tillman of South Carolina, Dolly Dolliver of Iowa, Sis Hopkins of Illinois— all first class Chautauqua talent, Class A entertainers, impersonators and lightning change artists.

In order to join the Senate Club you have to be a multi-millionaire or a mime. Any man who can do a good twenty-minute turn, or a two-hour stunt any time as the needs of the manager require, need not be discouraged.

Chauncey Depew was a fairish Class B vaudeville performer, until he lost his teeth. He lost them at the Auditorium in Chicago in 1901. He was born with false teeth, but this night he lost them in an impassioned moment—just as he was getting off a pun the teeth flew over the footlights. "I'm on," said a man in the fourth row, handing them to the leader of the orchestra and he handed them to the speaker, saying, "Chauncey, are these your grinders?" But it was of no use, Chauncey had lost more than his teeth, he had lost his nerve.

And that is just what public speaking is—a matter of nerve. When your nerve is gone, you are out. Public speaking means getting your goods in the show window at exactly eight fifteen P.M.

So Chauncey got the count—not even his money could save him.

Papa Hershey is pushing me hard for Chauncey's place. He says that Piatt and I would work together like Spooner and LaFollette.

Pop, however, insists that if he places me in the American House of Lords he is entitled as impresario to a twenty per cent commission on my salary. This is our only difference. I have offered ten per cent as a compromise, and if we can adjust the matter, I'll go.

The beauty of the Senate is that you do not have to be there, and your honorarium goes right along just the same.

Popsy has Beveridge working on a monologue for the Asbury Circuit this fall; and if I go to the Senate, Popsy, the man who has made us and not we ourselves, proposes to organize an All-Senator-Vaudeville and work the Chautauquas for fair, because that is what the Chautauqua is—a cross between a country fair and a camp meeting. Culture is what this country needs—culture! Bishop Galloway says, "I glory in the fact that I am a Jack-Screw in the hands of the Divinity being used to elevate the masses." And so I glory in the fact that I belong to a Jack's Crew, organized to elevate the Chautauquas.

RECIPE FOR BRINGING up your children to be kind and considerate: Be kind and considerate.

BERT LESTON TAYLOR

A newspaper columnist who affected to despise the entire "so-called human race," Bert Leston Taylor tended to be conservative in his politics and hopeless in his outlook. But perhaps "hopeless" is the wrong word; there is a certain pessimism in believing that the human race is not capable of improvement; but there is a certain optimism in believing that the human race is no worse now than it ever was. He wrote some clever little poems; but he was most famous for his newspaper columns., many of which consisted of stray observations collected from other newspapers, often sent in by his readers. Taylor's reaction to each new display of human idiocy was what his readers came back for day after day.

CANOPUS

When quacks with pills political would dope us,
    When politics absorbs the livelong day,
I like to think about that star Canopus,
    So far, so far away.

Greatest of visioned suns, they say who list 'em;
    To weigh it science almost must despair.
Its shell would hold our whole dinged solar system,
    Nor even know 'twas there.

When temporary chairmen utter speeches,
    And frenzied henchmen howl their battle hymns,
My thoughts float out across the cosmic reaches
    To where Canopus swims.

When men are calling names and making faces,
  And all the world's ajangle and ajar,
I meditate on interstellar spaces
  And smoke a mild seegar.

For after one has had about a week of
  The argument of friends as well as foes,
A star that has no parallax to speak of
  Conduces to repose.

A LINE-O'-TYPE OR TWO

THE VIEWPOINT OF Dr. Jacques Duval (interestingly set forth by Mr. Arliss) is that knowledge is more important than the life of individual members of the so-called human race. But even Duval is a sentimentalist. He believes that knowledge is important.

"The increase in the use of tobacco by women," declares the Methodist Board, "is appalling." Is it not? But so many things are appalling that it would be a relief to everybody if a board, or commission, or other volunteer organization were to act as a shock-absorber. Whenever an appalling situation arose, this group could be appalled for the rest of us. And we, knowing that the board would be properly appalled, should not have to worry.

Replying to an extremely dear reader: Whenever we animadvert on the human race we include ourself. We share its imperfections, and we hope we are tinctured with its few virtues. As a race it impresses us as a flivver; we feel as you, perhaps, feel in your club when, looking over the members, you wonder how the dickens most of them got in.

The man who tells you that he believes "in principles, not men," means—nothing at all. One would think that in the beginning God created a set of principles, and man was without form and void.

"Learn to Speak on Your Feet," advertises a university extension. We believe we could tell all we know about ours in five hundred words.

The fact that Abraham Lincoln, George Washington, and other great departed whose names are taken in vain every day by small-bore politicians, do not return and whack these persons over the heads with a tambourine, is almost—as Anatole France remarked in an essay on Flaubert—is almost an argument against the immortality of the soul.

The treeless plateau over which the train rolls, hour after hour, is the result of a great uplift. It was not sudden; it was slow but sure. This result is arid and plateautudinous, in a manner of speaking—not the best manner. It makes me think of democracy—and prohibition. To this complexion we shall come at last. To be sure, the genius of man will continue to cut channels in

275

the monotonous plain; erosion will relieve the dreary prospect with form and color, but it bids fair to be, for the most part, a flat and dry world, from which many of us will part with a minimum of regret. There will remain the inextinguishable desire to learn what wonders science will disclose. Perhaps—who knows?—they will discover how to ventilate a sleeping car.

HEYWOOD BROUN

Heywood Broun was a journalist and social reformer who ran for congress as a socialist and who married a famous feminist (Ruth Hale). Unlike many dedicated reformers, however, he was constitutionally tolerant. He was tolerant enough even to see the human side of intolerance.

And he was funny. He probably did more for the working class with his gentle but sharp humor than all the windy speeches of all the socialist agitators in America ever did. He held his own at the famous Algonquin Round Table, where he was known as positively the worst dresser of the lot.

Broun was not religious until 1939, when he surprised everyone by converting to Catholicism after long conversations with Fulton J. Sheen. It might have been a surprise to his friends, but in hindsight it seems in character. God was one of his favorite characters in the little fables he told in his columns; he desperately wanted to believe in a God who is more merciful than just, and his real problem with Christianity was that the Christians he knew were not very Christian at all.

Three months after his conversion, Heywood Broun died of pneumonia at the age of 51. Everyone who was anyone turned out for the funeral.

ART FOR ARGUMENT'S SAKE

We begin with a piece that very clearly shows where Heywood Broun's sympathies lie. He is all for economic justice and stuff like that, but he resents the politicized critics—left and right—who insist that nothing else matters.

277

ALL EDITORS ARE divided into two parts. In one group are those who think that anybody who can make a good bomb can undoubtedly fashion a great sonnet. The members of the other class believe that if a man loves his country he is necessarily well fitted to be a book reviewer.

As a matter of fact, new terminology is coming into the business of criticism. A few years ago the critic who was displeased with a book called it "sensational" or "sentimental" or something like that. To-day he would voice his disapproval by writing "Pro-German" or "Bolshevist." Authors are no longer evaluated in terms of æsthetics, but rather from the point of view of political economy. Indeed, to-day we have hardly such a thing as good writers and bad writers. They have become instead either "sound" or "dangerous." A sound author is one with whose views you are in agreement.

So tightly are the lines drawn that the criticism of the leading members of each side can be accurately predicted in advance. Show me the cover of a war novel, and let me observe that it is called "The Great Folly," and I will guarantee to foreshadow with a high degree of accuracy just what the critic of The New York *Times* will say about it and also the critic of *The Liberator*. Even if it happened to be called "The Glory of Shrapnel," the guessing would be just as easy.

The manner in which anybody says anything now whether in prose, verse, music or painting is entirely secondary in the minds of all critical publications. Reviewers look for motives. Symphonies are dismissed as seditious, and lyrics are closely scanned to see whether or not their rhythms are calculated to upset the established order without due recourse to the ballot. Nor has this particular reviewer any intention of suggesting that such activity is entirely vain and fanciful. He remembers that only a month ago he began a thrilling adventure story called "The Lost Peach Pit," only to discover, when he was half through, that it was a tract in favor of a higher import duty on potash.

A vivid novel about the war by John Dos Passos has been issued under the title "Three Soldiers." One of the chief characters was a creative musician who broke under the rigor of army discipline which was repugnant to him. Nobody who wrote about the book undertook to discuss whether or not the author had painted a persuasive picture of the struggle in the soul of a credible man. Instead they argued as to just what proportion of men in the American army were discontented, and the final critical verdict is being withheld until statistics are available as to how many of them were musicians. Those who disliked the book did not speak of Mr. Dos Passos as either a realist or a romanticist. They simply called him a traitor and let it go at that. The enthusiasts on the other side neglected to say anything about his style because they needed the space to suggest that he ought to be the next candidate for president from the Socialist party.

Speaking as a native-born American (Brooklyn—1888) who once voted for a Socialist for membership in the Board of Aldermen, the writer must admit that he has found the radical solidarity of critical approval or dissent more trying than that of the conservatives. Again and again he has found, in *The Liberator* and elsewhere, able young men, who ought to know better, praising novels for no reason on earth except that they were radical. If the novelist said that life in a middle-western town was dreary and evil he was bound to be praised by the socialist reviewers. On the other hand, any author who found in this same middle west a com-munity or an individual not hopelessly stunted in mind and in morals, was immediately scourged as a viciously sentimental observer who had probably been one of the group which fixed upon the nomination of President Harding late at night behind the locked doors of a little room in a big hotel.

The enthusiasm of the radical critics extends not only to rebels against existing governmental principles and moral conventions, but to all those who dare to write in any new manner. There seems to be a certain confusion whereby free verse is held to be a movement in the direction of free speech.

Novels which begin in the middle and work first for-ward and then back, win favor as blows against the bourgeois idea that a straight line is the shortest dis-tance between two points. Of course, the radical author can do almost anything the conservative does and still retain the admiration of his fellows by dint of a very small amount of tact. Rhapsodies on love will be damned as sentimental if the author has been injudi-cious enough to allow his characters to marry, but he can retain exactly the same language if he is careful to add a footnote that nothing is contemplated except the freest of free unions. A few works are praised by both sides because each finds a different interpretation for the same set of facts. Thus, the authors of "Dulcy" were surprised to find themselves warmly greeted in one of the Socialist dailies as young men who had struck a blow for government ownership of all essential industries merely because they had introduced a big business man into their play and, for the purposes of comic relief, had made him a fool.

Class consciousness has become so acute that it extends even beyond the realms of literature and drama into the field of sports. The recent "battle of the century" eventually simmered down into the minds of many as a struggle between the forces of reaction and revolution. It was known before the fight that Carpentier would wear a flowered silk bathrobe into the ring, while Dempsey would be clad in an old red sweater. How could symbolism be more perfect? Anybody who believed that Carpentier's right would be good enough to win, was immediately set down as a profiteer in munitions who would undoubtedly welcome the outbreak of another war. Likewise it was unsafe to express the opinion that Dempsey's infighting might be too much for the Frenchman, lest one be identified with the little willful group of pacifists who impeded the progress of the war. Eventually, the startling revelation was made by the reporter of a morning newspaper that he had seen Carpentier smelling a rose. After that, any belief in the invader's prowess laid whoever expressed it open to the charge, not only of aristocracy, but of degeneracy as well. After Dempsey's blows wore down his opponent and defeated him, it was generally felt by his supporters that the eight-hour day was safe, and that the open shop would never be generally accepted in America.

The only encouraging feature in the increasingly sharp feeling of class consciousness among critics is a growing frankness. Reviewers are willing to admit now that they think so and so's novel is an indifferent piece of work because he speaks ill of conscription and they believe in it. A year or so ago they would have pretended that they did not like it because the author split some infinitives.

One of the frankest writing men we ever met is the editor of a Socialist newspaper. "Whenever there's a big strike," he explained to me, "I always tell the man who goes out on the story, 'Never see a striker hit a scab. Always see the scab hit the striker.' "

"You see," he went on, "there are seven or eight other newspapers in town who will see it just the other way and I've got to keep the balance straight."

There used to be a practice somewhat similar to this among baseball umpires. Whenever the man behind the plate felt that he had called a bad ball a strike, he would bide his time until the next good one came over and that he would call a ball. The practice was known as "evening up" and it is no longer considered efficient workmanship. That is, not among umpires. The radical editor was not in the least abashed when I quoted to him the remark of a man who said that he always read his paper with great interest because he invariably found the editorial opinions in the news and the news on the editorial page. "That's just what I'm trying to do," he exclaimed delightedly. "I'm not trying to give the people the news. I'm trying to make new Socialists every day."

It is to be feared that even those writers who have the opportunity to be more deliberate than the journalists have been struck with the idea that by words they can shape the world a little closer to the heart's desire. Throughout the war we were told so constantly that battles could be decided and ships built and wars decided by the force of propaganda, that every man with a portable typewriter in his suitcase began to think of it as a baton. There was a day when a novelist was satisfied if he could capture a little slice of life and get it between the covers of his book. Now everybody writes to shake the world. The smell of propaganda is unmistakable.

With literature in its present state of mind critics cannot be expected to watch and wait for the great American novel or the great American play. Instead they look for the book which made the tariff possible, or the play which ended the steel strike.

A BOLT FROM THE BLUE

John Roach Straton was pastor of Calvary Baptist Church in New York, and one of the first radio preachers, if not the very first. It is not necessary to say anything more than that about him, because Heywood Broun draws his character with a few deft strokes.

JOHN ROACH STRATON died and went to his appointed kingdom where he immediately sought an audience with the ruler of the realm.

"Let New York be destroyed," shouted Dr. Straton as he pushed his way into the inner room. The king was engaged at the moment in watching a sparrow fall to earth and motioned the visitor to compose himself in silence, but there was an urgency in the voice and manner of the man from earth which would not be denied. "Smite them hip and thigh," said Dr. Straton and the king looked down at him and asked, "Is the necessity immediate?"

"Delay not thy wrath," said Dr. Straton, "for to-day on thy Sabbath sixty thousand men, women, and children of New York have gathered together to watch a baseball game."

The ruler of the realm looked and saw that 11,967 persons were watching the Yankees and the White Sox at the Polo Grounds.

"A good husky tidal wave would confound them," urged Straton, but the king shook his head.

"Remember the judgment you heaped upon Sodom and upon Gomorrah," suggested Straton.

The ruler of the realm nodded without enthusiasm. "I remember," he said, "but as I recollect it didn't do much good."

Dr. Straton's bright hopefulness faded and the king hastened to reassure him. "We can think up something better than that," he said, and had the visitor been an observant man he might have noticed that the streets of the kingdom were paved with tact. "Now there was the Tower of Babel," said the ruler of the realm reflectively, "that was a creative idea. That was a doom which persisted because it had ingenuity as well as power. That's what we need now."

Suddenly there dawned in the face of the king an idea, and it seemed to Dr. Straton as if he were standing face to face with a sunrise. The doctor lowered his eyes and he saw that the men and the women Sabbath breakers of New York were all upon their feet and shouting, though to his newly immortal senses the din came feebly. "Now," he said, with an exultation which caused him to slip into his old pulpit manner, "let 'em have it."

But the king with keener vision than Dr. Straton, saw that it was the ninth inning, the score tied, runners on first and second, and Babe Ruth coming to bat. "The time has not come," said the king, and he pushed the doctor gently and made him give ground a little. And they waited until two strikes had been pitched and three balls. The next one would have cut the heart of the plate, but Babe Ruth swung and the ball rose straight in the air. Up and up it came until it disappeared from the view of all the players and spectators and even of the umpires. Soon a mighty wrangle began. Miller Huggins claimed a home run and Kid Gleason argued that the ball was foul. The umpires waited for an hour and then, as the ball had not yet come down, Dineen was forced to make a decision and shouted "Foul!" while the crowd booed. One of the pop bottles injured him rather badly and there was a riot for which it was necessary to call out the reserves. Everybody went home disgruntled and a month later the Lusk bill abolishing Sunday baseball was passed.

And all the time the ball continued to rise until suddenly the king, thrusting out his left hand, caught it neatly and slipped it into his pocket. It was not a con-

ventional pocket, for there were planets in it and everlasting mercy and other things. For a long time Dr.
Straton had been awed into silence by the mighty miracle, but now he spoke, reverently but firmly.

"I beg your pardon," he said, "but you will observe
that there is a sign in the baseball park which says 'All
balls batted out of the diamond remain the property of
the New York Baseball Club and should be thrown
back!' "

The ruler of the realm smiled. "You forget," he answered, "that if I threw the ball back from this great
height it might strike a man and kill him, it might
crash through a huge office building, it might even de-
stroy the Calvary Baptist Church."

Then for the first time a touch of sharpness came
into the voice of Dr. Straton. "All that is immaterial,"
he said. "I think I know my theology well enough to
understand that law is law and right is right, come
what may."

"Oh, but it's not nearly as simple as all that," re-
monstrated the king. "There are right things which are
so harsh and unpleasant that they become wrong; and
wrong things which are, after all, so jolly that it's hard
not to call them right. Why, sometimes I have to stop
a fraction of a century myself to reach a decision. It's
terribly complicated. The problem is infinite. No mere
man, quick or dead, has any right to be dogmatic
about it."

"Come, come," said Dr. Straton, and now there
was nothing but anger in his voice, "I've heard all
those devilish arguments before. When I came here I
thought you were God and that this was Heaven. I

know now that there's been a mistake. God is no mol-
lycoddle."

He turned on his heel and started to walk away before he remembered that he was a Southern gentleman
as well as a clergyman and bowed stiffly, once. Then
he went to the edge of the kingdom and jumped.
Where he landed it would be hard to say. Only a carefully trained theologian could tell.

PROMISES AND CONTRACTS AND CLOCKS

"I AM ONE of those people," says the flapper in Beauty
and Mary Blair, "to whom life is a very great puzzle.
So many people seem to get used to living, but I don't.
I can't seem to get up any really satisfactory philosophy or find anybody or anything to help me about it. I
want everything, little or big, fixed up in mind before I
can proceed.

"Even as a very small child I always wanted my
plans made in advance. Once, when mother had a bad
sick headache, I sat on the edge of her bed and begged
her to tell me if she thought she was going to die, so if
she was I could plan to go and live with my Aunt Mar-
garet. I was an odious infant, but all the same, I really
wanted to know, and that's the way I am to this day! I
want to know what the probabilities are, in order to
act accordingly."

And without doubt she was odious, but only in the
same way that practically everybody else is odious, for
we live in a world which is governed by promises and

contracts and clocks. If there actually is any such thing as free will, aren't we the idiots to fetter it! The chances of doing things on impulse are being continually diminished. There are points in the city now where it is not possible to cross the street without the permission of the policeman.

"Stop," "Go," "Keep Off the Grass," "No Trespassing," "Beware of the Dog," "Watch Your Hat and Overcoat," "Positively No Checks Cashed," "Do Not Feed or Annoy the Animals"—how can a free and adventurous soul survive in such a world? Don Marquis has celebrated the exploit of one brave rebel, we think it was Fothergil Finch, who strode into the monkey house and crying "Down with the tyranny of the capitalist system," or words to that effect, threw a peanut into the baboon's cage. We know an even bolder soul who makes a point of never watching his hat and overcoat in direct defiance of the edict, but he says that the world has become so cowed by rules that nothing ever happens.

Even the usual avenues of escape have been beset with barbed wire. There was liquor, for instance. There still is, but the prohibitionists have been devilishly wise. By arranging that it shall be ladled out by prescriptions, no matter how lavish, they have reduced drinking to the prosaic level of premeditation along with all the other activities of the world. Things have come to such a pass that drinking has now been restricted to men with real executive ability. It is no longer the solace of the irresponsible, but the reward of foresight.

Once the easy escape from dull and set routine lay in stepping on board a steamer and sailing for distant and purple shores. They are not so purple any more. No traveler can feel much like a free and footloose adventurer after he has spent two weeks in conference with the State Department, presented a certificate confirming the fact of his birth, gathered together the receipts of his income tax payments and obtained a letter from his pastor. Even though he go to the ends of the earth the adventurer travels only by the express and engraved permission of the United States government. Oceans and mountain ranges cannot alter the fact that he is on a leash. Of course, to free souls the whole system is monstrous. The fact that a man suddenly feels a desire to go to Greece on some rainy Tuesday afternoon is no sign at all that he will still want to go two weeks come Wednesday. The only proper procedure for the rebel is to obtain passports for a number of places for which he has not the slightest inclination on the hope that some day or other through a sudden change of wind he may be struck with yearning.

Train journeys are almost as bad as sea voyages. Go into any railroad station in town and ask the man at the window for a ticket and he will invariably inquire "Where do you want to go?" No provision is made for the casual traveler without a destination. The query "What trains have you got?" meets with scant courtesy. Our own system is to shop for trains. It is possible to walk up and down in front of the gates and look over the samples before making a selection, but our practice is to take the first one. To be sure this has let us into going to a good many places to which we didn't want to go, but it has also saved us from visiting any number of others to which we ought to go. Moreover, confidentially, we have one trick by which we slash through the red tape of railroad precision. Only last Thursday we told the man with a great show of determination that we wanted to go to Poughkeepsie and bought a ticket for that place. Then, when the conductor wasn't looking we slipped off at Tarrytown.

Going to the theater, getting married or divorced are all carried on under the same objectionable conditions. "Seats eight weeks in advance" say the advertisements of some of the popular shows and others. How can anybody possibly want to do something eight weeks in advance? It makes taking in a matinée a matter as dignified to all intents and purposes as writing a will or doing some other service for posterity.

There are in this country statesmen who worry from time to time that people do not marry as young as they used to, if at all. How can it be expected that they will? The life force is powerful and may prevail, but nature never had within its intent a license, witnesses, bridesmaids, a plain gold ring, a contract with the caterer, a bargain with the printer and an engagement with the minister.

DOROTHY PARKER

"Dorothy Parker (I think) was suddenly, or at least found herself suddenly (I mean that she woke up to the fact) placed in a world that she didn't like."

So wrote Thomas Lansing Masson, and it would be difficult to come up with any better explanation for the observed phenomenon that is Dorothy Parker. She is always funniest when she is annoyed, and she is usually annoyed—which means that she is usually funny. Her cutting wit and her willingness to sacrifice anything to its blade have made her a sort of feminist heroine.

But there was obviously something more to Dorothy Parker than that. There was heart as well as hate. Her closest friend at the Algonquin Round Table was Robert Benchley, who in spite of his own cutting wit was known as the most selflessly generous of the lot. In fact, when Dorothy Parker was fired from Vanity Fair for annoying the theatrical producers with her biting reviews, Benchley immediately resigned in protest, in spite of the fact that he had no idea how he was going to feed his family. This is the secret of Dorothy Parker's popularity: she is not just a hating machine. Somehow her hate is of that rare and refined sort that inspires us to love her.

For the old *Life* magazine—the one that was a humor magazine—Parker wrote a series of *Hymns of Hate*, rants in free verse that distill Dorothy-Parkerness into its essence.

HYMN OF HATE

I Hate Books:
They tire my eyes

There is the Account of Happy Days in Far Tahiti;
The booklet of South Sea Island resorts.
After his four weeks in the South Seas,
The author's English gets pretty rusty
And he has to keep dropping into the native dialect.
He implies that his greatest hardship
Was fighting off the advances of the local girls,
But the rest of the book
Was probably founded on fact.
You can pick up a lot of handy information
On how to serve poi,
And where the legend of the breadfruit tree got its
    start,
And how to take kava or let it alone.
The author says it's the only life
And as good as promises
That sometime he is going to throw over his writing,
And go end his days with Laughing Sea-pig, the half-
    caste Knockout—
Why wait?

Then there is the Little Book of Whimsical Essays;
Not a headache in a libraryful.
The author comes right out and tells his favorite foods,
And how much he likes his pipe,
And what his walking-stick means to him,—

A thrill on every page.
The essays clean up all doubt
On what the author feels when riding in the subway,
Or strolling along the Palisades.
The writer seems to be going ahead on the idea
That it isn't such a bad old world, after all;
He drowses along
Under the influence of Pollyanesthetics.
No one is ever known to buy the book;
You find it on the guest room night-table,
Or win it at a Five Hundred Party,
Or some one gives it to you for Easter
And follows that up by asking you how you liked it,—
Say it with raspberries!

There is the novel of Primitive Emotions;
The Last Word in Unbridled Passions—
Last but not leashed.
The author writes about sex
As if he were the boy who got up the idea
The hero and heroine may be running wild in the Sa-
    hara,
Or camping informally on a desert island,
Or just knocking around the city,
But the plot is always the same—
They never quite make the grade.
The man turns out to be the son of a nobleman,
Or the woman the world's greatest heiress,
And they marry and go to live together—
That can't hold much novelty for them.
It is but a question of time till the book is made into a
    movie,

Which is no blow to its writer.
People laugh it off
By admitting that it may not be the highest form of
    art;
But then, they plead, the author must live,—
What's the big idea?

And then there is the Realistic Novel;
Five hundred pages without a snicker.
It is practically an open secret
That the book is two dollars' worth of the author's
    own experiences,
And that if he had not been through them,
It would never have been written,
Which would have been all right with me.
It presents a picture of quiet family life—
Of how little Rosemary yearns to knife Grandpa,
And Father wishes Mother were cold in her grave,
And Bobby wants to marry his big brother.
The author's idea of action
Is to make one of his characters spill the cereal.
The big scene of the book
Is the heroine's decision to make over her old taffeta.
All the characters are in a bad way;
They have a lot of trouble with their suppressions.
The author is constantly explaining that they are all
    being stifled,—
I wish to God he'd give them the air!

I Hate Books:
They tire my eyes.

ROBERT BENCHLEY

There is something wrong with a world in which Robert Benchley requires an introduction. A founding member of the Algonquin Round Table, he was also the only one of that extraordinary group about whom no one ever had anything bad to say. In addition to his writing, he created a series of deadpan faux-documentary movie shorts with titles like "How to Eat" and "The Sex Life of the Polyp."

In assembling his book *Our American Humorists* (1922), Thomas Lansing Masson asked Benchley for some biographical details. "After keeping at Mr. Benchley for weeks, nay months, he finally wrote out the following authentic biography of himself:"

OUTLINE OF MY LIFE.
R. C. BENCHLEY.

Born Isle of Wight, September 15, 1807.
Shipped as cabin boy on *Florence J. Marble* 1815.
Arrested for bigamy and murder in Port Said, 1817.
Released 1820. Wrote "Tale of Two Cities."
Married Princess Anastasie of Portugal, 1831.
Children: Prince Rupprecht and several little girls.
Wrote "Uncle Tom's Cabin" 1850.
Editor "Godey's Ladies Book" 1851-56.
Began "Les Miserables" 1870 (finished by Victor Hugo).
Died 1871. Buried in Westminster Abbey.

OPERA SYNOPSES

*Some Sample Outlines of Grand Opera Plots
for Home Study.*

I—Die Meister-Genossenschaft.

Scene: *The Forests of Germany.*
Time: *Antiquity.*

Cast

Strudel, *God of Rain*..Basso
Schmalz, *God of Slight Drizzle*...........................Tenor
Immerglück, *Goddess of the Six Primary Colors*
....Soprano
Ludwig Das Eiweiss, *the Knight of the Iron Duck*
....Baritone
The Woodpecker...Soprano

Argument

The basis of "Die Meister-Genossenschaft" is an old legend of Germany which tells how the Whale got his Stomach.

Act I

The Rhine at Low Tide Just Below Weldschnoffen.—Immerglück has grown weary of always sitting on the same rock with the same fishes swimming by every day, and sends for Schwül to suggest something to do. Schwül asks her how she would like to have pass before her all the wonders of the world fashioned by the hand of man. She says, rotten. He then suggests that Ringblattz, son of Pflucht, be made to appear before her and fight a mortal combat with the Iron Duck. This pleases Immerglück and she summons to her the four dwarfs: Hot Water, Cold Water, Cool, and Cloudy. She bids them bring Ringblattz to her. They refuse, because Pflucht has at one time rescued them from being buried alive by acorns, and, in a rage, Immerglück strikes them all dead with a thunderbolt.

Act 2

A Mountain Pass.—Repenting of her deed, Immerglück has sought advice of the giants, Offen and Besitz, and they tell her that she must procure the magic zither which confers upon its owner the power to go to sleep while apparently carrying on a conversation. This magic zither has been hidden for three hundred centuries in an old bureau drawer, guarded by the Iron Duck, and, although many have attempted to rescue it, all have died of a strange ailment just as success was within their grasp.

But Immerglück calls to her side Dampfboot, the tinsmith of the gods, and bids him make for her a tarnhelm or invisible cap which will enable her to talk to people without their understanding a word she says. For a dollar and a half extra Dampfboot throws in a magic ring which renders its wearer insensible. Thus armed, Immerglück starts out for Walhalla, humming to herself.

Act 3

The Forest Before the Iron Duck's Bureau Drawer.— Merglitz, who has up till this time held his peace, now descends from a balloon and demands the release of Betty. It has been the will of Wotan that Merglitz and Betty should meet on earth and hate each other like poison, but Zweiback, the druggist of the gods, has disobeyed and concocted a love-potion which has rendered the young couple very unpleasant company. Wotan, enraged, destroys them with a protracted heat spell.

Encouraged by this sudden turn of affairs, Immerglück comes to earth in a boat drawn by four white Holsteins, and, seated alone on a rock, remembers aloud to herself the days when she was a girl. Pilgrims from Augenblick, on their way to worship at the shrine of Schmürr, hear the sound of reminiscence coming from the rock and stop in their march to sing a hymn of praise for the drying up of the crops. They do not recognize Immerglück, as she has her hair done differently, and think that she is a beggar girl selling pencils.

In the meantime, Ragel, the papercutter of the gods, has fashioned himself a sword on the forge of Schmalz, and has called the weapon "Assistance-in-Emergency." Armed with "Assistance-in-Emergency" he comes to earth, determined to slay the Iron Duck and carry off the beautiful Irma.

But Frimsel overhears the plan and has a drink brewed which is given to Ragel in a golden goblet and which, when drunk, makes him forget his past and causes him to believe that he is Schnorr, the God of Fun. While laboring under this spell, Ragel has a funeral pyre built on the summit of a high mountain and, after lighting it, climbs on top of it with a mandolin which he plays until he is consumed.

Immerglück never marries.

II—Il Minnestrone
(Peasant Love)

Scene: *Venice and Old Point Comfort.*
Time: *Early 16th Century.*

Cast

Alfonso, *Duke of Minnestrone*.........................Baritone
Partola, *a Peasant Girl*...................................Soprano

Cleanso		Tenor
Turino	} *Young Noblemen of Venice* {	Tenor
Bombo		Basso
Ludovico	} *Assassins in the service* {	Basso
Astolfo	*of Cafeteria Rusticana*	Methodist

Townspeople, Cabbies and Sparrows

Argument

"Il Minnestrone" is an allegory of the two sides of a man's nature (good and bad), ending at last in an awfully comical mess with everyone dead.

Act I

A Public Square, Ferrara.—During a peasant festival held to celebrate the sixth consecutive day of rain, Rudolpho, a young nobleman, sees Lilliano, daughter of the village bell-ringer, dancing along throwing artificial roses at herself. He asks of his secretary who the young woman is, and his secretary, in order to confuse Rudolpho and thereby win the hand of his ward, tells him that it is his (Rudolpho's) own mother, disguised for the festival. Rudolpho is astounded. He orders her arrest.

Act 2

Banquet Hall in Gorgio's Palace.—Lilliano has not forgotten Breda, her old nurse, in spite of her troubles, and determines to avenge herself for the many insults she received in her youth by poisoning her (Breda). She therefore invites the old nurse to a banquet and poisons her. Presently a knock is heard. It is Ugolfo. He has come to carry away the body of Michelo and to leave an extra quart of pasteurized. Lilliano tells him that she no longer loves him, at which he goes away, dragging his feet sulkily.

Act 3

In Front of Emilo's House.—Still thinking of the old man's curse, Borsa has an interview with Cleanso, believing him to be the Duke's wife. He tells him things can't go on as they are, and Cleanso stabs him. Just at this moment Betty comes rushing in from school and falls in a faint. Her worst fears have been realized. She has been insulted by Sigmundo, and presently dies of old age. In a fury, Ugolfo rushes out to kill Sigmundo and, as he does so, the dying Rosenblatt rises on one elbow and curses his mother.

III—Lucy de Lima

Scene: *Wales.*
Time: *1700 (Greenwich).*

Cast

William Wont, *Lord of Glennnn*..........................Basso
Lucy Wagstaff, *his daughter*...........................Soprano
Bertram, *her lover*..Tenor
Lord Roger, *friend of Bertram*........................Soprano
Irma, *attendant to Lucy*.....................................Basso
*Friends, Retainers and Members
of the local Lodge of Elks.*

Argument

"Lucy de Lima" is founded on the well-known story by Boccaccio of the same name and address.

Act I

Gypsy Camp Near Waterbury.—The gypsies, led by Edith, go singing through the camp on the way to the fair. Following them comes Despard, the gypsy leader, carrying Ethel, whom he has just kidnapped from her father, who had previously just kidnapped her from her mother. Despard places Ethel on the ground and tells Mona, the old hag, to watch over her. Mona nurses a secret grudge against Despard for having once cut off her leg and decides to change Ethel for Nettie, another kidnapped child. Ethel pleads with Mona to let her stay with Despard, for she has fallen in love with him on the ride over. But Mona is obdurate.

Act 2

The Fair.—A crowd of sightseers and villagers is present. Roger appears, looking for Laura. He can not find her. Laura appears, looking for Roger. She can not find him. The gypsy queen approaches Roger and thrusts into his hand the locket stolen from Lord Brym. Roger looks at it and is frozen with astonishment, for it contains the portrait of his mother when she was in high school. He then realizes that Laura must be his sister, and starts out to find her.

Act 3

Hall in the Castle.—Lucy is seen surrounded by every luxury, but her heart is sad. She has just been shown a forged letter from Stewart saying that he no longer loves her, and she remembers her old free life in the mountains and longs for another romp with Ravensbane and Wolfshead, her old pair of rompers. The guests begin to assemble for the wedding, each bringing a roast ox. They chide Lucy for not having her dress changed. Just at this moment the gypsy band bursts in and Cleon tells the wedding party that Elsie and not Edith is the child who was stolen from the summer-house, showing the blood-stained derby as proof. At this, Lord Brym repents and gives his blessing on the pair, while the fishermen and their wives celebrate in the courtyard.

HOLT! WHO GOES THERE?

THE RELIANCE OF young mothers on Dr. Emmett Holt's "The Care and Feeding of Children" has become a national custom. Especially during the early infancy of the first baby does the son rise and set by what "Holt says." But there are several questions which come to mind which are not included in the handy questionnaire arranged by the noted child-specialist, and as he is probably too busy to answer them himself, we have compiled an appendix which he may incorporate in the next edition of his book, if he cares to. Of course, if he doesn't care to it isn't compulsory.

Bathing

What should the parent wear while bathing the child?
A rubber loin-cloth will usually be sufficient, with perhaps a pair of elbow-guards and anti-skid gloves. A bath should never be given a child until at least one hour after eating (that is, after the parent has eaten).

What are the objections to face-cloths as a means of bathing children?
They are too easily swallowed, and after six or seven wet face-cloths have been swallowed, the child is likely to become heavy and lethargic.

Under what circumstances should the daily tub-bath be omitted?
Almost any excuse will do. The bath-room may be too cold, or too hot, or the child may be too sleepy or too wide-awake, or the parent may have lame knees or lead poisoning. And anyway, the child had a good bath yesterday.

Clothing

How should the infant be held during dressing and un-dressing?
Any carpenter will be glad to sell you a vise which can be attached to the edge of the table. Place the infant in the vise and turn the screw until there is a slight redness under the pressure. Be careful not to turn it

too tight or the child will resent it; but on the other hand, care should be taken not to leave it too loose, otherwise the child will be continually falling out on the floor, and you will never get it dressed that way.

What are the most important items in the baby's clothing?

The safety-pins which are in the bureau in the next room.

Weight

How should a child be weighed?

Place the child in the scales. The father should then sit on top of the child to hold him down. Weigh father and child together. Then deduct the father's weight from the gross tonnage, and the weight of the child is the result.

Fresh Air

What are the objections to an infant's sleeping out-of-doors?

Sleeping out-of-doors in the city is all right, but children sleeping out of doors in the country are likely to be kissed by wandering cows and things. This should never be permitted under any circumstances.

Development

When does the infant first laugh aloud?
When father tries to pin it up for the first time.
If at two years the child makes no attempt to talk, what should be suspected?
That it hasn't yet seen anyone worth talking to.

Feeding

What should not be fed to a child?
Ripe olives.
How do we know how much food a healthy child needs?
By listening carefully.
Which parent should go and get the child's early morning bottle?
The one least able to feign sleep.

WHEN GENIUS REMAINED YOUR HUMBLE SERVANT

OF COURSE, I really know nothing about it, but I would be willing to wager that the last words of Penelope, as Odysseus bounced down the front steps, bag in hand, were: "Now, don't forget to write, Odie. You'll find some papyrus rolled up in your clean peplum, and just drop me a line on it whenever you get a chance."

And ever since that time people have been promising to write, and then explaining why they haven't written. Most personal correspondence of to-day consists of letters the first half of which are given over to an indexed statement of reasons why the writer hasn't written before, followed by one paragraph of small talk, with the remainder devoted to reasons why it is imperative that the letter be brought to a close. So many people begin their letters by saying that they have been rushed to death during the last month, and therefore haven't found time to write, that one wonders where all the grown persons come from who attend movies at eleven in the morning. There has been a mis-understanding of the word "busy" somewhere.

So explanatory has the method of letter writing become that it is probable that if Odysseus were a modern traveler his letters home to Penelope would average something like this:

Calypso,
  Friday afternoon.

DEAR PEN:—I have been so tied up with work during the last week that I haven't had a chance to get near a desk to write to you. I have been trying to every day, but something would come up just at the last minute that would prevent me. Last Monday I got the papyrus all unrolled, and then I had to tend to Scylla and Charybdis (I may have written you about them before), and by the time I got through with them it was bedtime, and, believe me, I am snatching every bit of sleep I can get these days. And so it went, first the Læstrygones, and then something else, and here

307

it is Friday. Well, there isn't much news to write about. Things are going along here about as usual. There is a young nymph here who seems to own the place, but I haven't had any chance to meet her socially. Well, there goes the ship's bell. I guess I had better be bringing this to a close. I have got a lot of work to do before I get dressed to go to a dinner of that nymph I was telling you about. I have met her brother, and he and I are interested in the same line of goods. He was at Troy with me. Well, I guess I must be closing. Will try to get off a longer letter in a day or two.

Your loving husband,
ODIE.

P.S.—You haven't got that bunch of sports hanging round the palace still, have you? Tell Telemachus I'll take him out of school if I hear of his playing around with any of them.

But there was a time when letter writing was such a fad, especially among the young girls, that if they had had to choose between eating three meals a day and writing a letter they wouldn't have given the meals even a consideration. In fact, they couldn't do both, for the length of maidenly letters in those days precluded any time out for meals. They may have knocked off for a few minutes during the heat of the day for a whiff at a bottle of salts, but to nibble at anything heartier than lettuce would have cramped their style.

Take Miss Clarissa Harlowe, for instance. In Richardson's book (which, in spite of my personal aversion to it, has been hailed by every great writer, from Pope to Stevenson, as being perfectly bully) she is

given the opportunity of telling 2,400 closely printed pages full of story by means of letters to her female friend, Miss Howe (who plays a part similar to the orchestra leader in Frank Tinney's act). And 2,400 pages is nothing to her. When the book closes she is just beginning to get her stride. As soon as she got through with that she probably sat down and wrote a series of letters to the London papers about the need for conscription to fight the Indians in America.

To a girl like Clarissa, in the middle of the eighteenth century, no day was too full of horrors, no hour was too crowded with terrific happenings to prevent her from seating herself at a desk (she must have carried the desk about with her, strapped over her shoulder) and tearing off twenty or thirty pages to Friend Anna, telling her all about it. The only way that I can see in which she could accomplish this so efficiently would be to have a copy boy standing at her elbow, who took the letter, sheet by sheet, as she wrote it, and dashed with it to the printer.

It is hard to tell just which a girl of that period considered more important, the experiences she was writing of or the letter itself. She certainly never slighted the letter. If the experience wanted to overtake her, and jump up on the desk beside her, all right, but, experience or no experience, she was going to get that letter in the next post or die in the attempt. Unfortunately, she never died in the attempt.

Thus, an attack on a young lady's house by a band of cutthroats, resulting in the burning of the structure and her abduction, might have been told of in the eighteenth century letter system as follows:

Monday night.

SWEET ANNA:—At this writing I find myself in the most horrible circumstance imaginable. Picture to yourself, if you can, my dear Anna, a party of villainous brigands, veritable cutthroats, all of them, led by a surly fellow in green alpaca with white insertion, breaking their way, by very force, through the side of your domicile, like so many ugly intruders, and threatening you with vile imprecations to make you disclose the hiding place of the family jewels. If the mere thought of such a contingency is painful to you, my beloved Anna, consider what it means to me, your delicate friend, to whom it is actually happening at this very minute! For such is in very truth the situation which is disclosing itself in my room as I write. Not three feet away from me is the odious person before described. Now he is threatening me with renewed vigor! Now he has placed his coarse hands on my throat, completely hiding the pearl necklace which papa brought me from Epsom last summer, and which you, and also young Pindleson (whose very name I mention with a blush), have so often admired. But more of this later, and until then, believe me, my dear Anna, to be

Your ever distressed and affectionate
CL. HARLOWE.

Monday night. Later.

DEAREST ANNA:—Now, indeed, it is evident, my best, my only friend, that I am face to face

310

with the bitterest of fates. You will remember that in my last letter I spoke to you of a party of unprincipled knaves who were invading my apartment. And now do I find that they have, in furtherance of their inexcusable plans, set fire to that portion of the house which lies directly behind this, so that as I put my pen to paper the flames are creeping, like hungry creatures of some sort, through the partitions and into this very room, so that did I esteem my safety more than my correspondence with you, my precious companion, I should at once be making preparation for immediate departure. O my dear! To be thus seized, as I am at this very instant, by the unscrupulous leader of the band and carried, by brute force, down the stairway through the butler's pantry and into the servants' hall, writing as I go, resting my poor paper on the shoulder of my detested abductor, is truly, you will agree, my sweet Anna, a pitiable episode.

Adieu, my intimate friend.
Your obt. s'v't,
CL. HARLOWE.

One wonders (or, at least, *I* wonder, and that is sufficient for the purposes of this article) what the letter writing young lady of that period would have done had she lived in this day of postcards showing the rocks at Scipawisset or the Free Public Library in East Tarvia. She might have used them for some of her shorter messages, but I rather doubt it. The foregoing scene could hardly have been done justice to on a card bearing the picture of the Main Street of the town, looking north from the Soldiers' Monument, with the following legend:

"Our house is the third on the left with the lilac bush. Cross marks window where gang of rough-necks have just broken in and are robbing and burning the house. Looks like a bad night. Wish you were here. C.H."

No; that would never have done, but it would have been a big relief for the postilion, or whoever it was that had to carry Miss Clarissa's effusions to their destination. The mail on Monday morning, after a spring-like Sunday, must have been something in the nature of a wagon load of rolls of news print that used to be seen standing in front of newspaper offices in the good old days when newspapers were printed on paper stock. Of course, the postilion had the opportunity of whiling away the time between stations by reading some of the spicier bits in the assortment, but even a postilion must have had his feelings, and a man can't read that kind of stuff *all* of the time, and still keep his health.

Of course, there are a great many people now who write letters because they like to. Also, there are some who do it because they feel that they owe it to posterity and to their publishers to do so. As soon as a man begins to sniff a chance that he may become moderately famous he is apt to brush up on his letter writing and never send anything out that has not been polished and proof-read, with the idea in mind that some day some one is going to get all of his letters together and make a book of them. Apparently, most great men whose letters have been published have had premonition of their greatness when quite young, as their child-

ish letters bear the marks of careful and studied attention to publicity values. One can almost imagine the
budding genius, aged eight, sitting at his desk and saying to himself:

"In this spontaneous letter to my father I must not
forget that I am now going through the *Sturm und
Drang* (storm and stress) period of my youth and that
this letter will have to be grouped by the compiler under the *Sturm und Drang* (storm and stress) section in
my collected letters. I must therefore keep in the key
and quote only such of my favorite authors as will contribute to the effect. I think I will use Werther to-day.
...My dear Father"—etc.

I have not known many geniuses in their youth, but
I have had several youths pointed out to me by their
parents as geniuses, and I must confess that I have
never seen a letter from any one of them that differed
greatly from the letters of a normal boy, unless perhaps
they were spelled less accurately. Given certain unin-
teresting conditions, let us say, at boarding school, and
I believe that the average bright boy's letter home
would read something in this fashion:

Exeter, N.H.,
Wed., April 25.

MY DEAR FATHER AND MOTHER:

I have been working pretty hard this week,
studying for a history examination, and so haven't
had much of a chance to write to you. Everything
is about the same as usual here, and there doesn't
seem to be much news to write to you about. The
box came all right, and thank you very much. All

313

the fellows liked it, especially the little apple pies.
Thank you very much for sending it. There
hasn't much been happening here since I wrote
you last week. I had to buy a new pair of running
drawers, which cost me fifty cents. Does that
come out of my allowance? Or will you pay for
it? There doesn't seem to be any other news.
Well, there goes the bell, so I guess I will be
closing.

Your loving son,
BUXTON.

Given the same, even less interesting conditions, and
a boy such as Stevenson must have been (judging from
his letters) could probably have delivered himself of
this, and more, too:

Wyckham-Wyckham,
The Tenth

DEAR PATER:—To-day has been unbelievably
exquisite! Great, undulating clouds, rolling in ser-
ried formation across a sky of pure *lapis lazuli.* I
feel like what Updike calls a "myrmidon of un-
hesitating amplitude." And a perfect gem of a letter from Toto completed the felicitous experience.
You would hardly believe, and yet you must, in
your *coeur des coeurs,* know, that the brown, eso-
teric hills of this Oriental retreat affect me like the
red wine of Russilon, and, indigent as I am in
these matters, I cannot but feel that you have, as
Herbert says:
   "Carve or discourse; do not a famine fear.
   Who carves is kind to two, who talks to all."

Yesterday I saw a little native boy, a veritable boy of the streets, playing at a game at once so naïve and so resplendent that I was irresistibly drawn to its contemplation. You will doubtless jeer when I tell you. He was tossing a small *blatch*, such as grow in great profusion here, to and fro between himself and the wall of the *limple*. I was stunned for the moment, and then I realized that I was looking into the very soul of the peasantry, the open stigma of the nation. How queer it all seemed! Did it not?

You doubtless think me an ungrateful fellow for not mentioning the delicious assortment of goodies which came, like melons to Artemis, to this benighted *gesellschaft* on Thursday last. They were devoured to the last crumb, and I was reminded as we ate, like so many *wurras*, of those lines of that gorgeous Herbert, of whom I am so fond:

"Must all be veiled, while he that reads divines,
Catching the sense at two removes?"

The breeze is springing up, and it brings to me messages of the open meadows of Litzel, deep festooned with the riot of gloriannas. How quiet they seem to me as I think of them now! How emblematic! Do you know, my dear Parent, that I sometimes wonder if, after all, it were not better to dream, and dream...and dream.

Your affectionate son,
BERGQUIST.

So don't worry about your boy if he writes home like that. He may simply have an eye for fame and future compilation.

RING LARDNER

There is a good bit of Artemus Ward in Ring Lardner. Like Charles Farrar Browne's bombastic but sly showman, Ring Lardner's characters speak to us in a voice we can hear from the page, and misspellings and comical neologisms make up a good part of the technique. Artemus Ward held onto a sense of self-important superiority, however; it was only in occasional flashes that we suspected his self-confidence was a mask. Ring Lardner's characters are perfectly comfortable not being at the top of the social or intellectual scale.

If Ring Lardner has one outstanding virtue, it is that his ear never fails him. He hears what real people all around him are saying, and he is able to absorb not just their way of speaking, but also their way of thinking.

Many of Ring Lardner's better-known books are still in print, so we have chosen a little essay that is not nearly so well known.

A SMALL VOCABULARY
MAY HAVE A BIG KICK

To the Editor:

The other night I was to a party where they had a argument in regards to how many wds. is in the average man or lady's vocabulary which they meant how many wds. does a person use in their regular every day conversation and one lady said 4 or 5 thousand and one of the men give her the laugh and said 700 was nearer the mark, and of course I didn't take no part in the argument as they was all my elders but that didn't keep me from thinking over the question and maybe some of my readers would be interested in doing the same.

Well, in the first place you would naturally suppose that a woman's vocabulary was a lot bigger than a man's on acct. of them talking so much more, but on second thoughts that don't prove nothing as you will notice that the most women say the same thing over and over and a woman might say 10,000 wds. per day but only 10 different wds. like for inst.:

"I wished we had a fire. The house is cold," which she is libel to say a 1000 times makeing a total of 10,000 wds. that don't mean nothing.

As a matter of fact, a man though he don't talk nowheres near as much, don't repeat himself nowheres near as often, a specially since they fixed it so he had to quit saying, "Give us another," so wile a man may talk 100 wds. a day to a woman's 10,000, still they's libel to be 50 different wds. amongst his 100 and some times even more than that, though if a man does say 100 wds. the chances are that at lease 50 of them is "Well."

Some men of course has more to say than others and they's been evenings in my career when I only said 2 wds. the whole evening namely "stay" and "pass" and a few afternoons spent outdoors when my conversation was just the numeral wds. "seven" and "eight."

When all is said and done I suppose the number of wds. a person talks depends on what line of business they are in, like for example a doctor talks practically all the time where as a engineer on a R. R. or a fisherman don't hardly say nothing, and even some people talks more than others in the same business like for inst. a elevator man in a 22 story bldg. has twice as much to say as a elevator man in a 11 story bldg. and a train man on a subway local has to name maybe 30 or 35 stations while a train man on a express only names 4 or 5, but as far as that is conserned for all the good they do, the both of them might as well keep their mouth shut.

A box office man in a N. Y. theatre only has to say 2 wds. all day, namely, "Seventeenth row."

A man that runs a garage can get along on even less, as all he has to do is say, "No," when people call up to ask is their car ready yet.

In the old days, barbers use to do a lot of talking. They had a vocabulary of about 1000 wds. which they would repeat them the same number of times per day as they had clients in their chairs, but the funny papers and etc. begin to kid barbers about talking so as now a barber is almost scared to even say your hair is falling out, but it's agony for them to keep their mouth shut and their wifes must get he-ll when they get home.

A traffic policeman's conversation varies according to what time of day it is. In the morning he only has to say "What do you think you are trying to do?" which is 9 wds. all together and only 7 of them different, but along in the afternoon when he ain't feeling so genial he adds 2 wds. makeing it:

"What the hell do you think you are trying to do?"

As for the motor man on a st. car they's generally always a sign that says don't talk to the motorman and

I use to think that meant you mustn't talk to him on acct. of it bothering him and takeing his mind off his work, but wile rideing on the front platform of st. cars in N. Y. and Chicago I come to the conclusion that he don't want to be interrupted.

The facts of the matter is that nobody likes nobody for their vocabulary and no man ever married a gal because she could say 5000 wds. besides yes or because she couldn't, and on the contrary one of my best friends is a man that don't hardly ever open his mouth only to take a fresh chew, but they say its nice for a person to know a whole lot of wds. even if they don't use them so when they are in church or rideing on a train or something they can amuse themselfs counting up the wds. they know.

As for a big vocabulary getting a person anywheres or doing them any good, they's a party liveing in our house that is 2 yrs. old and I don't suppose he has got a vocabulary of more than 200 wds. and even some of them sounds foreign, but this bird gets whatever he wants and I don't know of nobody who I would rather trade jobs with.

Which is about all the wds. I can write about wds., only to recommend to the reader a kind of a game I tried out the other day which was a couple of days after the party and the game was to try and think every time before I spoke and count the number of wds. I used and count how many of them was necessary and how many could be left out and of course I forgot a couple times and said things without thinking or counting them, but you would be surprised at the few number of wds. it is necessary for a person to say in

319

the course of a day and personally I come to the conclusion that a dumb mute ain't so much to be pitied after all and the people around him less.

Ring W. Lardner.

CPSIA information can be obtained
at www.ICGtesting.com
Printed in the USA
LVHW030854030821
694341LV00004B/387

9 781503 1841